Gods, Genes and Climate
An alternative history of the last 100,000 years

*Is it possible to create a single story
that explains all the mysteries of the ancient world?*

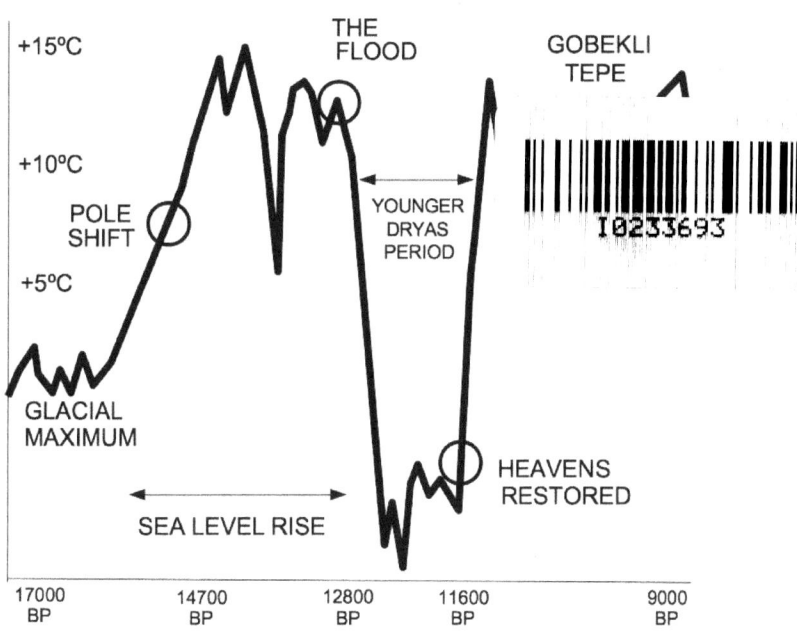

The graph in the cover image is a representation of how temperature in the fertile crescent may have changed between the last glacial maximum and the times when Gobekli Tepe was serially constructed. It is based on temperature assessments made from Greenland ice cores and ocean cores from the Cariaco Basin that is north of Venezuala, published by the US National Centers for Environmental information, National Oceanic and Atmosphere Administration,

Cover design is by Book Beaver, www.bookbeaver.co.uk.

Gods, Genes and Climate

By Roger Broadie.

© Copyright Roger Broadie, 2016.
ISBN: 978 0 9957142 0 5

Published by Fresh Insight Books, an imprint of Broadie Associates. Fresh Insight Books aims to present the edge of new knowledge in ways accessible to people not expert in the fields the books address.

Associated website: http://www.GodsGenesAndClimate.com

First published digitally October 2016.
First paperback edition 2 January 2017.

Gods, Genes and Climate

Contents

Introduction - Incredible ideas and crackpot theories............................1
Chapter 1 – Setting the scene..9
Chapter 2 - Arrival of the gods...19
Chapter 3 - Was Antarctica a potential home for our Adventurers?...34
Chapter 4 – Antarctica as a desirable home...49
Chapter 5 – What kind of society did our Adventurers have?............62
Chapter 6 – From new arrivals to residents...77
Chapter 7 – Sugar and spice and all things nice..................................80
Chapter 8 – The need for manpower; early development of humans. 87
Chapter 9 - Creating manpower..101
Chapter 10 – Developing manpower...109
Chapter 11 - Using manpower...119
Chapter 12 – Humans in Antarctica?..133
Chapter 13 – From myths and legends to written history..................138
Chapter 14 - The period 40,000 to 20,000 years ago........................146
Chapter 15 – Floods and The Flood..165
Chapter 16 – Moving house...180
Chapter 17 – Life for humans after The Flood..................................188
Chapter 18 – Did the gods return?..201
Chapter 19 - Humans and gods together..210
Chapter 20 - The gods' new home; 12,800 to 10,000 years ago.......217
Chapter 21 - 10,000 to 7000 years ago...227
Chapter 22 - 7000 to 3500 years ago..235
Chapter 23 - 3500 to 2000 years ago; the Middle East and Europe..245
Chapter 24 - 4200 to 2000 years ago in America..............................253
Chapter 25 - 2000 to 1000 years ago..257
Chapter 26 – So where are the gods now?..262
Appendix 1 - What kinds of evidence of the gods to look for..........274
Appendix 2 - Acceleration of the Earth's crust due to a comet.........275
Bibliography...280
Reference Index..288
About the Author..292

Introduction - Incredible ideas and crackpot theories.

If you want to start the story straight away please skip this introduction and jump straight to chapter one. If however you are a little uncomfortable with taking the ideas of aliens and Atlantis with any seriousness, even for the time it takes to read the book, this diversion about my struggles of mind over the last 40 or so years may be of help to you.

All my life I have been fascinated by those things that are on the edge of our knowledge, the facts that appear to have some substance but which scientists and scholars find deeply uncomfortable. It takes a brave scientist or scholar to rock the boat with radical new ideas, so their usual response to these uncomfortable ideas is to ignore them and hope they will go away. The scientific and scholarly communities often employ ridicule and mockery of people who insist on talking about them, so as to marginalise these facts and make them easier to ignore. When I was a young teacher I can remember being advised by a colleague to keep my interest in these things to myself. He felt, probably correctly, that it could have an adverse effect on my promotion prospects and career if it became known that my hobby reading was focused on 'ancient mysteries' and things that human beings observe that are not (yet) explained by science. As a science teacher I was expected to help my students understand the 'accepted wisdom' of the time, not to excite them about things that scientists avoided.

Now that I am of a relatively advanced age and don't need to worry about climbing the greasy pole, in order to support my family in the lifestyle to which they aspired to become accustomed, I no longer have these worries. And this stuff is important. If we don't take proper notice of things that don't appear to fit with our current view of the world, we won't advance in understanding. It is very much to the credit of those scientists and scholars who have been prepared to investigate things considered heretical by others, that our understanding has advanced. Often this has been at considerable personal cost, as for example for Galileo, whose heliocentric view of the world seriously conflicted with the Earth-centric view held by the Catholic church. He is not the only one to suffer for his belief in exposing the truth.

This book has come from the thought-journey that I have taken over many years. I was able to start early as we had a good local library only 15 minutes walk from the home where I grew up, in Withington, Manchester. This was in the early 1960s and already there were books available on UFOs and ghosts. In the late 1960s we entered the era of flower-power and the books available extended into areas such as the power of plants, the mysteries of ancient constructions like Stonehenge and the ideas of aliens on Earth put forward by von Daniken. Through the 1970s and 80s a steady flow of books appeared and I was able to afford to go searching for some older books that were harder to find (in the days before Amazon), such as the books by Velikovsky. You will discover what I drew from these and many others as you make your way through this book.

You will also find some reminiscences of times when I came to certain realisations. The moment when you decide that you have a good basis to fully believe in something is the moment when you start thinking differently about a whole range of other things. For example the careful study of numerous stone circles by Alexander Thom in the 1960s, convinced me that stone-age Britons were a lot more clever mathematically than I had been led to believe by my school teachers. And that impacted strongly on how I viewed other stone-age constructions. You will also find some diversions into scientific and scholarly avenues, to explore how the process of mankind acquiring new knowledge actually works in practice. What you are embarking on in reading this book is a process of following my logical and rational reasoning, which I hope you will also find logical and rational, even if the conclusions you end up with surprise you.

To return to the issue of the 'uncomfortable facts' that are the core of this book, it is necessary to acknowledge that some of the ideas proposed to explain uncomfortable facts do prove to be nonsense, which can justify ridicule. Books that offer ideas that you feel to have some truth when first read do sometimes prove later to be utter bunkum. I have been caught out by quite a few in my time. Or sometimes a few of the things they state as true prove so to be, while other things stated prove to be nonsense. But if my time is wasted by some books, I can justify this as helping me to draw the line about what I am prepared to believe might be true, though not yet explained. If a really powerful new idea doesn't at first appear to be crazy it is probably not radical enough to be important. And it is really exciting when a new and crazy idea proves to be true and opens up all sorts of new avenues of exploration.

Quite a few scientific theories that were well respected by scientists at the time are now known to be nonsense. The alchemist view that everything is made of earth, fire, air and water was well believed at the time, as was the phlogiston theory (look it up!). It is possible that some things physicists are currently working hard on, such as string theory, may prove to be wrong. There is as yet no scientific evidence that there is any truth at all in string theory. There are not even any proposals for ways to gain experimental verification of it. Yet research into string theory gets funded because it is possible to create sophisticated and complicated mathematics that suggests the theory might be true. These mathematical speculations build on the maths of theories that have been experimentally shown to be valid, but the maths is being extended way beyond what is verified experimentally. It is good to see that more scientists such as Lee Smolin are beginning to comment on and worry about this. A few times in the past the maths has been invented long before there was experimental verification of the physics the maths describes, for example the maths describing electromagnetic fields, so this is a valid way of proceeding as long as the maths does not get too divorced from verifiable reality.

In the fields of history and archeology speculation from accepted facts cannot be guided by maths, it has to draw on evidence that is very hard to understand. The speculations of the string theorists about multiple dimensions and parallel universes are fantastical, yet scientists act on faith that they may be true and invest huge effort. Speculations in history and archeology that draw on myths, legends and things we find in the ground that we can't explain can also be fantastical. If physicists can dream fantastic things and not be thought crazy I see no reason why those interested in history and archeology cannot also dream of things that may seem fantastic. We should be able to explore the observations that have stimulated the fantastic theories, without being considered crazy.

I like to keep an open mind and explore, fully prepared to acknowledge that I may have been a fool to half-believe things I can now see to be wrong. Hindsight is a wonderful thing! My 'skepticism threshold' alerts me when things being said in a book or blog are just too far away from agreed knowledge for me to believe them. You will have your own skepticism threshold; it is an entirely personal thing how far outside widely accepted knowledge you are prepared to consider ideas. I keep these 'way-out' ideas in the back of my head in case something crops up to suggest a new look might be a good idea, but I don't build them into any hypotheses I might be conjuring with. Those things on the right side of my skepticism threshold I hold in my mind as open possibilities, that might have a place in my model of what may have happened in the past. When evidence one way or the other becomes overwhelming I can decide to make those ideas a hard fact in my developing theories, or abandon them.

Some of these 'way-out' ideas, that at first scientists thought were nonsense, eventually make their way into acceptance and prove to be the basis of important new knowledge. People knew for a long time that the west coast of Africa and the East coast of South America looked like an uncomfortably good fit with each other, like jigsaw pieces. But it took many years for plate tectonics and continental drift to surface as a theory and as an explanation for how this jigsaw effect happened. Many thought it was completely impossible for continents to move around as they considered the Earth's crust to be solid. Now it is anyone who does not believe in plate tectonics who is thought the fool. Though there are some who suggest that the theory of plate tectonics is wanting in that it cannot explain various observed facts about the Earth (as you will see).

This book is the result of more than 50 years of mulling over uncomfortable facts that won't go away, supported by my wide eclectic reading of books and articles. If you want to take a similar journey I do encourage you to look for books with lots of notes and good bibliographies. The casual leisure reader has little time to verify the sources the author has used, but at least some sources are there if you want to follow them up. And the author has at least gone to the trouble of supporting their facts and arguments, which offers a little protection against time wasted.

This book is not researched in the same sense, of having statements tied back to specific sources, except for the new information on genetics which comes from specific studies. I am relying on the integrity of those authors who did provide that level of scholarly attribution. I want this book to be a story you can read without constant reference to notes. And I want to encourage you to make the journey yourself and read widely, assembling your own collection of what you feel is important and what should be ignored. I have used here only certain facts from all the books I have read, the ones that relate to this particular exploration and that are on the right side of my skepticism threshold. Other facts in those books may whet your appetite for further and different investigations.

You will find a bibliography at the end of this book but not quite a traditional one; I have used it to point out why, relative to this story, I feel the books listed are important. You are however likely to find that they are worth reading for other reasons too.

There is another reason for not using footnotes in this book. This book is a speculation, so many of the ideas don't link directly to specific sources. The ideas here are a synthesis often drawing on many sources. The facts in these various sources do not contradict my speculation, they could allow it to be true. If I come across really good evidence that makes some part of my speculation impossible then I will have to revise that part. In writing the book I have looked more carefully at many aspects of my developing overall theory of the last 100,000 years, often in trepidation that I am going to come across good evidence that will force me to change the story. So far I haven't found any scientific, historical or archeological facts that would make this story impossible.

Though you won't find footnotes you will find some web-links (more in the ebook version). I wanted to keep the story at an easily readable length so have avoided long explanations about things I refer to. If you need to know more to make sense of what I am saying then follow the links or do your own search on the Internet. I have added the links in full for the benefit of those using the ebook version, so apologies if they are hard to type. As things change on the Internet I am not going to apologise if you find any of these links broken. Neither am I going to make any judgement on how true the content of the sites I link to is. I have endeavoured to point you to sites that have reasonable credibility, but some contain both the credible and information I find unbelievable; again it is your job to judge this. The point of the links is to provide you with a starting point for your own explorations. Sites often suggest other search terms that will lead you to better sources. I find that the best sites are those put up by people who are themselves exploring in these areas. There is a growing network of people doing careful, scholarly and scientific exploration of ideas that are considered by established science and archeology to be 'way-out'. I am sure that at least some of the ideas they are propounding will prove in future to be true.

My attempt to fit together all the different bits of information that I have come across, and believe likely to be true, suggests that the current accepted wisdom about this period is at least incomplete and possibly significantly wrong. The accepted wisdom is that early modern humans (homo-sapiens) evolved from other hominins, through natural mutation and selection of the fittest to survive, maybe 200,000 years ago. Then rather suddenly around 60,000 years ago an evolution of early modern humans happened, creating higher level thinking. It is then postulated that they slowly developed technological and cultural capabilities as a race of hunter-gatherers, until rather suddenly in the few thousand years from 12,000 years ago (10,000BC) to 9,000 years ago (7,000BC) they developed both agriculture and city civilisations. Geologically the accepted wisdom is that the Earth has developed gradually, generally without sudden cataclysmic changes except for very occasional big impacts from asteroids.

These accepted views however don't provide explanations for various 'uncomfortable facts'. Some of these facts might seem 'small' compared to the huge weight of evidence available to support widely accepted theories, but it is often small discrepancies between a theory and what is actually observed that lead scientists to new breakthrough theories. For my story to work for me it has to provide a possible way of explaining *all* these uncomfortable facts.

To give you a preview of the diversity of facts I am trying to link in to the accepted history that we can be pretty certain is true, let me list a few for you, in no particular order:

- Frozen mammoths have been found in Siberia. There were frozen a long time ago and the really interesting finds are those animals that were quick-frozen, while still chewing plants. The species of plants they were chewing were temperate climate plants and do not now grow where the mammoths have been found. How did the mammoths get to be so rapidly deep-frozen and how could temperate climate plants ever have grown in Northern Siberia?

- Ancient mariners' maps have been investigated that appear to show the coastline of Antarctica as it really is (or would be) when free of ice. The US Navy has compared them to what we now know of this coast and they agree. It appears that someone, in the days before we had sensing equipment to look through thick ice, must have seen this coast without ice. How and when? Or are these maps just fanciful suppositions that by chance happen to match the real ice-free coast?

- Why did cro-magnon man suddenly appear around 60,000 years ago? There is quite a discontinuity in this. Hominins had been slowly improving the stone tools they used over many hundreds of thousands of years, then suddenly in a matter of only a few thousand years, much more sophisticated stone tools appear. We also pretty suddenly get the beautiful artwork in caves. So was this a natural sudden evolution or were there some other factors involved?

- The next thing we have lots of evidence of is that civilisations sprang into being in Mesopotamia and surrounding countries extremely rapidly around 9,000 years ago. Where did these civilisations come from? What happened with human societies in the preceding 30,000 years? Hunter-gatherer societies that existed in this period were quite sophisticated; what stopped them developing cities earlier. What was the stimulus that caused mankind to change from the very sustainable and effective hunter-gatherer lifestyle to cities and a farming lifestyle?

- Pyramid building in Egypt appears to go backwards in competence and scale. The great pyramid is a masterpiece of construction, much more complicated and better constructed than later pyramids, but appears very early relative to when most pyramids were constructed. Why did the Egyptians lose their pyramid building expertise?

- The so-called sarcophagus in the kings chamber of the great pyramid appears to have been drilled out with an ultrasound drill. No-one can come up with any satisfactory theory on how the kinds of drills that we know could have existed in dynastic Egypt could have made the marks that are found in the hard granite of this object.

- The Sphinx is heavily water-worn, much more so than experts expect given the date they believe it was built. That area of the planet does not seem to have had heavy and persistent rainfall that could have caused this water-erosion in the few thousand years since archeologists believe the Sphinx was created.

- Around the world there are ancient complex astronomical observatories. Newgrange for example may have been built to track the 8-year cycle of Venus. Why was there a such a concern to make observations to a far higher accuracy than is needed to predict the seasons?

- It is said that one factor that helped the Spanish conquer the Incas In South America, is that they had a legend that a bearded God would appear in ships from the East. Where did this legend come from?

- How did they cut, move and place those stones? I am talking here of the really massive stone blocks around the kings chamber in the great pyramid, and the even larger blocks in Lebanon at Baalbeck.

- How were the intricately cut and interlinked blocks in Cusco in South America assembled. And how were the very finely and precisely cut stones at Punku Puma made? We could not manage some of these feats today, so how did they come about?

- The origin of some plants is very obscure, such as how the edible banana was derived from its non-edible cousins. There is some strangeness around Emmer wheat too, in that it has been found in graves around 20,000 years ago but only seems to have been first cultivated around 12,000 years ago.

- There must have been a major worldwide flood during the time that mankind has existed on the Earth, given the huge number of flood legends from all around the world. While local reasons have been proposed in various places, such as the flooding that created the Black sea, no good theory is accepted as to what might be the cause of a flood that almost eliminated human beings from the planet, as the legend would have us believe.

- Where do all the stories of gods and god-kings come from? Isolated societies tend to have shamanistic worship and beliefs focused on the spirit world, that do not have gods as individuals. Were all the stories of the Sumerian, Greek and Roman Gods just that, stories that were invented. Or is there something else behind them?

- There are some languages, an example being the Basque language, that don't seem to fit into the neighbouring language families from which it could be expected they have arisen. If the Basques didn't develop their language starting from neighbouring languages, what language did it develop from?

That's probably more than enough to be going on with and to give you a feel for how widely we will range in this book. The challenge is to construct a hypothesis of the history of the world that accommodates and helps to explain all the facts that we have good evidence for.

So let's proceed with the thought experiment. What set of circumstances could make all the above acknowledged facts fully understandable and lead us to the truths behind them?

****

Chapter 1 – Setting the scene.

This is a story that has been growing in my mind for many years. It is a story of our origins, where we came from and who we are. We know quite a lot about the origins of mankind, our prehistory and written history. Though written histories can contain inaccuracies or even downright lies, and interpretations of the archeological record can be flawed, there seems to be a deal of truth in the commonly accepted story that we teach children in school.

But the commonly accepted story is not the whole story. Recent discoveries such as the bones of ancient hominins discovered in the Rising Star cave are revealing to us more intriguing insights, not least the lengths they apparently went to in disposing of their dead. Advances in genetics that are enabling us to explore the DNA in ancient bones are particularly important in revealing more about how mankind developed. We also know that the accepted story is not the whole truth because there are mysteries that are not satisfactorily explained. My brain will not allow me to push these to one side as most scientists and scholars seem to be able to do. I need a story that explains all that we see around the world, including the mysteries.

Our story must explain and provide a context for all those known facts that scientists generally ignore. It must be based, as far as possible, on verifiable facts that cannot be disputed. But if we wish to step outside the commonly accepted version of the past and to create an innovative and new scenario, there will inevitably be some ideas that are not accepted. If they were, then others would probably have brought together the elements of this scenario before me.

The critical thing is to keep the new and non-accepted ideas to a minimum. If we then find that a whole mass of verifiable ideas and facts can be linked and better explained by accepting just a very few hard-to-believe ideas, this will suggest that these hard-to-believe ideas might just be true. This will then make them worthy of more serious and widespread investigation.

There are just three of these hard-to-believe ideas that I am asking you to accept for a while, as you read this book.

The first hard-to-believe idea, is that technologically advanced alien beings might have arrived on Earth some time around 100,000 or more years ago.

The second hard-to-believe idea, is that these aliens might have had very long lives compared to the lives of human beings.

The third hard-to-believe idea, is that the North and South Poles might not have been where they are now, and moved from about 17,000 years ago.

You will see as we progress through the book why I think it is worthwhile conjuring with these three ideas.

There is a central conundrum in these ideas. 'Technologically advanced' means that these beings that arrived had full knowledge and control of all the elements of the periodic table and particularly metals. It means that they had access to large amounts of energy and could achieve things that we are not yet technologically capable of. We can clearly see from our own history what we have had to do to reach our own technological level. Our acquisition of metals and energy has come at the cost of major disruption and damage to areas of the world.

The central conundrum is that we have almost no evidence of an ancient civilisation prior to the copper age that was mining for metals or energy sources, as we have. As I am proposing these technologically advanced beings were on the Earth for many thousands of years, yet we cannot see where they got the resources needed for their technology, I shall have to explain why this is so. The long timescale is also part of this conundrum. If we are to believe that these beings had a civilisation that lasted tens of thousands of years, without a population explosion comparable to that which mankind has achieved through technology, which would surely have left widespread evidence around the world, again I shall have to explain why. It will be necessary to explore the mind-set of these beings. We will have to speculate about how a technologically advanced group of beings could exist on the Earth for so long, without leaving obvious and indisputable evidence for them having been here. If we can't imagine how this could be possible, we will not be able to believe in their existence. So some of the chapters will explore this.

However we had better start by considering just how outlandish and improbable are the three central ideas that I am asking you to believe.

How likely is it that aliens came to the Earth?

Great fun can be had by making mathematical guesstimates. It's best to have a calculator to hand and you need to be comfortable handling large numbers. If you can use a spreadsheet with simple formulae it can make handling numbers in the millions and billions much easier, as it saves having to count lots of zeros. Having references sources can make your guesstimates more accurate but doing it without references makes the discussion more fun, as you can have good arguments about the numbers involved. It's an excellent way of getting people to develop a better idea of the relative sizes of numbers, both big and small. In a way, having the power to search the Internet for answers makes it more of an exercise than a game. I think it's best to play the game and argue it through, and only if you really want to find a more correct answer to then go and find out what the numbers really are, and how close you got with your guesstimate.

A good question to start with in trying this approach is 'How many piano tuners are there in Chicago?' What do we need to know to answer this? The logical sequence of questions is:

- How many people live in Chicago? Well it's not as big as London which I think has around 8 million people living in it. I used to live in Sheffield and knew that its population was around 500,000. Chicago is bigger than Sheffield but not as big as London. Shall we guess 5 million people in greater Chicago? It's probably not the right number but it will do as a starting point.

- How many of them have pianos? Well in my early youth, when most families did not have a TV, a sing-song around the piano was one of the few home entertainments available. Even quite poor people in the first part of the 20th century had a piano, now it is far fewer. And pianos have been replaced by keyboards, which don't need the services of a piano tuner. It might be that one in twenty families have a keyboard, but perhaps only one in a hundred have a piano. This statement of course makes you realise that we shouldn't be starting from overall population, but from the number of families. If we reckon that the average family is 3.5 people (don't forget there will be a sizable number of people living on their own, to bring the average down), then the number of families in Chicago is 5 million divided by 3.5, which is 1.43 million. So if one in a hundred of these families has a piano, that's 14,300 pianos.

- How many people bother to get their piano tuned and how often? Well probably most will want their piano tuned. If you are going to give a piano house room, you probably want it tuning. How often is a more difficult question. Once every 3 years? Or once every 5 years? If we balance the estimates a bit, and take the bigger estimate for people who use the services of a piano tuner, 100%, and the smaller estimate for how often of once every 5 years, that means 2800 pianos being tuned every year.

- How many pianos can a piano tuner tune in a year? Well it takes a couple of hours to tune a piano and they will have to travel between houses, so let's guess they manage 3 a day, during their working week. A year minus holidays is perhaps 47 weeks, which is 235 working days, so each piano tuner can tune 705 pianos a year.

- And finally we can answer the question, by dividing the 2800 pianos needing tuning every year by 705, giving us 3.97 piano tuners in Chicago. Which is probably 4 piano tuners, one of whom got ill for a day or two.

Obviously the answer is wrong, but around 4 might be in the right ball-park and almost certainly is the right order of magnitude. It would be quite a good bet that there are more than 0.4 and less than 40 piano tuners in Chicago.

What is the point of this diversion you may ask? It is because some people, particularly Frank Drake and Carl Sagan, have taken the trouble to ask the question 'What is the likelihood of aliens visiting Earth' and made estimates – but in reality more guesstimates. To get an answer you need a series of questions about how many planets capable of sustaining life there are and so on. Frank Drake produced an equation to aid the search for extraterrestrial intelligence, SETI. The Drake Equation estimates how many intelligent civilizations capable of extraterrestrial communication might inhabit our galaxy. The equation is:

$N = R^* \times fs \times fp \times nE \times fl \times fi \times fc \times L$

N is the number we are looking for, intelligent civilisations in our galaxy capable of sending radio messages.

R^* is the average star formation rate in the galaxy (in other words the number of stars averaged out as stars die and are born over billions of years).

fs is the fraction of "suitable" stars capable of supporting a habitable planet.

fp is the fraction of suitable stars that actually do have planets.

nE is the average fraction of "Earth-like" planets amongst these planets, capable of supporting life.

fl is the average fraction of Earth-like planets with life.

fi is the average fraction of life-bearing planets evolving at least one intelligent species.

fc is the average fraction of life-bearing planets with intelligent civilizations capable of interstellar communications.

L is the average lifetime that a civilization remains technologically active and will use radio communication.

As this is an equation where most of the multipliers are fractions, the answer is going to get smaller and smaller as each new factor is taken into account. However the number we start with is very big. Estimates of the number of stars in the Milky Way (which is our galaxy) vary between 100 billion and 400 billion.

Carl Sagan, the astronomer, was heavily involved in the early stages of SETI and he wrote about the likelihood of aliens visiting Earth. This was at a time when there was a lot of interest in UFOs and even governments were taking notice of them to some extent, with the US Air Force setting up Project Blue Book (see http://www.bluebookarchive.org/). He went one step further than the Drake equation to estimate the fraction of technologically active civilisations that could travel across space. I see that Wikipedia now states that Sagan reckoned the likelihood of aliens visiting Earth was 'vanishingly small', but that is not what I remember from his book. It was a library book that I read in my teens, so I no longer have it to hand, but my memory of it is that his conclusion was that it was quite possible the Earth had been visited by aliens once during the time that humans have been on Earth, in other words once during the last 50,000 years or so. This was admittedly at one end of the range of possibilities, the other end being just one visit tens or hundreds of millions of years ago. However a reasonable possibility is just that, even if it is at the extreme end of the range of possibilities.

I will admit that his conclusion made me rather happy. There being a tiny possibility of aliens having found the Earth leaves it open for my very logical mind to continue to hold on to this idea. There is also the thought, that Sagan did not consider, that should interstellar visitors have found the Earth at any time in the last 5 million or so years, they would have noticed early varieties of hominin and might have been able to guess from their own evolutionary history that Earth was in the early stages of evolving a technologically capable species. They could have beamed this information back to their home planet so that Earth could be put on the list of places for a future expedition to visit. There is no fundamental reason why a species that has gained interstellar technological capability should not survive for millions of years. And if the moral imperative that was driving their civilisation was a desire to spread intelligent life throughout the universe, it would make a lot of sense to create a target list of planets where home species might benefit from a push towards civilisation at the right time, when a species that had evolved on the planet was ready for this.

Some people who speculate about aliens visiting Earth propose that they visit regularly in flying saucers. Though various manifestations in the sky have been interpreted as flying saucers and things like ball lightening and crop marks make for fascinating reading, I will leave those to another book. We are talking here about a visit where aliens came, stayed and walked on the Earth. No doubt the 'thought police' exerted some pressure on Carl Sagan so that he reduced his estimates as it became more unpopular for scientists to take UFOs at all seriously. But given that astronomers vary by a factor of 4 in their estimates of the number of stars in the Milky Way, which is almost half an order of magnitude disagreement between them, then I think it is quite in order for us to believe that aliens from another planet just might have visited Earth during our prehistory.

There is a possibility, so our story can continue!

Long lives.

There is more discussion later in the book about just how possible lives considerably longer than current human life spans are, so I am only going to touch on it briefly here. Three-score years and ten has been the guideline for the length of human life for a long time, barring accidents and illness. In centuries gone by average life-span was considerably less than this as many died young, though a few people lived into their 90s. When I was young living to 100 was remarkable, to the extent that everyone in the UK who lived to 100 would get a congratulatory telegram from the Queen. It is no longer remarkable; many more people are now living considerably beyond

100 years. The oldest person in the UK is 112 and was recently on the TV news, as she has just had a hip replacement to keep her mobile for some more years. I guess she must still be reasonably healthy and fit for the doctors to have agreed she could handle the bodily stress of an operation.

These however are small extensions to life. I would like you to imagine beings that lived so long compared to human lives that in human eyes they appeared immortal. I suggest to you that any being that was alive when your great, great grandparents were alive would fall into this category. However with each generation being 20 years or less when there were no contraception methods, this probably only amounts to 150 years. If a being lived for some hundreds of years it would certainly be considered immortal, as the time when it was born and was young would be lost in the mists of time. It is only since we have had written records that we have been able to grapple with such long periods of time and work out clearly how long ago things happened.

We must also bear in mind the strides being made in genetics. Our understanding of genetics is only a few decades old. It is impossible to predict what life extension genetic manipulation and genetic cures may make possible by the end of this century. It may be a joke to suggest that the first person to live forever has already been born, but maybe not. There is a lot of work now going on to understand ageing processes and to discover how the cells in the body can be made to regenerate.

We can't say how likely really long lives are, just that it is looking more and more likely as our understanding of the body and genetics grows. For the purposes of reading this book, I would like you to imagine that the alien beings that arrived on Earth had a life-span of at least 1000 years. That may stretch your credulity but I believe it is imaginable.

The North and South Poles being in different places.

Of my three initial ideas this one, though it may sound the most unbelievable to you, is actually a very viable theory. Albert Einstein considered that the theory behind this is worthy of serious investigation. The theory was produced in the 1950s by Charles Hapgood. He wrote about it in detail in his book "The path of the Poles".

One of the main problematic facts that Hapgood's theory provides an explanation for is how areas at the Equator have rock structures that show they were glaciated in the past, while areas close to and even at the poles have rocks that could only have been created by tropical seas and tropical vegetation.

The current theory of 'ice ages' states that ice cover at the poles has varied over millennia. At some times there was much reduced ice at the poles and at other times the glaciation extended much further towards the Equator. The geologists do know with some certainty that the temperature of the Earth has varied considerably over the millions of years during which the rock strata we see have been created. You might imagine that it was when the Earth was cold that ice ages happened and that when it was warm they declined. However this may not be true. To create glaciers you need snow and that needs lots of water in the atmosphere, which comes from evaporation from the oceans. And this happens more when the Earth's temperature rises. I think it would be best to describe geologists' current understanding of glaciation and 'ice ages' as confused. They would certainly agree that there is no solid consensus. Except that they all agree that the poles have always had some ice and the Equator has never been frozen and glaciated. So how can it be explained that the rocks show otherwise, rocks now at the Equator were covered in glaciers and rocks now at the South Pole could only have been formed in a tropical climate.

Geologists do have the theory of continental drift which moves the continents, but this is far too slow to explain the different layers of rock built up at the Equator and poles. So it cannot be the explanation for how the rocks that undeniably exist came to be formed. They presumably allow this contradiction to persist in their theories because they don't like the idea of Earth crust displacement, though some geologists have suggested, like Hapgood, that displacement of the crust might be a possible explanation of what the rocks show.

Hapgood proposed that the crust of the Earth can move over the internal core of the Earth. I will discuss this at some length at the appropriate point of our story. For the moment let it suffice to realise that this would be a very much faster process than continental drift. Hapgood marshaled a considerable amount of indisputable evidence in support of his theory. Though this has yet to convince geologists the theory appears to me to be quite viable. Read his book and make your own mind up if you don't want to take my word for it.

So of my three 'unbelievable ideas', one is just possible according to a reputable scientific calculation, one is looking more and more possible as we learn more about genetics, and one is based on a well worked-out theory that Einstein considered worthy of exploration. I think we can therefore proceed to create a scenario on the basis of these three ideas, with at least a chance that the ideas might have some truth behind them, and hence that the scenario we create just might be true.

How many aliens might have come to Earth?

It is time to get into the scenario, to exercise our imaginations and to apply some logic.

Imagine that some aliens – intelligent and very capable creatures of some kind - arrive at the Earth, somehow, from somewhere. Let's not worry about where they have come from or, for the moment, what kind of creatures they are. The only thing we need to note at this stage is that they must be pretty clever and technologically advanced to have achieved what we haven't yet, at least inter-planetary travel, probably inter-star travel, or even inter-galaxy travel. It will help to think about what kinds of people we would send on such a trip if we did have the capability. We would send our more intelligent and fit 'alpha' human beings. We would select them to have a range of knowledge and skills so that between them they could manage all the demands of the expedition, including any novel demands that could not be predicted from afar. If the intention is to set up home at their destination and stay for a long time, the group will be both male and female and large enough to be able to satisfactorily produce progeny, to continue the society when the older members die.

There will be a reason of some kind why they have come to the Earth, but let's also leave proper discussion of this on the side until later. We are going to take this story step-by-step and make logical deductions about what would happen at each stage. These will be based on what we know about the Earth, with a little speculation thrown in from some of those uncomfortable questions and facts scientists tend to ignore.

We will assume that it was a limited number of these beings that arrived, a group. You can decide for yourself how big a group. If it had been a mass invasion of aliens come to take over the Earth entirely for their own ends, human history would probably not have played out as it has. The aliens would probably still be here controlling us as slaves, or they might have hunted us to extinction. The group that arrived might be anywhere between say four as an absolute minimum up to over a thousand. The number will make a difference to how the story develops and just to make our thinking more tangible I am going to guess that the group is more than twenty and less than fifty. We know from the amount of knowledge that we currently have that to understand all that needs to be understood for survival in new places, to the depth of knowledge necessary, a team is needed. Having a doctor and a dentist is a good idea, someone technical who can keep the spaceship going, someone who understands how to grow food, someone good at exploring and so on. At least twenty in the group allows me to assume that any knowledge or skill needed by the group is available. Within the limits of the knowledge of their civilisation they will be able to do anything they need to. The Pilgrim Fathers who boarded the Mayflower to colonise America were a group of around 100. Our more technologically advanced group will have access to huge amounts of information. A smaller group than the Mayflower group they could have a sufficient range of skills to survive and be a big enough group to be able to breed sustainably,

I have set 50 as an upper limit as I am assuming they arrived in some kind of spaceship, rather than by matter transport or wormhole travel, which goes rather beyond the technological level of aliens I am attempting to consider here. It is possible to imagine a spaceship holding hundreds, just as we can pack hundreds into ocean liners, but given that the spaceship would also have to give space to food production and whatever leisure and work activities the aliens engaged in while traveling, and storage for all that they wanted to bring with them, 50 sounds about reasonable to me as a maximum. It is enough for diversity but not too many to make the group unmanageable. Fifty is about the maximum number of people that can be sensibly gathered in one room for discussions. The politics of groups and how to keep harmony and a common direction of effort will have been one of the big considerations in the decision on how many people, and which people, were chosen for the expedition.

So that we are not distracted by the term 'aliens' and all the imagery and baggage that term brings, I am going to refer to this group as our Adventurers. Whether pure adventurers, a scientific expedition, some kind of missionaries or a group sent by some power to manage development of the Earth, their journey to Earth would certainly be an adventure.

****

Chapter 2 - Arrival of the gods.

The spaceship that our Adventurers have arrived in must have been able to sustain them in the near vacuum of space and the thin upper atmosphere of Earth. The craft may be a flying saucer of other-worldly design, but will still be understandable as a craft of physical form, made of something strong and containing the tools, drives and other equipment necessary to make it work. Picture it as you wish and then imagine yourself inside it with our Adventurers, circling the Earth. Imagine what you and they see and what you will all be thinking.

A craft with physical form will need to take some notice of physics. It might take advantage of physics we as yet know nothing about, such as anti-gravity - there are some 'uncomfortable facts' available to us that suggest this might be possible - but to move the craft will take energy of some kind even if the force of gravity has been removed. And an anti-gravity machine would presumably need some energy to power it. It's always good to avoid wasting energy, so probably our Adventurers' first reaction on arrival at the Earth will be to park. It's actually pretty easy to park around Earth. Just get the craft to the same place that our geo-stationary satellites occupy and they can then sit there using no energy, having a look down at their potential new home. With a tiny bit of energy just to get moving a bit faster than the Earth rotates, they can make their parking slot slowly orbit the Earth so they can get a really good look at all parts of the Earth. What will they see with their eyes and their sensors?

The reason our Adventurers came will dictate what they look for to some extent, but this will not be the over-riding consideration. The first step will be to check that the Earth is habitable for them, and stable enough to provide a home. They will need to assess dangers and food sources. Only once these are satisfactorily settled will they be able to concentrate on things that will make achievement of their aims easier.

What will our Adventurers be thinking on arrival at Earth?

You may have noticed that in introducing this story I am starting to make some deductions that take us beyond our starting assumption of 'alien creatures of some kind'. I am also indulging in some anthropomorphism, assuming our Adventurers are a bit like us, have eyes and would like to have a good look before landing on the Earth. I am going on to assume that they have similar basic needs to us, of food, shelter and society. I have also assumed intelligence that is not unlike our own, even if more advanced. Unless I do this the book will just be a piece of science fiction. We are going to be reasoning logically, in other words using human logic, thinking about what we would do in similar circumstances. So we may as well assume our Adventurers will do things somewhat similarly to what we would do in a similar situation, even if they do have green skin and purple eyes.

One of my starting assumptions is that they are creatures with long lives, maybe very long lives. This assumption fits well with them being intelligent and very capable. Development of high levels of knowledge and skill takes a long time, requiring a long childhood and years of study before they become fully qualified adult workers. The time human beings spend being educated has grown substantially over the last century and we are now starting to worry that by having people retire in their 60s we are losing a lot of skills and knowledge that older people have acquired.

I like the assumption of very long lives because it implies that our Adventurers may have been able to sustain their society and their purpose over the long timescales that fascinate me – the last 100,000 years. This long life assumption also brings a perspective that may help us make more sense of what evidence we should be looking for. Some societies of people with short lives make a mess of their environment as their leaders personally have little concern about what the world will be like in two or three hundred years. As a result such societies leave huge amounts of evidence of their destruction of parts of the Earth behind them. But if you know you will still be alive in hundreds of years you are likely to be much more concerned about the impact things that are being done now will have, over long timescales.

The human race has been making a mess of the Earth for many thousands of years. There are many extinctions and environmental disasters that are the work of human beings and others that may have been our fault. Short-lived peoples, with the exception of some whose over-riding philosophy is that they are custodians of the Earth for future generations, tend not to care too much whether they improve or damage the environment for their offspring. They have short-term desires and drives. When the Europeans who had invaded North America tried to buy land off the native Americans the concept that it could be bought and owned made no sense to them. They just could not imagine that land could be owned like possessions and be bought and sold. Though they might have fought other tribes for the right to live in an area, this did not mean that they owned the land, they were simply custodians of it. Would that more of our current societies on Earth acted as custodians of the Earth rather than consumers of all it can give. Short-lived beings also tend to breed an awful lot to secure their old age and to ensure their lineage carries on. This can rapidly lead to overpopulation and more destruction of the environment. If mankind were to become extinct and eventually other intelligent creatures were to appear on Earth, they would have no trouble deducing that intelligent beings were here. We have made huge holes in the ground and have constructed objects that will survive for millennia. We are leaving behind concentrated radioactive sources that will be active for tens of thousands of years. The fact that our Adventurers have not left this kind of evidence of their presence is a key fact we must take into account and explain, and maybe long lives is part of that explanation.

We have no way of knowing if the assumption of a 1000+yr lifetime for our Adventurers is correct but I shall carry on as if it is. The main implication at this point in the story, as they circle the Earth, is that they would make a much more careful study of the Earth than human colonists did before deciding to establish themselves somewhere. The colonists' decisions were made on the basis that the place chosen was acceptable enough to be a home for a few years, had sufficient resources to support them and some things they wanted. Our Adventurers would be looking for the very best place on Earth to set up home and would be considering all aspects of support for their lifestyle over thousands of years. They would also consider their ability to explore the Earth and to gather from elsewhere on the Earth all the things they might possibly want in the future, that their chosen location did not have – the choice of home is always a compromise.

So with this mindset we will now consider what our Adventurers can see as they circle the Earth.

What can our Adventurers see?

No matter what technology our Adventurers might possess, including any technology that we do not yet know about, they will have had to take the Earth as they found it and work with it. They could change it only through processes that will work here on Earth. Major changes would either take a long time, if you created a change that had a cumulative effect (think climate change from carbon dioxide for example) or would take massive manpower which we assume our small group of Adventurers do not have (think for example about clearing large areas of forest). They would very largely have to live on the Earth as they found it, at least for the first period of their time here.

The first thing to do is to ask the basic questions. Is Earth habitable? How hot is the planet and does it have the necessary requirements for our Adventurers' form of life? I have to assume that our Adventurers are life forms that find our Earth pleasantly habitable, at least in some parts of it. Were they beings that liked to live with a sulphuric acid atmosphere at several hundred degrees they would pretty quickly have moved on, maybe to Venus. This story is about them staying, and about them possibly having lived alongside humans, so I may as well assume that they breath our kind of atmosphere and live in our kind of temperatures. This pretty much guarantees that the liquid that sustains their life form is water, as it is the only abundant liquid on Earth. NASA has done work on hypothetical types of biochemistry that you can look up on the internet. This work looks at liquids such as ammonia and methane as the solvents that could enable other kinds of lifeforms to exist, but we needn't worry about those kinds of life-form here.

For reasons that we will come to later, I am also going to assume that our Adventurers are carbon-based life forms. All animals on Earth are carbon-based so it is a reasonable assumption and it is the realms of science fiction to imagine our Adventurers being silicon-based life forms. There is huge diversity of carbon-based life-forms on Earth, so you can still speculate as wildly as you like on what our Adventurers look like and how many limbs or eyes they have. Again we needn't worry about that for the moment. However they would have had the same needs as the carbon-based animals we see around us; water, food and the ability to maintain a body temperature that enables their bodies to work and which avoids overheating.

Our Adventurers will of course see land and seas, mountains and plains, some land covered by ice but also lots of land not covered by ice, even if they have arrived in the middle of a period when there was more than usual glaciation. There is a great deal they will be able to find out about Earth before they land. They will no doubt have the sensors to be able to fully map the Earth visually, thermally and for radiation. Our satellites with cameras pointed at the Earth can take pictures down to a resolution of under half a metre (see http://hothardware.com/News/Worlds-HighestResolution-Satellite-Imagery/). It's a pretty good bet that if the military have released images from these satellites, they are probably experimenting with cameras that are able to see much more. You can however only see the top of things, so wherever there is forest cover you can't see what is on the ground. Before mankind got going on changing the Earth, particularly by grazing sheep and other livestock over wide areas, there was a lot more forest than there is now. Our Adventurers will also be able to map terrain, even terrain under forest using radar, and they will soon have a 3D map.

They will be able to see some animals, at least down to the size of the pre-cursors of modern sheep and goats. Large herds will be visible as well as large individual animals. A big difference compared to the animals you can see now from space would be the megafauna, very large animals in very large herds. The best known is the woolly mammoth but there were also large numbers of woolly rhinoceros and musk ox in Eurasia and bison in Siberia It is quite likely that hominins (precursors of mankind and early forms of human) played a rather big part in the extinction of large animals, alongside climate change and maybe that little episode of flooding there are so many myths about. We know from fossils that there were many very large animals alive 100,000 years ago.

It was not just humans that aided the extinction of megafauna, there is good evidence that neanderthals were successfully hunting woolly mammoths. But through into modern times we can see the effects of humans on the bison in America, with the remaining herds now being a fraction of the size they were when Europeans first arrived in America. Large herds of megafauna would certainly have existed in the natural tundra areas of the Earth, but large herds would also have played a big part in keeping areas clear of trees in the more forested parts, by trampling young trees and foraging on them. This behaviour may have allowed our Adventurers to see larger animals in dense forest and jungle areas, as they would have created paths and clearings as elephants do today in Burma.

Whether or not they could see early pre-cursors of human beings would depend on whether these beings were spending some time on open plains rather than living in the forest. It is thought that homo-erectus existed from about 1.8 million years ago. Evolutionary biologists theorise that apes coming out of the forest and existing on plains was either a cause or a benefit of the upright stance that gives homo-erectus its name. As we know from their stone tools that these human pre-cursors were hunting large animals, they would certainly have been out in the open when engaged in this. The opposing theory, that our upright stance was caused by wading in water would place hominins on the coast and river edges, where again they would have been visible.

Our Adventurers will be able to infer from the diversity of landscape and animals they can see that there is a well developed flora and fauna that make the Earth an interesting place to explore. They will also deduce that exploration and setting up home will need to be done carefully as there are potential dangers from the flora and fauna. If a group of homo-erectus or neanderthals can trap and kill a woolly mammoth through cooperative action, they might be capable of creating some nasty surprises for our Adventurers.

While doing this mapping our Adventurers will of course also notice the weather, which is important. An otherwise very pleasant land might be an impossible place to live if there are regular large storms. They will notice the tides and how storms and tides interact. They will plot the weather systems and soon understand why some areas are desert and others have lush vegetation. Human beings who set off in ships to colonise parts of the Earth had far less information to inform their decisions of where to go. Our Adventurers will not want to make the mistakes that many human colonisers did and land themselves in hostile environments, such as some did in Panama (they didn't survive long!). Our Adventurers' planning of where to land will have been meticulous.

Their view of where to settle will also be informed by investigations of how stable a planet the Earth is. It is reasonable to assume that having come from their own planet that they have good geological insight. Mechanisms like continental drift and plate tectonics will be well known to them, as will the propensity for active volcanoes to occur around the plate edges. They will probably have good understanding of how planetary temperatures relate to ice formation and weather systems. There are mechanisms at work on Earth that we still imperfectly understand, as witnessed by all the arguments around climate change. These include interactions with wind and water currents that alter the climate that might be expected just by looking at latitude. For example, the climate of Western Europe, particularly Great Britain and coastal areas, is so much more balmy and warm than the latitude of these areas might suggest partially because of the Gulf Stream. We are only now beginning to worry that global warming might disrupt this. The water near the North Pole is warming and is not sinking as strongly as it did in the past, and hence might not drive the Gulf Stream so strongly in the future. However there is also research that suggests the Gulf Stream is not the major cause of Western Europe being warmer than the East coast of the USA and that a bigger cause is the position of the Rocky Mountains and what happens to air-flow as the Earth rotates. We have much to learn that our Adventurers may have been able to work out.

In any event global weather and climate is not as constant as we like to assume. The 1920s and 30s were a particularly balmy period in Britain. The rich built swimming pools in their gardens, drove around in convertible cars, and fitted external plumbing to houses without fear that it would freeze up. Yet only 70 years or so earlier the river Thames had frozen over, during the 'little ice age' of Victorian times. As I am assuming our Adventurers have very long lives they will want to be sure that the place they locate themselves will have as much stability of climate as they can arrange and will remain at a habitable temperature through these variations over time.

When did our Adventurers arrive?

To understand what our Adventurers are looking at, while we consider their possible thinking and conclusions, I will have to postulate when they arrived. If we were to go back hundreds of millions of years this would affect things like how far Africa and America had been pushed apart by the formation of the mid-Atlantic ridge. Over the past tens of millions of years it would dictate whether the earth is heavily glaciated and hence what height sea level is and how much ice cover there was. We are assuming that they arrived some time in the last million years, so we don't have to imagine a world too different from the map we now see as regards the placing of the landmasses relative to each other.

But there will be differences in ice cover. The last million years is part of the pleistocene era, during which ice cover grew and retreated a few times. The current 'ice age' of considerable glaciation is reckoned to have been going on for the last two and a half million years, with several interglacial periods. We are currently in an interglacial period with the ice having been melting and retreating between about 20,000 years ago and 11,000 years ago, since when it has been stable up to the recent global warming and further reduction in glaciation. As I have taken the history of the last 100,000 years as the subtitle of the book, we may as well look at what our Adventurers would see 100,000 years ago, in order to consider where they might have established home.

You will find it useful to lay your hands on a world atlas before reading much further, and if you can a globe, ideally a globe that you can remove from its mountings so you can look at it from any direction with ease. I hope you will find it interesting to think through for yourselves what decisions you would make if you were in the Adventurers' position, looking at the Earth. One of my key starting assumptions, which we are about to discuss, is the 'unbelievable idea' that the North and South Poles may have been in different positions when they arrived. An atlas or globe will help you consider what the implications of that could have been, as well as giving you more insight into world geography from the perspectives I will suggest.

During the Pleistocene era the extent of ice coverage varied. It is thought that at its maximum ice covered maybe 30% of the Earth's surface, at other times less than that but still with considerable ice coverage at the poles. The ice sheets tied up huge volumes of water in the ice, causing sea level to drop by as much as 100m (approx 300 ft) from current levels. If you use your atlas to look at the depth of seas you will see that it is possible that the North Sea, Adriatic Sea, Baltic Sea, Yellow Sea, East and South China Seas, Persian Gulf and significant sea areas around India were in large measure dry land. Coastlines would have looked quite a lot different.

If you look at where most modern cities are the majority are less than 100m above the current sea level. Low and level land by the sea is the most productive land and it is possible to take advantage of marine food sources in addition to land food sources. It is very likely that human beings and earlier forms of hominin occupied these lands, that were then exposed but which are now covered by sea. As so much water is locked up in ice at a glacial maximum, there is also less rainfall, so the interior of continents could be considerably drier. This is another reason hominins may have preferred to live near coasts. Our Adventurers no doubt understood that sea levels can rise and fall quite considerably as ice coverage varies and hence would avoid coastal sites where this would be a problem.

It is also possible that the heights of land above the sea might differ for reasons other than sea level rise from the melting of ice. We know land height changes slowly, for example in the way that Great Britain is slowly rising in the North now that it is no longer covered by thousands of feet of ice. The North is rebounding and this is making the South of Great Britain sink, which has created the Solent where once there were just river valleys reaching the sea to the south of the Isle of Wight. The height of land might also change rapidly. Earthquakes can cause uplift of several metres. Some people have proposed that the Earth has cataclysmic periods where uplift of land and mountain building could have been much greater and faster. If you want to look at this an Internet search on 'cataclysmic geology' will bring you lots of links to follow up.

There is however one cataclysmic change to the Earth's surface that we are going to consider now. The one that Einstein thought worthy of investigation.

Earth Crust Displacement – could it happen?

Earth crust displacement (ECD) is an idea, written about in depth by Charles Hapgood in his book 'The Path of the Pole', first published in 1958. ECD is also discussed more simply in Rand Flem-Ath's recent book 'Atlantis beneath the ice' with specific reference to Antarctica and Atlantis. The idea is that the whole crust of the Earth might be able to slip over the interior of the Earth.

'The Path of the Pole' has now been reprinted and can be bought. It is well worth a read if you want to look at the wide range of evidence that ECD can happen. This is a controversial theory that you won't find quoted in standard geology text-books, despite the fact that numerous geologists over the last 100 years and more have suggested ECD as a possible explanation of geological features of the Earth that they cannot otherwise explain. The Wikipedia entry very cautiously talks about this theory by Hapgood as "….if true, (this) would require major revisions to the history of exploration, settlement, evolution, and technological advancements of the time.". This very cautious wording makes clear the reasons why the scientific community has not investigated ECD in any deep way.

The several geologists who have in the past considered ECD have done so to explain how glaciers could have existed in India and Africa, areas which are now close to the Equator. The evidence for glaciation in these areas is clear and given that the Equator has never been frozen, these are hard to explain. It is extremely well established that areas of the Earth have over millions of years been in different climatic zones of the Earth. Coal can only form where lush vegetation can grow, yet coal is now found near the poles. Rock with fossils of creatures that can only live in tropical seas has been found near the South Pole.

The only theory that Geologists generally accept to explain how continents can have been in these different climatic zones is continental drift. But this is completely inadequate to explain the many movements of continents between being at the poles, at the Equator, and at positions in between, that are required to explain how the layers of rock that we find in the Earth were formed. Einstein is on record as saying that he considered the idea of Earth crust displacement worthy of exploration, and indeed wrote a foreword for Hapgood's book. The probable reason for the majority of geologists being unwilling to accept this idea of Earth crust displacement is that it is very scary and would (will?) cause a major revision of current theories in geology. It proposes a feature of the Earth that could happen again at any time, which would cause havoc with our civilisations if it happened anything more than extremely slowly. And there is some evidence that it might be able to happen really rather fast.

We don't know a great deal about how the interior of the Earth operates. Geologists are fairly sure that the rocky crust of the Earth is 5km-10km thick under the oceans and 30km-50km thick under the continental shelves. And we know that the layer below the crust is molten lava, because it sometimes escapes through volcanoes. The mantle underlying the crust is made of rock that is denser than that of the oceanic and continental crust, so the crust is actually floating on the mantle. The theory of continental drift states that the continental plates move slowly over the mantle and that magma rises in the mid Atlantic and creates new ocean floor, pushing the Americas away from Africa. Hapgood has a rather different explanation for the volcanism in the mid-Atlantic ridge, which is part of his evidence base for ECD. We do know that the Pacific crust is being pushed down under the west coast of America, causing an earthquake zone particularly in California. Suggesting that ECD happens does not deny the theory of tectonic plates and continental drift, it just brings another factor into play that could move the continents to different climatic zones, possibly much faster than continental drift acts.

We know a bit about the inside of the Earth deeper down, but not a lot. Deep inside the Earth the pressure is immense so no matter what the Earth is composed of at that depth, we are pretty sure it will be solid in the centre due to the pressure. Between the core and the outer layers there are theories that the rock may be molten, but a lot more viscous than the mantle below the crust, again. Some geologists consider that there are very slow convection currents in this viscous material, that might drive continental drift, but we really don't know. We do know the mantle under the crust can quickly become molten when a volcanic eruption reduces the pressure.

I should also mention the Earth's magnetic field. We know a bit about this, though we don't know what causes it. Magnetic North, the point at which the Earth's magnetic field lines converge back into the Earth is not precisely at the true North Pole, which is the centre of the axis of rotation of the Earth. Magnetic North wanders about over time. If you look at the bottom of a UK Ordnance Survey map you will find directions for calculating how many degrees off true North a compass will point (relative to when the map was printed). The magnetic North Pole is currently moving by around 40 miles a year (see http://news.nationalgeographic.co.uk/news/2009/12/091224-north-pole-magnetic-russia-earth-core/), faster than it has ever moved since it has been tracked, so you can't trust the calculations suggested by old maps to know precisely where Magnetic North now is. As there is no agreement as to how the Earth's magnetic field is created there is also no understanding of why it moves. The point of mentioning the magnetic field is that Hapgood uses evidence of the past magnetic field of the Earth, that is captured in rocks as they form, to support his theory. Because the angle that the field dips down into the Earth varies from horizontal at the Equator to vertically down into the Earth at the poles, you can tell how close to the pole the rock was when it formed.

A second area of evidence that the crust may have moved relatively recently, that Hapgood uses, comes from ocean core samples. The sediments on the ocean floor vary depending on ocean temperature and whether that part of the ocean was close to glaciers or river mouths at the time. The sediments also include fossils of the creatures and plants that lived in the sea, or on land that became submerged under the sea, at the time. Again these vary depending on latitude and temperature. Sediment cores can be drilled that show how the sediments have changed over thousands of years. This, combined with the evidence from magnetism, enabled Hapgood to propose several pole-shifts and positions for the poles over the last 100,000 years.

The third set of facts that might be evidence of ECD depend on whether you believe what is there to be seen. This is the existence of very ancient world maps that have been pretty conclusively shown to depict the coast of Antarctica - without ice. The current Antarctic ice sheet extends many miles into the sea beyond the actual rock coast, so the shape that you see from the sea or air today is different to the real coastline. This is particularly so of the area of Antarctica closest to South America, where a long peninsula sticks out some 1200km from the roughly round shape of the Antarctic continent. The experts who have looked at the maps include the US Air Force cartography section which one has to assume is expert at mapping. If they and others who have studied the maps are right, either this part of the Antarctic coast was clear of ice at a time when sufficiently competent people where around to map it, or some people alive before historical times from which we have records could peer through the ice with sensors. Or the maps show somewhere else and we are all deluded in thinking they might show Antarctica, which is the usual line taken by people who don't want to believe they do show Antarctica. These ancient maps, such as the Piri Reis map, were explored by Charles Hapgood alongside his investigation into geomagnetism in rocks and were a key stimulus for his work. He wrote about this in his book "Maps of the Ancient Sea Kings".

To understand how and why ECD may happen we need to consider the physics of the Earth as a whole. If you want to get an idea how complex and anti-intuitive this might be, have a play with a gyroscope. You can easily find gyroscope videos on YouTube showing you what they can do. However it is much more fun to play with one because the force with which a gyroscope resists having its orientation changed is quite remarkable; it defies what your intuition tells you should happen. The Earth is of course a gyroscope. You might not think it is spinning fast enough but try a little maths. The Earth's diameter is 12742 Km, so its circumference, 2π x radius is 40,035 Km. Each spot on the circumference at the Equator takes 24 hours to complete a revolution, so each spot is moving at 1668 Km/hr. For comparison, if you have a gyroscope with a diameter of 5cm, circumference 15.71cm, if a spot on the circumference was to travel at the same speed as a spot on the surface of the Earth the gyroscope would have to spin rather fast. 1668 Km/hr is 166.8 million cm/hr. This is 2.78 million cm/minute. Divide this by the circumference of the gyroscope and we get a revolution speed of 176,957 revs per minute! Gyroscopes, even those used in navigation instruments, do not spin anything like as fast as this.

As well as the Earth's surface moving a great deal faster than a toy gyroscope the Earth is a solid sphere and very heavy. What this means is that the Earth has a very large angular momentum. I'll leave you to explore how angular momentum is measured if you want to, suffice it to say that it is the size of the angular momentum of an object which dictates how big the gyroscopic forces are. The 'bottom line' of this discussion is that the Earth's gyroscopic forces are very large. The force needed to change the direction of the Earth's spinning axis is immense and any such force applied to the Earth would probably cause it to break into bits. Any change in the Earth's axis of spin could only happen extremely slowly over immense periods of time. Change in the axis of spin cannot be an explanation for why the positions of the poles relative to the continents change and hence why ice caps have appeared in places which are not now at either of the poles. The poles, being the points on the spin axis of the Earth, do not change. The question is whether the crust moves over these pole points.

If a very large force were applied to the crust, as the core of the Earth is essentially an immoveable object which will fiercely resist any change to the way it rotates, the force would have to be dissipated in some way other than changing the axis of rotation. Possible ways the energy this force imparts could be dissipated are as heat, ejection of large amounts of material from the Earth into the atmosphere, or the force could accelerate the crust and make it move over the core of the Earth.

There are two possible candidates for what could apply a large force to the crust:

1. An imbalance of mass on the surface of the Earth, caused by changes in the weight of the crust at different places on the Earth's surface, causing a gyroscopic force. Practically this could mean changes in the distribution of glaciers, this being a relatively quick way for weight distribution on the crust to be changed. Mountain-building processes with the crust being pushed up or allowed to sink lower by changes in the mantle under the crust could also affect this, but the consensus of most geologists is that these are slow changes. Hapgood discusses mountain building in his book and his views differ from those of most geologists.

2. An asteroid or comet crashing into the earth.

In any movement of the crust, just as for the movement of any object over the underlying surface, the force needed to get something moving is greater than the force needed to keep it moving. An imbalance of mass on the Earth might build up considerably beyond what is necessary to create the force needed to keep the crust moving, overcoming sliding friction, but not cause slip until the force became large enough to overcome the initial friction. So when it did slip it might accelerate relatively quickly initially. Once the crust started moving, immense heat would be generated where it slips over the underlying mantle, which would tend to melt this, reducing the friction opposing the slippage.

And there is of course the option to imagine that both causes of a force on the crust might happen together.

Scientifically we need to understand not only how movement of the crust might be started, but how the force of the moving crust is then resisted and the kinetic energy of the moving crust absorbed into the Earth, slowing and stopping it, to leave the poles in a new position. The Earth is not in fact a perfect sphere. It is oblate with the diameter across the Equator being greater than the diameter from pole to pole, by about 25 miles. It bulges at the Equator because of the centrifugal force of rotation counteracting the gravitational forces that otherwise would make the Earth completely spherical. If there was a larger than usual mass on the Earth's crust at higher latitudes (nearer the poles) the centrifugal force would tend to push this mass towards the Equator.

If the crust that runs round the shorter pole to pole circumference of the Earth was slid round to be on the Equator, it would have to stretch by 25 miles. It would split at one or more places and lava would come flowing out. Hapgood sees strong evidence for this in the way that the cracks in the Atlantic floor have happened. Crust moving from the Equator circumference to the poles would do the converse, it would need to be compressed to occupy less distance. You may think rock is pretty strong and hard to split or fold but it is not. Rock is very strong when you try to compress it, but really pretty weak when you apply a pulling or stretching force or bend it. Note this thought for reference later in this book.

Both these effects, stretching and compressing rock, would tend to resist the slipping of the crust, slowing it. Then, if the unbalanced mass on the crust reached the Equator, if it went beyond the Equator the gyroscopic forces would reverse and push against the moving crust, further slowing it down until it stopped.

We don't know the answers as to what is going on inside the Earth but there does not seem to be any physical impossibility to the idea that the Earth's crust can slide over the interior core of the Earth in certain extreme circumstances. The physical processes Hapgood proposes all make perfect sense, the only unknown being just how molten and fluid the rock below the crust is, and hence just how much force would be necessary to start the crust moving. Overall I feel it is quite permissible and reasonable to conjecture that the Earth's crust can and does occasionally slip.

Earth Crust Displacement – how would this make the Earth different?

In this chapter we are considering what our Adventurers are looking down on, if they arrived before the poles of the Earth came to their current positions on the Earth's crust. From this point of view the major difference to how the Earth looks now would be where ice cover was and on the climate of different areas of the Earth.

Hapgood reckoned there were three displacements of the poles in the last 100,000 years with the most recent shift ending around 12,000 years ago. Prior to this Hapgood reckons the North Pole was in the Hudson Bay area of Canada and the South Pole was on the edge of Antarctica towards Australia. The current received wisdom is that research on the ice sheets of Antarctica has completely discredited the theory. However while I can find research that clearly indicates that the half of Antarctica opposite to the Antarctic peninsula has been covered by ice for millions of years, I have yet to find any conclusive research that proves the Antarctic Peninsula was similarly ice-covered 100,000 years ago.

The ECD theory could also provide some insight into other troubling facts, such as those frozen mammoths in Siberia. Just how did they come to be deep frozen while still chewing vegetation that could not have been growing if Siberia was then as cold as it is now? Was Siberia suddenly moved from warmer climes into frozen climes, accompanied by incredibly severe weather conditions that completely covered the mammoths in snow, never to be revealed again until dug up more than 10,000 years later?

We will return later to the impact of an Earth crust displacement and another possible source of evidence of what happened 12,000 years ago. For now all we need to realise is that if Hapgood's view is true, our Adventurers would have seen at least part of Antarctica free of ice and therefore as a candidate for where they might set up home.

****

Chapter 3 - Was Antarctica a potential home for our Adventurers?

Antarctica is a very big continent. It is around 5,500 km from the tip of the Antarctic peninsula to the Shackleton Shelf on the other side of the continent. This is comparable to the distance from the north of Greenland to Florida.

If the poles were in a different place, some 2000km from where they now are, this also would have meant that there was much more land at the North Pole. Any movement of the pole of this magnitude would move it out of the Arctic ocean to a point on land. Hapgood's view is that the North Pole was then positioned over Canada. More land at a pole means a greater depth of ice – compare the depth of the ice-sheet at the South Pole to that at the North. At the North Pole, in its current position, ocean currents can keep the pole area a bit warmer. However the fact that the ice is floating on water is the main reason for there being less ice, as this stops it building up to the several kilometre depths found in ice sheets on land.

It is worthy of notice while discussing ice cover on the Earth that there is currently a big ice cap on Greenland but not on parts of Northern Europe that are at higher latitudes and closer to the North Pole than Greenland. How is it that the European ice sheets melted at the end of the last glacial maximum but the Greenland ice sheet did not? Or were these northern latitudes of Europe not covered by ice to the extent that Greenland was and is?

It is known that ice cover prior to 20,000 years ago was very extensive over Canada, the northern part of the USA and some parts of Northern Europe. Try as a thought exercise, or practically if you have a globe or atlas to hand, taking the size of the Antarctic ice sheet and mapping it over the northern hemisphere, centred at the current North Pole. You will find that it covers the northern part of Canada, down to the southernmost point of the Greenland ice cap, most of Norway, Sweden and Finland and all of Siberia. The rest of Russia including Moscow and Leningrad and all of the rest of Europe would be clear of ice.

However, during the last period of glaciation up to 20,000 years ago this is not what the ice coverage was. Most of Siberia was clear of ice but the whole of Canada and the USA down to New York and Chicago were covered by the Laurentide ice sheet, which extended right across the USA and joined up with the ice sheet over the Rocky Mountains. Over in Europe the whole of Britain, Scandinavia and the northern part of Western Europe were ice-covered, including the northern part of Russia, but as already mentioned, not Siberia. This area is comparable to the size of the current Antarctic ice sheet and you will find that the centre of this ice sheet was somewhere around the Baffin Bay area! The ice cover in the last ice age, up to around 20,000 years ago, rather suggests to me that the North Pole at this time might have been a couple of thousand miles from where it is now.

At the South Pole, if the centre of the ice cover were moved a similar distance to the North Pole moving to Baffin Bay, the South Pole will be seen to be on the coast of Antarctica opposite to the Antarctic peninsula. Most of Antarctica would be still covered with ice, but Alexander Land protrudes a very long way from the main bulk of Antarctica. A way to think about this relative to the current world is that the tip of Alexander land might have had a climate comparable to living in Florida or the South of France, even though the area from the current South Pole to the side of Antarctica opposite to Alexander Land could still be covered with an ice sheet. Antarctica is a very big continent.

Where to land and make home?

To recap, 100,000 years ago, the time when we are imagining our Adventurers arriving, was a time of extensive glaciation and much lower sea-level. The view of the world that our Adventurers would see would be a main interconnected land-mass and a couple of island continents. The interconnected land mass is essentially all the land on the Earth except for Australia, Antarctica and the various small islands that exist. The Americas would have been connected to Siberia as the Bering Straight would be a land area, which is known to people who study how the world looked in this period as Beringia. Siberia is joined to Asia which of course joins onto Europe. This is all connected south to China and New Guinea and connected south west to Africa.

Australia would probably still be a separate continent but might not have been – the Torres Strait is less than 200 metres deep. Even if it was separate there would only be a small amount of sea between Australia and New Guinea with such a low sea level. We do know that the ancestors of the

Australian Aborigines arrived there probably 40,000 years ago, so human beings did manage to cross over. Japan might be separate but maybe joined to China at it's northern end. Madagascar would still be an island but it's pretty close to Africa, so might also have been accessible to early hominins. Greenland would be under the northern ice cap.

And then there would be Antarctica, sitting in the middle of what would appear to be the world ocean. We have rather artificially split this world ocean into Atlantic, Pacific and Indian oceans. We view maps of the world from our northern hemisphere viewpoint, as countries in the northern hemisphere led the world explorations that happened in the last five centuries. The ways that we map the world and the projections we use to map a sphere onto flat pieces of paper tend to make us unaware of how big a landmass Antarctica is and how separate it is from the other land-masses of the Earth. If you have a globe you will be able to see this more clearly, particularly if you can as suggested take it off its stand and look at it equally well from any direction.

I strongly recommend to you the game of looking at maps the 'wrong' way round. Have a look at MacArthur's Universal Corrective Map of the World. Search for this online and you will find images of it. This map has Australia in the middle, at the top. It will take you some time to realise where your home country is on this map, as the world appears upside-down and transposed East to West. If you live in the UK, try looking at the map of Europe upside down. You will then see a straggling peninsular at the bottom right of Europe, that is actually an island that nearly touches mainland Europe at one point. This peninsula of Europe has a large conurbation in the way of anyone from further along this peninsula who wants to get to mainland Europe. If I want to get to Europe from my home in Northern England I can quite quickly get to London, but it then takes me hours to get through or around London. You will quickly realise from this way of looking at Europe why Great Britain is becoming marginalised in European development. As another experiment in looking at maps the wrong way round, orient a topographical map of Europe with the North Sea, the Channel and Britain at the top and Germany at the centre, and you will instantly see why Hitler completely ignored the French Maginot line in the second world war, and just attacked straight through Belgium to the coast, to the great consternation of the French who of course viewed Europe from a France-centric viewpoint.

We are prisoners of the 'usual' map projections. Our adventurers would see the world in the round, and orbiting whichever way they wished would have seen the surface without the distortions created when mapping a round object onto flat sheets of paper.

Our Adventurers, being very long-lived beings, will no doubt have taken a long-term view of where to set up home and taken their time deciding. There will have been a number of considerations guiding their thinking, which we will now work through.

Considerations on what makes a good home.

Our Adventurers, having made a full study of the Earth, would be ready to get out of the confines of their transport. The question they would have had to answer is which bit of the land on Earth will be most conducive to a safe, pleasant and long life? Our assumption that they have very long lives means they need to take a very long-term view of this. For human beings, the chance of being swept away in freak floods that only occur on average every 500 years may be a chance worth taking. Perhaps that is why we have built on so many flood plains in the UK, though one suspects the real reason is a combination of the opportunity for builders to make more money than if they built on brown-field sites and purchasers who did not take the trouble to check such things. That is until recent extreme weather and the threat of climate change started to make checking this a priority. For beings living hundreds of years things that happen rarely and those that change slowly over time such as sea level would have to be taken fully into account.

What then are the consideration that will inform the decision of where to live? All animals need the same basic things; shelter, security, water, and food - in that order if you arrive with only the clothes on your back. Intelligent beings will add to these some considerations about what they want to achieve and where they might need to travel to. We have a little experience of landing on planets. In going to the Moon and Mars shelter, food and water were taken with the astronauts to the moon and not needed by the robots on Mars, leaving only security to consider. The sites of the Moon and Mars landings were decided upon to some extent because of the investigations the teams behind them wished to carry out, though the first consideration was given to the problem of landing safely. This led these landings to be in rather boring places that were flat and without too many rocks to tumble over, or steep slopes to tumble down.

I think it is safe to assume that our Adventurers would be able to land wherever they liked, so we can consider any land mass. I am going to ignore them landing and setting up home on or under water. This would involve them continuing to live in a high-tech construction of some kind and would not allow them to take advantage so easily of the food production, availability of water and opportunities for comfortable shelters that the land areas of Earth can offer.

Though shelter and security from dangerous animals has to be the first consideration should you find yourself suddenly in a new place, technologically advanced people with tools and resources can arrange this in many different ways, even in hostile environments. So our Adventurers probably looked at the issues of water and food first, in narrowing down the options of where to set up home. They could leave working out how to achieve shelter and security as the next deciding factors. Access to water and food would be in the gift of the Earth.

Where to find good water and food.

It seems strange writing the title of this section putting water first, as we normally refer to 'food and drink'. But water is much more critical to life than food. We have, not so long ago as I write this, had the story of an Indian woman pulled out of the ruins of a collapsed factory 17 days after it collapsed. She had no food but she did have a source of water. Without it she would not have survived for more than two or three days.

Drinking water can be obtained three ways, by removing the salt from seawater, by catching rain, or by getting water as it flows to the sea, rain having fallen somewhere else. Distilling or de-ionising seawater takes energy, either the energy of the sun or energy from another source, leaving you ultimately reliant on the energy source. Water from the sky depends on rainfall, which depends on which way the winds blow. These shift as a result of how the high-altitude winds like the jet-stream shift. On the Earth as it is now (rather than with poles possibly shifted by 2000km, as I am conjecturing might have been the case) Australia is sub-tropical with abundant vegetation on its East coast but it is very dry on its west coast where they have periodic droughts. The eastern side of North and South America has sub tropical well-vegetated areas in Florida and Brazil, whereas Spain and Southern France, though also at sub-tropical latitudes are a mediterranean climate with much more sparse vegetation, because they don't normally get that much rain. The jet stream usually brings most of the rain into Europe over Ireland, Britain, France and the Benelux countries, making Ireland the 'Emerald Isle' of lush green grass. Some years the jet stream moves, bringing icy winds from the North down over Britain and pushing the damp winds from the Atlantic further south.

Having access to copious amounts of water can overcome a lack of rain. In the Mediterranean the Romans took advantage of this and developed aqueducts. If your water catchment area includes mountains that have snow cover on their peaks all year round you can rely on a steady flow of water even in hot and dry Summers. Our Adventurers would surely be similarly capable of channelling water from afar if necessary, so they would be able to choose to live in an area that is sub-tropical even if the rain was not very reliable, provided they could channel water from snow-covered mountains. Living in sunshine makes one happier than living under dark clouds and in rain, so surely the best of all worlds would be a place with sufficient general rainfall for a variety of natural vegetation but plenty of sun and a secure water supply fed from the mountain snows and glaciers in high mountains. It is not surprising that property prices on the Cote d'Azur are extremely high. Lots of rich people want to live there because of its lovely climate.

As to food it is wise to have food growing close to home, even if you prefer to eat foods grown a long way away. Sometimes it may not be possible to get these. As a civilisation we have played with this in the western world, spending large amounts of time and money on bringing foods from far-off countries. Only now are people beginning to realise that adding air-miles is not very sensible. In a reasonably temperate climate it is possible to grow a very wide range of foods and there are ways to preserve foods for the winter when it is too cold for food plants to grow. The several crops a year that can be grown in tropical climates is useful if you have many mouths to feed, but our Adventurers are only a small group so this would not be an issue.

Human beings and animals have adapted to live in some of the most inhospitable areas of the Earth, where the range of food on offer is limited and hard to grow reliably. Those who live nearer the poles often live largely on fish, because plants don't grow in the long cold winters very well. Those who live in desert regions have to depend on the few animals that can live there and on the plants that have become adapted to take advantage of the water sources available. Our Adventurers would have no need to be so adaptable. They obviously have the capacity to live wherever on Earth they wish and could choose an area where growing food is easy.

So with all the choice in the world what kind of climate would you choose to live in, to have available the best food and sufficient water? Temperate climes would be a possible home but involve more dependence on root vegetables and hard fruits than you might desire. If you go instead to a sub-tropical climate you can have soft fruits and a wider variety of vegetables, but some vegetables would be plagued by pests and find the climate too hot. Go too far into tropical zones and growing plants and fruits may become harder; the plants might need irrigation, or if growing in tropical forest may need to be protected from non-food plants that would over-grow them. For my tastes in food I would prefer to be on the borderline between temperate and subtropical areas. A few hundred miles of transport could then bring me blight-free potatoes from Scotland and peppers and oranges from the Mediterranean. Or with some care these can be grown at the mid-point between the two.

In the world as it is now, there would be plenty of choices like this in both northern and southern hemispheres. Antarctica obviously would not currently be a choice. If however the poles were not in their current place, but instead were shifted by 2000 kilometres things would be different. Using my assumption that the North Pole was then in the Baffin Bay or Hudson Bay area, in the northern hemisphere Europe and Africa would stay at pretty much the same latitudes. North America would be a lot colder and covered by ice and Siberia would be warmer. There would be sub-tropical areas in middle America and in China. So there would still be lots of northern hemisphere choices.

In the southern hemisphere South America would be across the Equator and hence would be fully tropical and Australia would be much nearer the South pole and probably heavily glaciated. This leaves only the southern part of South America, the very southern part of Africa and the Antarctic peninsula as suitable temperate to sub-tropical climate choices in southern latitudes. But overall that leaves a range of options. It is time to consider whether other considerations might narrow down that range of options.

Where to find good shelter and security?

Having narrowed our choice of home down by reference to climate, food and water, we can now consider shelter and security.

With advanced technology shelter is relatively easy to arrange. It just needs a workforce to build the home of your choice and the tools and energy to get and manipulate the raw materials. Security from the weather is simply a matter of placing of your habitation and its design. I am sure we can assume our Adventurers could design their home to arrange this, having come from a society sufficiently able to design a craft to bring them here. We will have something more to say later about what kind of buildings they might have created.

As to the placing of a home, as most of us live in cities we have rather lost the art of placing a home well. Unless we are rich we just have to buy the best we can find that is affordable. I live in Calderdale in Yorkshire, an area of deep cut valleys that rise from the rivers to the moorland above. As I drive around I can see where the farmers of old chose to build their manor houses. The steep valleys are very wooded and damp, the moorland is exposed to lashing winter rain and snow. But sufficiently high above the rivers the trees thin out and there is more open space and there, a little below where the good grass turns into moorland tussock grass, you see the old farmhouses. They are usually in the lee of the sloping land below the moor, with a view, good air and protection from the worst of the weather, and sufficient hill above them to give them a regular supply of good water from their local stream.

However these kinds of considerations are relatively minor details. There is a much more important consideration that those of us who live in modern cities can pretty much ignore - security from animals. In past times this was much more important. In some countries people have traditionally built their villages on stilts planted in lakes. At first sight this seems an extraordinary length to go to, but it protects against attack by large land animals and pesky small ones. There are three kinds of problem in arranging security from other living things, little animals that nevertheless have a big impact on your life, big animals that want to hunt and eat you, and intelligent animals that may present all sorts of reasons to be a problem to you.

Little mammals and reptiles are reasons to live in temperate climes, or not far into sub-tropical climes, but definitely not in tropical climes unless you have no choice. There is huge diversity of smaller animals in tropical forest, quite a number of them are dangerous and it is hard to stop tropical forest from encroaching on your house, making it more accessible to these animals. Temperate areas suffer from plagues of small animals too, such as mice or lemmings, but these are occasional problems not full-time dangers.

Insects are a bigger problem and can make life miserable. You will find yourself plagued by the midges on the west coast of Scotland as the day gets towards dusk, and by aggressive mosquitos all day long in Summer in parts of Northern Scandinavia. Insects being cold-blooded require heat to get going, so the hotter it is the more they can be active. And the more they can breed. Having some relatively cold weather in the Winter kills insects, so they have to grow their population again the following year. But some like the Scandinavian mosquitos have rapid population explosions when it gets hot in the Summer. Being by the sea sometimes help to reduce insects as they breed on land and sea breezes blow them further inland. To minimise insect pests I would look to live relatively close to the sea in a temperate or only just sub-tropical area. I would prefer the inland areas close to my home to be more hilly or mountainous rather than flat and boggy, as many insects breed in pools.

Big animals that want to eat you are a different problem. You can of course clear areas and build fences, but these need looking after. Just as horses and sheep seem to prefer the grass on the other side of the wall or fence, most animals will explore to find ways around obstacles put in their path. A rather better solution is to find an island that you can completely clear of anything that is very dangerous, which is sufficiently separated from the mainland that the big animals are unlikely to swim across and re-establish themselves. Even with an island, tropical vegetation would make it very hard to be sure all the really dangerous animals had been killed. Temperate woodland can be hard to hunt in, but nothing like as hard as tropical forest. We can however surely assume that our Adventurers had imaging technology and night-sights and could achieve the task if it was a relatively small island. There are quite a number of good candidate islands, in the Caribbean, the Mediterranean and elsewhere in the world. However if we carry on with the possibility of moved poles, another island comes into play as a possibility, Alexander Island just off the Antarctic peninsula. This is about the same size as Ireland and hence could be cleared of big and dangerous animals without too much difficulty, given advanced techniques to lure and trap predators.

There is also another consideration about big animals, which is whether they are there in the first place. We know that expanses of sea can stop animal migrations, but short stretches of sea do not do so to anything like the same extent. Some kinds of animals may have migrated from the main land-masses of the world to Australia in the very distant past, before continental drift separated the continents. Once there was sufficient sea between New Guinea and Australia to stop animals swimming across, Australia was left to develop its land animals in complete isolation from the rest of the world and they developed very differently.

Antarctica is thought to have been part of the single world continent Pangea that existed hundreds of millions of years ago. Wikipedia reckons that Pangea started to split up about 200 million years ago. This was the Jurassic period when dinosaurs dominated the Earth. It is possible that after this split Antarctica may have remained separated from all the other continents by large areas of sea. Then when the extinction event that killed off the dinosaurs happened 65 million years ago, Antarctica could have been left with animals that developed very differently to those in the main Earth landmass, as Australia's did. And maybe without large and dangerous animals.

We have pointed out above that in the last ice-age when sea level was very low, all the Earth's main land-masses except Australia and Antarctica where connected, so animals that evolved could migrate easily. The main connection is east-west and animals could travel at the latitudes they were happiest living in. Africa and South America are the only parts of this land-mass where migration involves moving through the equatorial tropics, which was impossible for many animals. Jared Diamond's book Guns, Germs and Steel has a lot to say on this matter of what kinds of animals developed where, and the impact of this on the development of mankind.

The point to draw from this for our story, is that ridding Antarctica of any very dangerous animals might not have been necessary, or might have been a considerably easier task than on the main land masses.

Security from hominids and hominins.

Intelligent animals are a different kind of problem altogether. They might decide to try to kill you just because they don't like you. Or because they have taken a fancy to the bit of land you are occupying or to something you have that they don't. There are plenty of examples in human history to indicate that human beings are very dangerous animals indeed. To discuss this needs a section all of its own.

If our Adventurers arrived 100,000 years ago, there would have been a variety of hominids and hominins in various places on Earth. 'Hominid' is used to describe all creatures in the family of great apes. 'Hominin' is used to describe the human-like creatures, including early modern humans and all those creatures of varying intelligence that preceded or lived alongside anatomically-modern humans. Great apes have not aggressively expanded the areas in which they live to anything like the same extent as the hominins, so they would probably not have been much of a problem. Monkeys are a nuisance but not in the same class of security risk as hominins.

Mobile hunting bands of hominins would probably have been detectable during our Adventurers' initial survey of the Earth from space. The very facts of there being several species and that they were widespread on Earth would probably indicate to our Adventurers that these hominins were rather good at competing with other animals and in time might evolve some more. The techniques that animals use to protect themselves against predators tell you quite a lot about the nature of the animals. Animals that live in herds on the plains have evolved to work with the disadvantage that slower older and younger animals may fall prey to big cats or wolves and this sacrifice protects the rest of the herd for a while. The herd has to be big enough to survive this loss. Animals that live in forest survive by being able to evade predators by climbing or jumping around. Small animals burrow so as to be able to hide in places larger animals can't get to easily. Predator animals use their fighting skills to survive attacks by other similar-sized predators and their hunting skills to see and avoid larger predators they could not run from. Birds fly if they can get off the ground fast enough, and there only have to worry about flying predators.

To our Adventurers the hominins would clearly be seen to be taking a different strategy, the use of intelligence, ability to work together and weapons. They may have existed in groups but we have no evidence they lived in large herds. It appears they came out of the forest to a considerable extent, as they lost a lot of their climbing abilities as they evolved. There is no evidence that they burrowed but they certainly did make use of caves if they were available. And though their bipedalism gave them a fair turn of speed, they would not succeed in outrunning a big cat. They must have used a combination of avoiding predators and standing and fighting as a group if cornered. And not being fast enough to chase food animals they must have used their cunning to trap and injure them, so that they could close in on them and kill them. The picture that archeologists have traditionally painted of beings such as homo-erectus is that of creatures not far removed from apes but this may be a very wrong way to view them. Michael Cremo and Richard Thompson in their book Forbidden Archeology document finds that are little discussed in archeological circles, but which could take the start of sophisticated tool-making back to millions of years before the accepted dates. Beings such as homo-erectus might have been very considerably more intelligent than they are commonly imagined to be.

Our Adventurers could of course take the same strategy as as can be done with big animals to gain security; find an island and kill all of them that are on the island. However these intelligent animals are not stopped that easily. They are inquisitive and clever. Somehow hominins reached Australia, long after Australia had separated from Pangea. To do so they probably had to cross some considerable area of sea. They might have found a way to float across rather than swim. Having experienced the crossing of small channels between islands, a nice enclosed sea like the Torres Strait might pose little problem on calm days. This might then tempt them to be more adventurous and cross more open water. It would all depend of course on how evolved the hominins were, or how evolved they might have become during the time our Adventurers expected to be on Earth.

There is increasing evidence that the hominins of 100,000 years ago were a lot more capable than the experts have so far believed. Neanderthal stone tools have been found on Mediterranean islands off Greece, and possibly also on Crete. The Greek islands are only a few kilometres from the coast, but Crete is 40km from the nearest mainland, which is a distance that could not be managed by swimming, even if sea level was considerably lower and the distance a little less. If neanderthals were on Crete our Adventurers would have been able to see them there, and would know clearly that they already had seafaring capabilities.

The survey our Adventurers made of these hominins would indicate that they were widespread across the Earth. They seem to have come out of Africa and while evolving into various sub-species to have spread across Asia and Europe and down into S.E. Asia. There is argument about when human beings reached the Americas but there was no insuperable problem for them in doing so. With sea level so low due to all the ice tied up in ice sheets Asia was joined to North America. However the way may have been blocked by the North American ice sheets at the time our Adventurers arrived. The Anzick child found in Montana appears to be of a family from which all people in North and South America are descended. This discovery suggests that humans only started moving into the Americas after the last glacial maximum, when the ice started melting. However there are competing claims of evidence to show humans were there long before that, with new evidence emerging to support this claim.

From what they could see and deduce our Adventurers could speculate that should these hominins develop and build boats they would be able to cross reasonable distances of sea. There would not be many places on the Earth that these intelligent and dangerous animals could not get to. With the Earth as it appears now, with Antarctica fully covered in ice, our Adventurers would have to choose the best island in the rest of the Earth. They would need to keep a close eye on any developing capability of hominins enabling them to get across the intervening sea. Madagascar would have been quite a good choice as the sea channel from Africa is quite wide and the climate is not equatorial though it is tropical. However if the poles were in a different position and some of Antarctica was free of ice, then it would present a choice of complete separation from these dangerous hominin animals. Antarctica is separated from all the other land-masses of the Earth by around 1000 km of sea. And the sea around Tierra del Fuego, the closest other land mass, is reputed to be a very hostile sea.

Is it possible that this argument, of safety from early forms of mankind, could be the critical argument for the decision on where to live? Did our Adventurers settle in Antarctica?

Security from flood and transport considerations.

There is one remaining element of security that our Adventurers would need to be sure of, security from changing sea level. We are looking at this together with the issue of transport, as the two are intimately inter-linked.

If the politicians we have now were due to live for the next two hundred years they would be a lot keener to make effective policies on global warming. They would need to take seriously the longer term projections on the sea level rise that is resulting from it. Our Adventurers would know that sea level could change. Our researches have shown us that glaciation on the Earth changes over time, with some inter-glacial periods where lots of the ice melts and sea level rises. Our Adventurers would surely have known this too. They would have looked for a home sufficiently high to avoid being flooded by the sea any time in the next many thousand years.

They are also likely to have been aware that over long timescales there is a considerable risk of tsunamis, caused by earthquakes under the sea. The coast may be pleasant for a holiday but it is quite a dangerous place to live, particularly in areas of the world close to tectonic plate edges which are most volcanically active. Even away from these volcanically active areas there are problems. London has already had to resort to construction of a barrier on the Thames, which may need to be made even higher fairly soon, because of how tides, rising sea-level and winds interact in the North Sea. Winter storms and hurricanes regularly blow into the East coast of North America causing massive destruction and considerable flooding to coastal areas.

But there is a compromise to be considered here. Our Adventurers would have wanted to explore the Earth, maybe just to take advantage of what it offers or maybe because that was one of their main reasons in coming. No doubt they will have the capability to do this by air, but this takes fuel even if they have technology such as anti-gravity. Flight in their machines may have involved sources of energy that are not easy to come by on earth, certainly without mining or drilling. Landing places will be in short supply in any well wooded areas, which probably in these times covered a lot of the temperate zones. They would have been thinking about long-term sustainability of methods of transport, so would probably look at exploring in transport that uses sustainable energy, the sun and wind being the most favoured sources. Growing chemical energy and then releasing that energy through burning is a very messy process needing a lot of effort and trouble, as is extracting fossil fuels. By far the most comfortable way to explore, particularly if you are not pushed for time as we short-lived humans are, and can time your journey to avoid bad weather, is by sea.

If you decide on a home sufficiently high in hills or mountains to be some hundreds of feet above sea level, to avoid rising sea level, tsunamis and floods, it may quite possibly be a long way from the sea. Any journey would then need a long land journey before you could start your sea journey. To overcome this you would need to look for places in the world where mountains rise close to the sea, such as Norway or New Zealand. Or Antarctica.

There is also the matter of where you might want to get to. If you want to explore the whole Earth by sea, would you place your home somewhere in the northern hemisphere? If you did, then to get to a lot of the other parts of the northern hemisphere by sea, you have to go round all those bits of land that jut out across the Equator, particularly South America and Africa. There would have been no Suez or Panama canals to help you. If on the other hand you put yourselves somewhere in the southern hemisphere, such as the southern tips of Africa or South America, you can sail all the way round the world in a straight line. Which you could also do if the poles were not where they now are and you could set up home in Antarctica, which is right in the middle of the world ocean. Then to get to anywhere in the northern hemisphere you can just go out and back from Antarctica.

Taking the considerations of both travel and height above sea level together, our Adventurers may have looked for a home in the southern hemisphere, where the land rises quite rapidly from the sea. Antarctica, if the Antarctic peninsula was well clear of ice, would have been a good option. Antarctica is a very mountainous continent, and on the peninsula and Alexander Island, the land rises to over 1000m within a very few kilometres of the coast. Though we cannot now see all the lie of the land due to ice cover, it is surely possible that our Adventurers could have found a sufficiently high place for their habitation, sufficiently close to the sea for their exploration needs.

These issues of security from sea level rise and ease of transport, combined with the considerations of being safe and secure from the potentially troublesome hominins would to me be the final part of the argument.

From here on in this book I am going to assume that Antarctica is where our Adventurers set up home. We will return to the issue of Earth crust displacement and moving poles in a later chapter, and will introduce the fourth kind of evidence that might point towards it having happened. We will have moved forward in the story many years when I come back to discussing this, into almost historical times. But we have a lot to discuss before we get there. We need to think about what kind of lifestyle our Adventurers hope to develop and how they might have achieved it. Without a full mental picture of what our Adventurers were doing we won't know what kinds of evidence of them being here to look for.

****

Chapter 4 – Antarctica as a desirable home.

Deciding that our Adventurers set up home in Antarctica has one big downside. Since we are also assuming that Earth crust displacement has since then shifted the poles to where they are now, any evidence our Adventurers left behind in Antarctica is destroyed or made inaccessible by ice. This is not much fun. We want to play with possible evidence for their existence that we can find, and this will now have to be evidence in the rest of the world, not their home base.

But before we start looking around at the rest of the world, which we will do in later chapters, it would be sensible to consider what their home in Antarctica was like and what it provided for them. This will form a basis for discussing why they ventured away from Antarctica and what they possibly hoped to gain by doing so.

Climate, flora and fauna in Antarctica.

Let us look in more detail at the nature of Antarctica when our Adventurers arrived so that we can assess what they may have found when they landed there. Alexander Island, which we have proposed as a site that our Adventurers might have chosen as their home, would be some 4500km from the then South Pole. This equates to the kind of climate and vegetation we now find in the northern part of the USA, or in Europe this would equate to a similar climate to the middle of France. If they went right to the end of the Antarctic peninsula this would have given them the opportunity to settle up to another 750km away from the pole if they wished, which would have given them a Mediterranean climate, or compared to the USA the climate of the Carolinas or Florida.

What flora and fauna would they find in Antarctica? Our Adventurers would of course be self-sufficient in food grown in their craft, so they could take their time deciding if they would like to use Earth plants and animals as part of their diet. When the Pilgrim Fathers landed in America they knew that they had to successfully plant and grow crops in their first year there, and discover very quickly what edible food they could gather and animals they could hunt. They did not carry food-growing technology of the like we can expect our Adventurers to have.

The flora and fauna our Adventurers found would quite likely be very different to what they would have found in the rest of the world. Examples of places with very different flora and fauna are really all we need in order to think about the possibilities. The best way we can get some idea of what the flora and fauna of Antarctica may have been is to compare it to other lands that are separated from neighbouring lands by large stretches of water. Australia has maintained a very different flora and fauna with less then 200km of sea between New Guinea and Australia, less than a quarter of the distance from Antarctica to S.America. Madagascar also has very different fauna, with only 300km to the African coast. Perhaps the best comparator is the Galapagos Islands, that are a similar distance from S.America that Antarctica is. There Darwin found many completely unique species. It seems that it is only necessary to have a few hundred kilometres of water to stop most species migrating. Small seeds will no doubt get carried on the wind and many birds do fly such distances, but land animals and most plant seeds cannot travel such distances across sea.

One thing to note about Australia is that though many of the animals there are marsupials they appear to have evolved to fill similar ecological niches to animals in the rest of the world. This suggests Antarctica could have had a range of small and large animals to fill the diverse ecological niches that would have existed in such a large continent, prior to its complete coverage by ice.

This does not however say anything about how useful the flora and fauna might have been to our Adventurers. Kangaroo steak is not the same as beef steak and it is rather harder to keep kangaroos in fields that are easy to access when you want to slaughter some animals. There is an excellent discussion of the difference in animal populations in the different continents in the book Guns, Germs and Steel, by Jared Diamond. He points out that Europe had much more useful animals than either Southern Africa or the Americas. Particularly, Europe had many more animals that it was possible to domesticate. These animals did not reach Southern Africa because they could not cross the tropics, and they did not reach North America through Asia because the way was blocked by ice, and then by the Bering straight. South America anyway has the same problem as Africa, the inability of animals to cross the tropics, so useful animals that did exist in North America could not get to South America.

The species of animals available to be hunted and farmed makes a big difference to available food sources. Jared Diamond explores the difference between Europe and America as places to live, to understand how Europeans developed faster and were able to almost destroy South American civilisations, despite them being considerably advanced. It appears to be a matter of the luck of the draw. Europe was blessed with cows, horses, sheep, pigs and goats that could all be domesticated. South America has only the llama. Australia did not develop large grazing animals like cows, only the kangaroo and wallaby. In Europe and Asia no matter where an animal originated, it could spread anywhere from the Bering Straight to the Atlantic coast as there were no extremes of climate in the way. So societies right across Europe benefited from the animals that were the precursors of our modern domesticated animals.

In choosing Antarctica, for reasons of security and ease of travel to other parts of the Earth, our Adventurers might have compromised with regard to access to the best animals for food. The other key theme of Guns, Germs and Steel I will leave you to conjure with on your own, or better still read the book. Germs can cross between species. To some extent the closer species are to each other in their biological make-up, the easier it is for diseases to cross between the species. The more that animal species co-exist with humans in close proximity the more likely this is to happen. Is there also something here that might have guided our Adventurers to a land where there were no hominins?

Creating the comforts of home; animal products.

The temptations of good food are very strong. If one's native land does not provide tasty animals and plants and you have the ability to import them or the food they produce, human beings have often done so. For example Mediterranean wine has been imported into Great Britain for thousands of years. Poor people cannot afford to import luxuries but the very rich can. Mankind has made mistakes in the process of importing desirable animals, because they have a tendency to escape, no matter how well guarded. Rabbits cause Australians many problems, as they have no natural predators in Australia. This led to the creation of the longest continuous fence in the world, the Western Australia rabbit-proof fence. Originally 1833 Km long, there are now over 3000Km of rabbit-proof fences protecting the farms of Western Australia from this pest. It can be best to leave animals and plants in their existing habitats even if they are useful.

We can however assume that with due caution our Adventurers could have introduced animals to Antarctica that were not originally there, provided the animals could tolerate the climate there and be controlled. The lack of good animals for food would not have been a reason to abandon the idea of living in Antarctica; this would have been a small consideration compared to the considerations discussed in the last chapter.

There is however a limit to what you can import and grow locally. Certain things that Europeans have found very desirable cannot be grown in Europe. A lot of the reason for the creation of colonies, and certainly the main reason for the slave trade, was to gain access to things that had to be grown in tropical climates. We will discuss these in more detail later. For now we will just stress again that choice of a home is inevitably a compromise; you can't have everything you want growing on your doorstep.

Creating the comforts of home; furnishings.

Our Adventurers, though they may have arrived in a very large craft, would have only been able to bring limited supplies. If they wished to build and furnish homes outside their craft they would need a range of materials drawn from what they had around them.

In our current western world we use a lot of metals and plastic. This is because these are easier to process automatically in large volumes than natural products. We create factories with largely automatic machines to process the raw materials into metal and plastic, then more factories and machines to process the metal and plastic into the goods that individuals want. To get similar products from natural materials such as leather and wood takes a lot more human input. Our society finds it worthwhile to put in the large initial effort to mine metal ores and to drill for oil to make plastic, and to create the factories to process these, because we have to provide millions of products for our millions of population. And greedy people who want to make large amounts of money, greater than they have need for, have persuaded us to become consumers who throw things away, often before they have reached the end of their useful life, and buy new and flashier products. Our Adventurers were only a small group and would hence need products only in very low volume. They are therefore unlikely to have gone down the route of using metal and plastic for anything that could be made out of wood, leather, plant fibres or stone. The only reason to use metal or plastic would be if they had qualities not possessed by any other materials –

electrical conductivity for example. We use electricity for light or heat, but these can be achieved satisfactorily in much more natural ways. You don't need much wood for heat if you live in a mediterranean climate. And you don't need much light at night unless you have to work in the night and have not developed ways of entertaining yourself before sleep that can be done in low light. For thousands of years humans have managed with flames for light at night. I am sure our Adventurers could have done so as well. If they had very long lives they probably did not live life at the frenetic pace many of us now do.

We can look back at the stone age to see what our ancestors used in their small societies, before the profit motive and the need to provide products for large populations arrived. We can see what extensive use they made of natural materials. Generally speaking they also made things to last if they could. This carried on all the way into historical times. You can see in the wills of people in the middle ages, that a leather jacket might be bequeathed from father to son and even on to his son, being repaired as necessary but the leather itself lasting decades, longer than the life of a person. Now our clothes have become almost throw-away items. We have even stopped darning socks!

There is one major difference between how our stone age ancestors created what they needed and how our Adventurers could. Our Adventurers would surely have had some powerful tools. However this does not make much difference in how you process animals and plants into useful materials, particularly if you have lots of time and are only creating enough to serve the needs of a small group. Animals are fairly easy to skin and chop up and crops are fairly easy to gather and prepare. It is only in the last 100 years or so that mankind has used big powered machines for this work and the main reason, just as with metals and plastic, is to increase the quantity of food or other products being gathered and prepared.

Even the difference created by access to metal is not as large as you might imagine. The phrase 'stone-age' tends to create an image of brutish creatures with the most primitive of tools. But it wasn't like that at all. Stone tools in the period we are discussing, from 100,000 years ago, were becoming extremely sophisticated. Some of the pressure-flaked flint tools that have been found are exquisitely fashioned and would have been very effective. Flint can be extremely sharp and when hafted well into a carefully fashioned wooden handle flint knives, choppers and scrapers would have been almost as effective as our modern knives in the butchery of animals. Obsidian tools can be sharper than metal scalpels, which is why obsidian had a very special place in stone age culture (see Collins' book on Gobekli Tepe).

But having powerful tools does make a difference in how easily you can use wood and stone. If you have powerful cutting and lifting technology it is a lot quicker to build a log cabin from large tree trunks than it is to build it with lots of smaller branches that have to be inter-woven and connected. Or if your cutting and lifting technology can manage the much harder and heavier material of stone, then you can build much sturdier buildings even quicker, as the individual pieces can be larger than tree trunks. I will leave this idea to be explored later; this chapter is mainly about food and other products our Adventurers may have desired.

Farming versus hunting and gathering.

I feel that there is a tendency to consider hunter-gatherer lifestyles as antiquated and the people who persist in these lifestyles to be primitive. With our current high population densities we have no other option but farming. For a successful hunter-gatherer lifestyle you need to have control of a large area where you are not competing with others for the food it contains. If you can do this, there is a lot to commend the life of hunting and gathering.

Plants that look after their own surroundings are good as they take less effort to manage. They take a little while to get established but don't forget that we think in human lifetime terms when it comes to time. If you were to live a lot longer, then the time it takes for an apple tree or olive tree to start to produce fruit is not such a concern. Trees and bushes between them produce some wonderful things, like coffee and oranges, olives, bananas and walnuts.

If you were a hunter-gatherer with the additional advantage of power-tools, it would take very little effort and time to stop neighbouring or invading trees from crowding a favoured food-source tree or bush, and to make space for it to naturally produce more of its kind. Every year when the harvest is ready you can spend a little time discouraging competitor trees and bushes. You can also, in a fairly low maintenance way start to cultivate things that grow lower to the ground or in the ground, while still leaving them to look after themselves and reproduce naturally rather than farming them. The hunter-gatherer life style is estimated to have needed fewer hours per day of work to get food than the farmer life-style. There is some evidence of ancient diets that suggests that hunter-gatherer societies would also promote the growth of useful plants over competitors to some extent, presumably by cutting back plants they found of no use and spreading the seeds of useful plants around. I hope that if you go picking blackberries or elderberries that you drop a few further along in places the bushes have not yet reached.

The one problem with the hunter-gatherer lifestyle is the seasons. Gathering works well when the plants are growing strongly and seeding, from say April to September in the northern hemisphere, but in Winter you have to fall back on hunting to some extent. With care it is possible to store seeds, fruit and nuts. Iron-age villages that have been investigated in England often have pits that are interpreted as storage pits for this purpose. Many fruits and vegetables are naturally designed to last over Winter, so that in the Spring the food in the fruit or nut can encourage re-growth of the plant by fertilising the ground for the growth from a new seed. It is the later part of the Winter and the beginning of Spring that you have to plan for, the 'green gap', when stored food is becoming rotten and new crops have not yet grown sufficiently to eat. At this time root-crop tubers prove very useful food sources.

Domesticated animals are still a food source in the Winter, because they can eat grass and leaves that we can't. In the western world we think of domesticated food animals living in fields, but in Africa they are herded, as reindeer are in Scandinavia. With some care, for example through providing watering places, animals can be persuaded to gather where you can easily find them. There is no clear dividing line between farming and a hunter-gatherer lifestyle until you get to the point of creating field systems. We should not be surprised if our Adventurers and humans extensively managed how plants and animals survived and grew in their hunting-gathering area, and yet left no evidence of their presence from the approaches they used to ensure a supply of food.

However before we leave the matter of food, there are two things we should bear in mind that we will come back to in later chapters. I have painted a picture of an idyllic environment with easy access to an interesting diet and useful plant and animal resources, through expenditure of minimum effort. If our Adventurers were not satisfied with this and set about doing things elsewhere in the world there must have been some reasons.

The first issue is that when using animals for food there is the messy business of getting it from them. Who is going to milk the cow morning and evening, deal with calving and clear the manure? Who is going to herd the reindeer and the sheep and look after the pigs? Some of the processes to create desirable things from animal products, such as butter-churning, require rather hard and long work. There are many people in the current world who keep animals because they enjoy doing so. But there are also farmers who enjoy the products they get from their farm, who employ farm labourers to get what is needed, to process it and to bring it to them.

The second issue is all those delicious and useful things that will only grow successfully in tropical climates, and how to obtain a regular supply of such things.

Why did our Adventurers come?

We are moving in this story towards later chapters, where we will explore the kinds of impacts our Adventurers might have had on humankind and what changes they might have made to the Earth. These will be influenced considerably by the drives that brought them here in the first place, though as time went on those drives may have altered. Human beings have different drives at different stages of their lives and we have a rather limited time to accomplish them. A lot of human life is taken up by learning, establishing a career, creating a family and by declining years when health is failing. If our Adventurers had much longer lives the time taken by these might have been a much smaller percentage of their lives, leaving much more time for pursuit of their personal desires and interests.

We are discussing many tens of thousands of years. But even if our Adventurers lived 10,000 years, there would have been at least 10 generations of Adventurers in the last 100,000 years. It is probable Adventurers that humans may have been in contact with in the last 10,000 or 20,000 years will have been the descendants of the original Adventurers who arrived, maybe several generations on from the original Adventurers. They may have continued with the same drives that brought their parents to Earth but they may also have developed other drives and reasons for remaining here.

If it was us going the other way to a planet around another star, at some point in the future when we are sufficiently technologically advanced, there are several reasons that might be behind such a trip.

It's rather hard to envision a mass migration to another planet because we have made such a mess of our own. I have already ruled out some kind of matter-transfer and have assumed our Adventurers arrived in some kind of craft. Though the physicists are beginning to contemplate the possibility of matter transfer and can already instantaneously change matter at a distance through entangled particles, that is a long way away from being able to matter-transfer a human being and have them arrive at the other end as a functioning being. Without some kind of matter-transfer, sending a whole world population to another planet would involve huge numbers of spacecraft. Traveling to another planet is almost inevitably going to be an expensive business that can only be afforded for the few. And any planet whose inhabitants had made a complete mess of it would likely be in crisis and unable to afford thousands of spaceships. That our Adventurers' planet was in crisis must however be a possible reason. We can see on our own planet that the population is outstripping the available resources and it is not clear that we will succeed in getting it under control. Even water is in short supply in many places and minerals such as the rare earth minerals, many of which are vital in highly technological products, are getting increasingly expensive as demand outstrips supply.

I suspect however that a civilisation that has succeeded in establishing interplanetary and maybe inter-galaxy travel, has probably been through the kinds of problems the Earth currently faces and survived. Looking at the history of technology development on Earth, it is easy to see how it is accelerating. The major population increase from better food and medicine and fewer wars has happened only in the last couple of hundred years. Another 200 years of technology development is going to bring unprecedented levels of change and in this period we will surely manage to start reducing the population pressure and develop lifestyles that put far less pressure on the resources of the Earth. Hans Rosling, who is extremely expert at analysing and presenting data, is already seeing signs of this. He believes the population of Earth could be stabilised at 9 billion by 2050. Watch his TED talk "Global population growth, box by box" on YouTube, it is an absolute delight. We might thereafter achieve a decline in world population if having children ceases to be the only way people can guarantee a satisfactory life in old age. A period of 400 years to move from the little technology we had in 1800, to a technological level we still can't imagine in

2200, is really a very short time in the life of mankind, and probably was a short time in the history of our Adventurers.

There is another reason why I suspect a lifeboat for a species whose planet was dying is an unlikely scenario. In this case one of the prime activities on arrival for those on board would be breeding in order to re-establish the species on a new planet. In that case we would surely find the Earth filled with aliens, which we don't. Unless of course we are the aliens and our Adventurers were human beings from another planet - an idea I will develop a little more in a later chapter.

More likely is that our Adventurers were a selected group who set off on an expedition of some kind. The two most likely scenarios I believe are adventuring or an expedition for scientific or moral reasons. Their mode of transport could have been a conventional spaceship traveling at say half the speed of light. There is a planet with Earth-like mass circling Alpha Centauri B which is only 4.3 light years away. If our Adventurers lived as long as Noah is supposed to have done, a 10 year journey would be only 1% of their life. If someone proposed to you an extremely exciting expedition but with the slight downside that to get there would take 9 months in a luxurious ocean liner, you might well think it would be worth your while to spend 9 months that way. This is our human equivalent to our Adventurers committing 1% of their life in a 10 year journey. Early world explorers were often away for over a year and in Victorian times plant-hunters engaged in expeditions involving months at sea and years away from home. If we devised a means for interplanetary travel, that could get groups to distant planets in a suitably small fraction of their lifespan, there would be quite a lot of volunteers to go.

If the reason for coming to Earth was simply 'to have an adventure', our Adventurers will have set about doing on Earth what they like to do when adventuring. Human beings who go adventuring go to find new places, new peoples and new animals and plants that they haven't seen before, or to find thrills that can only be experienced in certain places. Quite often however people who go adventuring are also deeply interested in the things they go to find, scientifically, commercially or religiously. Often this is the reason that the funds have been provided to get the adventurers to where they are going, in the expectation that they will report back information, or send back things desired at home. Scientific expeditions are really just adventuring with a deeper reason than just going to see and play in new places.

Pure adventuring as a reason to come to Earth sounds a little unlikely to me. Having adventures is something that you do at intervals during your life, before returning home. Our Adventurers have probably made a one-way journey; the process of traveling at close to the speed of light will have changed their time relative to that of their families back on their home planet, as defined by Einstein's theories of relativity. If they went back they might be going back to a radically different society and their families and friends might be dead. This does of course depend on how fast they travelled, as the time dilation rapidly increases as you get close to the speed of light. At 50% of the speed of light time for the travelers would slow by about 10% compared to the time for the people back home. But for people with very long lives this is not as much of a problem as it would be for us. When our Adventurers set out for Earth, if they had come from Alpha Centauri the people back home would have to wait around 15 years to receive a message back - the 10 years spent traveling amounting to 11 years on the home planet, plus the 4.3 light years for a radio signal to travel back.

Our Adventurers probably came intending to stay, since going back would be time consuming and considerable time would have passed on their home planet. It would be a life choice to spend their lives in a small group engaged in an interesting project. If the trip was funded by their society rather than them personally, there would likely have been a moral purpose rather than a desire to have things sent back, unless what was required back was of small volume and not needed for many years, or was purely information. Societies do send out people to effect change in the place they travel to for moral purposes. Christian missionaries travelled the world with the moral purpose of saving the souls of the peoples they found by converting them to Christianity. Many modern-day missionaries are often medical or educational rather than religious, with a moral purpose of bringing health to those who suffer from illness and deprivation. In these two examples we can see quite different effects on the peoples who are influenced, which will give us some hints as to what we might look for on Earth as the impacts our Adventurers had on mankind. Religious missionaries from Europe quite often managed to convert native societies to Christianity. They left them with a set of myths, stories and beliefs – the religion - that persist to this day. Medical missionaries leave behind them healthier societies able to grow more strongly and rapidly, which is why it is rather useful if medical missionary work is alongside educational work. It appears to be education, particularly of women, that is the best guard against societies growing to the point where over-population causes poverty and medical problems.

It is of course quite possible that amongst the group of Adventurers that arrived there were several different drives. Some may have come to have fun and explore, some to find a new home and society, some for scientific reasons and some with a moral purpose of helping the native inhabitants to improve. There is a range of different kinds of impacts we could look for.

Possible impacts on the Earth and human beings.

The process of finding a new home and society is akin to establishing a colony. It is possible to imagine that a group that had learnt the lessons of the dangers of over-population might have been satisfied with only occupying one continent, leaving the rest of the world to develop by itself. If that continent were Antarctica, there may be all sorts of remains and evidence of the impact of our Adventurers on the landscape of Antarctica, that we could find if only the ice were not there, and very few remains elsewhere in the world. Indeed you will find many books that take advantage of this idea to speculate wildly. In my view finding such evidence is an impossible pipe-dream. Glaciers don't just sit on the Earth and cover things up, they move. You may remember geography lessons at school about the typical shape of valleys that have been scoured out by glaciers and how the hanging valleys on the sides show how deep the glacier was. Over the time-scales we are talking of any evidence of our Adventurers on Antarctica will have been scoured from the land and buried in the sea as icebergs calved from the ends of the glaciers.

That our Adventurer's main colony and home was in Antarctica would be an explanation for why we don't see major impacts on the landscape of the rest of the Earth that could be attributed to them. The lack of this is an important piece of evidence in its own right. An alternative explanation is that our Adventurers had a lifestyle that did not require activity that would leave easily visible evidence on Earth. Most of the highly visible human impact on the Earth that would last over thousands of years is due to mining, quarrying and construction of roads and industrial facilities, and to a much lesser extent farming involving terraces. A small group that could fly, which had realised the benefits of using natural materials for products and energy rather than metals and oil, and which could choose agricultural land that did not need terraces, would leave very little evidence of their existence behind them in the ground.

If the purpose in coming was scientific, their colleagues back on the home planet would surely have wanted to hear what they found out, even though this might come back to later generations than those who organised the trip. Though we have some long-term scientific expeditions on Earth, such as the scientific stations in Antarctica, most such expeditions set out to spend a period of time in the place they are investigating and then to return home. They do not tend to be long-term. And it is hard to see what kind of scientific benefit could be gained by an expedition to a planet with much lower technology, except to satisfy curiosity about different kinds of planets.

Missionaries on the other hand often go out to places with a view to spending their whole lives there, supporting and helping the 'natives' in whatever way they feel is appropriate. As this story develops you will see that I propose our Adventurers were on the Earth for many thousands of years. We cannot rule out a kind of contact more like the Starship Enterprise's five year mission, but it doesn't fit the story very well. The scenario that I think is the best fit is that they came to establish a small society that would nurture and develop planet Earth over a long period of time, and study the Earth.

These drives and higher purposes for coming will of course be overlaid on top of the basic drives of survival and comfort, so let us leave them on one side for the moment and return to the basic drives and what these may have caused to happen.

****

Chapter 5 – What kind of society did our Adventurers have?

In later chapters I will be asking you to consider why things we can find around the world might be evidence that our band of Adventurers existed and impacted on mankind in various ways. And as I mentioned in the introduction we will have to understand how a technologically advanced group could exist on Earth without leaving the kinds of evidence that our technological civilisation is leaving on the world. Or if they did indulge in mining, extraction of metals from ores and the use of large amounts of energy, how the evidence of this has disappeared.

If we are going to do this successfully we will have to get inside the minds of our Adventurers and think like they do. So bear with the excursions I am going to take in this chapter. Before you can think like our Adventurers you need to challenge some of the ways that people in our modern societies think. We accept a lot of things that we do as societies as just the natural way that things are and the ways that things must inevitably happen. But this is not true, it is possible to think and act differently.

We also need to understand our Adventurers' mindset in considering how to interpret things we might find. When archeologists come across evidence that they don't understand, they usually tend to explain it as something that has come about through 'ritual practices' and 'belief systems'. They would have us believe that ancient peoples were in many ways deluded about the true state of the Earth and the universe and about many things that impacted on their lives. Hence they see them creating rituals and places for rituals not on the basis of logic but on the basis of faith. This may be true, but it may not be.

It does appear to be true that human beings are hard-wired to engage in complicated rituals. From a very young age babies will copy things they are shown how to do by an adult, that have no purpose at all. The scientists doing these experiments feel that the reason is probably that engaging in a complicated ritual that has no real-life purpose gives people a sense of belonging to a group. Hence the rituals get passed down. The young people engage in the rituals because the adults treat them as important so they become self-perpetuating. In the western world even non-religious people engage in various rituals at Christmas, the origins of which are lost in the mists of time. Why do we bring holly and ivy into the house? Religious people of course engage in the rituals of their particular faith.

It is also true that human beings can be very superstitious, particularly when they don't understand the reasons why certain things happen. We can certainly see examples of people around the world who even today clearly do not understand and believe what has been discovered about the nature of disease. They put reliance in ritual practices or treat disease as god-given and therefore untreatable, making it much harder for medics to convince them of what they should do to avoid the pathogens causing the disease. And it is quite possible to look at many current religious practices and to see how much they are based on blind faith, rather than the kinds of personal experiences that can be experienced through shamanic worship. So the explanation of 'ritual practices' to explain archeological sites may contain much truth.

But rather than just resorting to the 'blind faith' of the people of the time to explain the existence and purpose of archeological sites that have been found, it is possible to think that sites may have been created for very rational reasons and with very logical approaches. We should consider this particularly for sites where there might have been interactions between humans and our Adventurers. How the humans used these sites may well have involved ritual practices but our Adventurers may have had very rational reasons for creating the site. And how the humans reacted to the presence of our Adventurers may have been very rational. However we must note that the rational reasons of our Adventurers may have been seen quite differently by humans, maybe because our Adventurers wanted them to interact with the site for reasons other than the core reason the humans believed the site had been created for. Or simply because humans are different and at that stage of mankind's development would not have been able to understand what the site was for.

So let us try to get into the mindset of our Adventurers.

What size of society did our Adventurers create?

Before we consider how our Adventurers might have impacted on the societies that mankind created in the past it will be useful to consider what kind of society our Adventurers may have wished to establish amongst themselves. I am assuming, as discussed in the last chapter, that they have come to stay for a long time, with a purpose in mind, probably something to do with advancing the development of planets as well as securing fulfilling lives for themselves. The Pilgrim Fathers set out to create a new life in a new place, and to build a new society. Building a new society in the way that they wanted to was a key agenda for the Pilgrim Fathers. They wanted religious freedoms that they could not have in England and they had a clear moral code that they all agreed with. Our Adventurers would also no doubt have had some clear ideas about the kind of society they hoped to form once they had discovered an appropriate planet, a society that they would then gift to their descendants.

The Pilgrim Fathers would have thought about the new society that they hoped to establish within the constraints of their lives and the technologies of the time. They no doubt planned to grow their society to a size that would give them the capabilities, security and comfort they desired. Their models will have been the villages and towns in England, with populations of a few thousand. The largest city they could know about was London, with a population of perhaps 250,000 at that time. Plymouth, from where they set sail to America, was a small walled town with a dozen or so streets. Its population would have been only one or two thousand, maybe just hundreds. The Pilgrim Fathers would also have had in their heads a model of what they felt the ideal family should be. Parents needed to be supported in their old age by their children, and as children often died they probably thought ideal families would have many children. Though they must have desired to grow their population to give them greater food and physical security as well as protection in old age, growth would not be very fast given the high death rate amongst children.

They would have conceived of the society they wished to build relative to their own lifetimes, that at a maximum were likely to to 70 years or so and quite likely to end when they were in their 40s or 50s. In societies where people have little technology, where medical science is not well advanced, and where lifetimes are a few tens of years, it is sensible to conceive of an ideal society having at least several hundred members, possibly several thousands, or growing to be many thousands of members if they could expand the area they occupied. They would have been aware that every new mouth would have to be fed so the size of their society would be limited by the food growing or gathering area they could control. Since medieval times in Britain there had been clear ideas about how much land was necessary to support families, as seen in the medieval strip-field systems.

Our Adventurers did not have these problems. I have assumed long lives of hundreds of years so replacement of people dying would be only a small concern. They would only need to produce enough children to grow their society to the population density they desired and then to keep it at that level. That would mean only a couple of children over their long lives. Procreation would be a short episode in their lives that they would choose to undertake, instead of being a major part of life as it is for us. They certainly had high technology and very likely extremely good medical science. The survival rate of any children they had was likely to be 100%.

With very powerful weapons they did not need to fear overwhelming numbers of neighbours unduly. Besides they could choose their home well to avoid this danger. They could afford to consider an ideal society as being one with far fewer members than human beings consider necessary. It is quite possible that before setting off they had thought through what their ideal size of society should be. They were going to live as a society on their craft as they travelled and having achieved that for several years it is not likely that they had strong urges to breed and to expand their society beyond their ideal of appropriate size. They would surely have separated sex and procreation so that procreation had become a very positive choice, with no procreational 'accidents' happening. The two main factors defining ideal numbers would have been ensuring a sufficient range of skills across the society and a population density low enough for sustainable living without degrading their environment.The only reason to grow their numbers more than this would be if they wished to colonise new areas of the planet. However we have already noted that there is little evidence to suggest major colonisation. More likely is a small society in a single very well chosen place on Earth.

You might think that to have sufficient knowledge and skills in their society would require many thousands of people. However we as a world society are getting close to the point where if we want to do something we can learn how to do it 'just in time'. You have at your fingertips the whole of the Internet. And with data-storage now pretty cheap, if you want to you can site-suck whole websites onto your own local storage. It is possible to imagine a society where the need for new knowledge declines in importance, because just about everything that is needed to be known for the society to function at a very high level has already been discovered and recorded. Further development of knowledge beyond this point would then only be possible in very arcane and specialist areas, or as a form of creativity. I think we have already reached this point with regards to cookery. Every year's crop of new cook-books is essentially a re-hash of cook-books that have been published before. The arcane cookery developments undertaken by Heston Blumenthal are really only of interest to pleasure seekers or possibly to supermarket bosses who want ever-cheaper ways to make food last for ever on the shelves, while still keeping a taste we can be persuaded to believe is good. If all the members of your society can learn to do anything that needs doing, and how to do just about everything is stored in the society's library, it would be possible to have a huge range of skills with a very much smaller population.

They would need to manage the size of their society actively. Some people in human societies seem to enjoy having lots of children. In western society where support of the old is to a degree provided by the state, there is no need to have more than 2 or 3 children. In my family records there is a photograph from a branch of the family that went to New Zealand in the 19th century, showing mother and father and then all their 13 children, in descending height. Mother and Father obviously enjoyed sexual intercourse and there were no contraception techniques available. They were opening what to them (but not the Maoris!) was new territory, so there was plenty of room for expansion of their society.

Our Adventurers would be likely to know that societies growing rapidly can cause problems when there isn't land available to expand into, and would see societal growth as a bad thing. We can look back in history and see how societal pressures caused events in world history. Viking societies grew as the families had many children and food was plentiful. When the eldest son took over the family farm, his brothers had the choice of working for him or going somewhere else. The possibilities of new places to live close to their family home, that could sustain a farm, were soon exhausted so younger sons looked elsewhere. Expanding societies in this way works well when there is space available, it ceases to work well once all good land has been taken. The result was that the younger sons of the Vikings looked around for other places where they could live, where the people already there could be killed or displaced. They sailed across the North Sea to the UK and down the coast to France. They went down the major rivers of Northern Europe and then dragged their boats to the Danube and Volga and found their way into Eastern Europe. Today there are still good links between Turkey and Northern Scandinavia, which seems strange until you realise how connected they are by the rivers.

Expansion of societies such as the Vikings can of course be the cause of wars. Human populations on Earth would be much more comfortable and suffer far less strife if world population was only a fraction of what it now is and was managed to stay at a safe and comfortable level.

The point of this discussion is to establish that it is quite likely that our Adventurers made a conscious decision to keep their society quite small. There may also have been in their heads the thought that at some stage they might move on to another planet, in which case the number who could travel in the spaceship would have been a limit. Letting their society grow to more than this might lead to terrible problems if only some could move on and some had to be left behind. Note that a very small society helps to explain why we cannot find any large-scale mining or energy-extraction damage to the Earth from this period in time. If they did have needs beyond what they could achieve sustainably and through re-cycling, these needs will have been very small.

My conclusion therefore is that their society could have been as small as a few tens of people, or might have been a few hundreds, but was unlikely to have been allowed to grow into the thousands. Not that this was necessarily easy to manage, as we will see!

Sex and procreation amongst our Adventurers.

There is of course another reason, apart from a rational desire to grow the group, why societies grow. People like sexual relationships and this can over-ride the dictats of the society. People in a close relationship also quite often wish to have their own children, even if they have already had children through a previous relationship. In the modern world we have a current example of the balancing act between the dictats of a society and personal desires. China exerted huge pressure on its population for two parents to raise only one child. This did work with most but has however had some unexpected results, such as the big imbalance between male and female children that has resulted. Given the greater importance of having a son to support the parents in old age, the parents have found devious ways to prioritise having sons over having daughters. The result has been referred to as the Little Emperor problem. One of the 'Inevitable Surprises' looked at in Peter Schwarz's book of the same name is that the Chinese are starting to marry their way around the world. With insufficient girls at home for all the boys, the Chinese boys are starting to look elsewhere for wives.

If our Adventurers were similar to human beings in their sexual lives there would no doubt be similar happenings to what we see in human societies. There would be relationships and the personal conflicts these can sometimes bring. Just because our Adventurers had long lives and their society exerted pressure to keep the society to a certain size does not mean that they would necessarily avoid having children. There are four possibilities for how the size of the group of Adventurers changed in the many years after they arrived. The impacts on Earth and on mankind will differ, depending on what happened. Our Adventurers' society may have declined and eventually died out, it may have remained stable, grown slowly, or it may have grown rapidly. For the story to continue on to look at the impact on human beings, we have to choose which we believe happened.

I do not believe their society grew rapidly, because we don't see lots of aliens inhabiting the world or any large amount of evidence that they did. Any of the other three scenarios might have happened.

If their society was a stable group of Adventurers, remaining at the same group size as when they arrived, we will have to consider where they went and why they are not still here. They could however all have just decided to go at some point and left on their spaceship. That would just leave us the task of deciding when they left.

Their society might have been stable or growing during the development of mankind, but then declined and eventually died out, explaining why they are not still here. In this case we can look for impacts on mankind as we developed. If we can find such impacts we will need to consider what might thereafter have caused the society of our Adventurers to decline in numbers and what the possible causes of them dying out might have been. Was it anything to do with us? And if they were impacting on mankind and then ceased to, we may be able to detect, from how mankind behaved and developed, when this dying out of our Adventurers happened.

Or their society might have grown to some extent, beyond the capacity of their spaceship. This would mean that if some did leave some would have remained behind and they or their descendants could still be here. Or again we will have to explain when and why those remaining died out.

How stable a society?

Much of the world history of mankind has happened because of instabilities in societies. I have mentioned the instability that caused the Vikings to raid and conquer. That was caused by plenty of everything except land to live on. Other instabilities happen because of the lack of things, particularly rain and water supply. Power and greed have also been a factor, with empires being grown by conquest because leaders wanted more power and their followers liked the benefits gained at the expense of those they conquered. It seems to be a natural part of animal societies that there are power relationships, rivalries and fights to gain dominance. If our Adventurers were animals – and we have assumed they are carbon-based life forms so assuming they are animal in some ways does not require a great leap of thought – it could be that they too had to manage internal rivalries in their society. These would have created tensions and acted against the stability of their society.

Alongside population growth and rivalries within societies, the other development in human societies that is troubling us on Earth is 'growth', by which is meant 'economic growth' and consumption. There seems to be an innate human desire to have more. To provide for this desire for more, most countries in the world base their economies around the idea that every year gross domestic product will increase. Politics focuses on increasing the 'standard of living' of its populace, through growth of the country's economy. This is very sensible when much of the population of a country is living in poverty and with malnutrition. But it does not make a lot of long-term sense when people already have food, homes and many physical goods. If everyone on the planet consumed to the same level as the average American the planet would be very short of resources and problems like global warming would become acute and very threatening.

There is some light for us at the end of the 'growth' tunnel, in that some products such as computers now use less raw material and energy as they are smaller and more efficient. Communication with others no longer needs large black telephones and telephone wires strung across the country. Information travels along glass fibres or wirelessly, methods which are a lot cheaper to make than copper wires and have less impact on the resources of the Earth. Sand to make glass is plentiful whereas copper ore is not. But we are still wedded to the idea of always having more.

There are however now a few people who are changing their mindset, realising that more things and more travel does not necessarily bring happiness. And there are people realising that once devices have improved to a certain point having a new one does not bring much greater advantage. The classic car movement is an expression of this. 30 year old cars can travel just as easily at the speed limit as new cars, with as much comfort and without using very much more fuel. There are markets for all sorts of products that are made to a high quality in long-lasting materials, but these products tend to cost more initially. Even if overall it is cheaper to buy a £100 handbag properly made of leather that will last 10 years, instead of ten £25 bags from the local market that each break in a year, many households can't afford the initial outlay for good products, and manufacturers make more money by selling products that break and have to be replaced. Fashion and our desire to be seen to be 'cool' and up to date also play a big part in maintaining this mindset of consumption.

A factor that may be driving this change to a mindset of being satisfied with what you have got and not wanting more is that average life-span is increasing. Older people tend to be far more selective in what they acquire and much clearer about what they need. Now that I am past 60 I have rather got over the desire to own a sports car in order to impress a future mate, though I must admit having one for my own personal driving pleasure in addition to my 'sensible' transport still appeals. Many older people are de-cluttering, getting rid of things they acquired largely for the sake of increasing their possessions and to try out new things. They tend to look harder at whether acquiring something else will add value to their lives. Our Adventurers, with much longer post-education and post-procreation lives may have been a lot more comfortable with what they had and might have very largely overcome the need for more, that is having such a damaging effect on the planet now. This would be another reason for why we cannot see large amounts of evidence that our Adventurers were here on Earth.

For our society to get into this mindset there would have to be radical changes to how our societies operate. We would have to build high quality housing that can be maintained and renovated over hundreds of years, instead of putting up cheaply-built houses that need replacing even before they are a hundred years old. For transport we would have to start thinking of cars as things that we maintain and repair over many years, instead of being something to replace every few years. The business models of car manufacturers will need to change alongside this. Lifestyles will also need to change with people being satisfied with devices that do the job satisfactorily over a long time, without upgrading every two years to a new model to get new and whizzy features, as we do with our mobile phones. This is essentially a model where the current frenetic pace of technological change slows and reaches a plateau, with new technology only being adopted slowly after careful exploration of the real-life and societal benefits that it brings.

Our Adventurers would probably have thought very differently about this to the way we do. Their planet may have been through a phase of over-population such as we are experiencing now, and through a phase of rampant profit-motivated capitalism, and they may have learnt about these in their history lessons. Their politics would probably be based around ideas of satisfactory sufficiency, stability instead of growth, and benefit to society from technology being the driver of its adoption, rather than profit. They will have spent some years in a very carefully controlled society in their spaceship, where sustainability must have been the key driver and the kind of 'growth' possible on a planet would have been impossible. In this kind of society renovation would be first choice rather than replacement and recycling of anything that had to be replaced would be the norm. A 'throw-away' society would be anathema to them, so don't expect them to have left artefacts lying around for us to find.

This argument matters when we get to look at the impact of our Adventurers on Earth. Ensuring economic 'growth' has made a big mess of various areas of the Earth as more and more people have demanded things, and hence the resources to make them have had to be found. Though we may find it hard to imagine living very long lives without replacement of things that require use of the non-renewable resources of the Earth, I think it is likely that our Adventurers knew how to maintain a stable society that made only very limited non-renewable demands on the environment.

They must have found their satisfaction from being guardians of the Earth, in designing the very best tools and equipment and in looking after these things to ensure they continued to perform at their best. Either that or the ways that they impacted the surface of the Earth, their quarries and mines and landscaping, have not yet been identified as their work and are currently being considered to be the work of mankind.

Weapons and society.

If we took a random selection of human beings, with the mindsets we have in our current world, and put them onto a new and hospitable planet, we can imagine what they might do to that planet over tens of thousands of years. The history of the world over the times that we count as historical times, and going even further back into the archeological record, is largely a story of power and greed. We see empire after empire growing, grabbing as much land as it can, building magnificently and enabling its elite to live in luxury, and then declining for various reasons. There are some notable exceptions. In our current time we have the example of the Amish (see http://www.amish-heartland.com/), who live a simple life and reject much of the development they see around themselves in the modern world. I was actually quite astounded to find several websites about the Amish way of life. It will be fascinating to see whether they adopt the technology of the Internet which can be used to promote communication, collaboration and community which are values they aspire to. They have adopted horse-drawn technology and metal agricultural equipment, while avoiding the kind of rampant consumerism that surrounds them in the USA. They of course are able to have the lifestyle they choose because they are protected by American society that stops warlike people grabbing their lands. Since the Earth became fairly full of people and the ability to travel developed, the strong and warlike have tended to dominate. Though even in the jungles of New Guinea and the Amazon tribes fight each other.

It is worth asking whether this will always be so or whether human beings could change. There are some who suggest that the development of weapons was a step towards a better society, because they gave the physically weak the opportunity to harm and kill at a distance. In animal societies power goes to the biggest and strongest animals. In human societies, once we got to the point where leaders could gain power through their political skills rather than brute strength, some leaders have been only average height or even smaller, and we have had women leaders though they have less physical strength than men. These leaders' physical security has been secured by employing others to protect them. It is also more possible to have revolutions if oppressed peoples can obtain weapons comparable to those in the hands of the powerful. So perhaps the secret of societies that are peaceful in the very long-term is keeping the society small enough, in a large enough area, to avoid conflict over space and resources, to manage rivalries politically but also to have weapons, the use of which is controlled. Though the situation on Earth is far from satisfactory, we are slowly as a world community realising that some weapons such as nuclear and chemical weapons are too de-stabilising and must be banned with worldwide consent, so it becomes almost unthinkable to use them. European societies have in the main decided that guns should not be in the hands of everyone. Perhaps one day taser devices that can protect against bears might be produced and people in the USA be persuaded to adopt those instead of guns, though I don't hold out much hope of the National Rifle Association agreeing to that any time soon.

Development of weapons, putting progressively more power into the hands of individuals is not the only thing that has happened in human societies over the years. Robert Wright in his book Nonzero suggests that there has been progressive development in human societies' desires and abilities to work together. He suggests that collaborating in various ways produces more benefits for societies than competing and fighting; that it is not just a matter of dividing up the 'cake' of what the Earth offers with the most powerful tribes or nations getting more than others, but that the 'cake' can grow if societies collaborate, so there is more for all. Hence the title 'non-zero', one society grabbing a benefit does not completely cancel out benefits for others. For this to happen there must be a developing awareness among the people in societies that working together is better in the long run than fighting.

This awareness must come from the history of the societies and must become embedded in their customs. Wright acknowledges there are frequent reverses. Well organised collaborative societies get destroyed and the people are forced to revert to much more primitive living with fighting over resources. But overall, over the thousands of years we know about, there has been a positive trend. People are becoming more collaborative. We can see this trend in modern history. 300 years ago the world was a collection of nation states who battled each other and took ownership of lands they could conquer, in order to extract products they wanted, be it gold, rubber, tea or cotton. We now have a world where nation states, while not yet in decline, are passing more power to collaborative political organisations. The existence of the European Union has successfully prevented France and Germany fighting in warlike ways, though they still fight politically. The United Nations is slowly getting more power to intervene to stop conflicts. It learnt a lot about this in Bosnia and it is now learning more about how to do this through the Middle Eastern conflicts, though as I write this we still have thousands of people being killed in Syria and millions displaced from their homes because countries in the United Nations cannot agree how to intervene effectively. The only intervention in Syria that appears to be being successful is Syria's agreement to abide by the chemical weapons convention and the steps being taken to remove their manufacturing capability and stocks of such weapons. We also have North Korea threatening nuclear war while the Chinese government, who hold most political power over the North Korean government, appear not to be intervening very effectively with them. They perhaps view North Korea as useful in some way in their power battle with the USA.

It is however becoming just about possible to imagine a world where societies have such established ways of resolving conflicts with neighbouring societies that they can hardly imagine resorting to violence to resolve them. If the society mindset against war is sufficiently strong on both sides, warmongering individuals would not be able to exercise sufficient persuasion to cause war. The problems with the use of weapons would then focus on individuals who act alone. We can see in our current world a dangerous trend in the weapons available to individuals. Sometimes these are lone individuals but increasingly the danger is groups that persuade individuals, with religious or political ideas, to sacrifice their own lives in order to kill others. We have also had such groups getting hold of chemical weapons. There are occasional scares that they also have biological weapons such as anthrax or nerve gas. While the received wisdom is that they do not yet have nuclear weapons, there is certainly the possibility of them getting hold of plutonium and creating a 'dirty bomb', that would contaminate a large area with highly radioactive substances. One of the problems with states like Sadam Hussein's Iraq and Mahmoud Ahmadinejad's Iran, that did not permit their nuclear facilities to be inspected is that they could be a route for individuals or groups to obtain the materials for a nuclear bomb.

The point of discussing this is that our Adventurers, according to our story so far, established a society on Earth that survived as a stable society for tens of thousands of years. They must surely have understood nuclear technology and the dangers of chemical weapons. It is inconceivable that they could have reached the technological level of inter-star travel without understanding nuclear physics. The idea of chain reactions is not complicated. The only complicated thing is how to squash sufficiently radioactive materials into a small enough space to make them explode as a bomb, rather than just heating up uncontrollably into a huge and unstoppable fire spreading radioactivity in the smoke cloud - as was happening at Chernobyl until the firefighters sacrificed themselves in adding materials to slow the chain reaction.

As our Adventurers' home planet obviously survived the discovery of how to make atom bombs and had managed to control this, at least up to the point where our Adventurers departed, we can expect our Adventurers to have beliefs about how societies should be organised that reflect the dangers of hugely powerful weapons. They must also have had ways to identify and deal with the individuals who alone or in groups might resort to using weapons to destabilise their society.

This will obviously effect how their society operated on Earth. If our Adventurers had split into factions, taken control of different areas and fought between themselves we might expect to see some evidence of this, particularly if they got around to using very powerful weapons such as nuclear explosions. I feel we are unlikely to find evidence of a war amongst our Adventurers. Though we might just find evidence of a lone individual who overstepped the bounds of their society and used banned weaponry, such as nuclear weapons. I will leave this thought hanging in your heads until we start to look at things that might be evidence of our Adventurers on Earth. However at the start of their time on Earth, and maybe for the majority of the time we are discussing, I think we can expect them to have behaved as a single, well organised and peaceful society.

How did our Adventurers achieved self-fulfillment?

Without wars and fighting to distract them and occupy their time, our Adventurers must have found other ways to pleasantly fill their time. For people who are curious and inquisitive, going through life is a learning experience. If you undertake an activity it is likely that you first of all learn how to do it, then you learn how to do it better, then you consider how to extend the activity in new enjoyable ways.

In a life of three-score years and ten there are many new activities that it is possible to undertake when you become tired of the old activities. There seems to be always something new to learn. If life is several hundred years long, to keep oneself entertained and amused it would be necessary either to have many different activities that you can progress to, or to have a few activities that are extremely absorbing and interesting, such that you can pursue them for hundreds of years without getting tired of them. These thoughts really relate to later chapters where I will suggest what impact this had on humans, but I am introducing them here as we first need to get a feel for the impacts of long life on the society and activities of our Adventurers.

One area of possibilities for activities that are absorbing long-term is visual art. The infinite variety and the creativity involved in art can absorb many hours and give great delight. Composition and creation of music also seems to be a lifelong, ever-developing passion. Another possibility is cultivation. Those people who cultivate plants get to see genetic variations appearing unexpectedly. They can manipulate these and create new varieties of plants and animals. A fourth possibility is science and technology, pushing the boundaries of understanding and creating new things. We have, mainly in the last 300 years or so, but starting 6000 years ago, been through the kind of science that involved big impacts on the physical structure of the Earth. We have mined metal ores and non-renewable energy, we have dug canals, built railways and then roads, and quarried extensively. We have built rocket-pads and sent numerous satellites into space. And in so doing we have not found any satellites or other evidence of this kind of activity left by a group such as our Adventurers. So we have no evidence that they engaged in this sort of science. But we are now moving into a period where much of the development in science is focussed on living things and manipulation of materials at the molecular level. These activities have far less impact on the structure of the Earth and will leave no physical evidence behind that will survive for thousands of years. If our Adventurers had scientific capabilities at and beyond this nano-material stage, we can imagine them able to produce high technology products without the large factories and industrial facilities that we find necessary. And hence they would leave little direct evidence of their scientific and technological capability. We would only see this by looking at how objects on the Earth have been cut and manipulated.

I will leave you to wonder how these different ways for the Adventurers to keep their minds active might have played out in how the Earth developed, except to note that studying the development of mankind over hundreds and thousands of years would have been fascinating. I will just note for now that I don't find it either impossible or surprising that a small technologically advanced society could live on the Earth without making the kinds of landscape changes and leaving the kinds of evidence that human beings have made. We are probably going through a necessary phase in development of a technological society. Our Adventurers came to Earth having already been through that phase. They may have made a similar mess of their own planet to the mess we have made of ours. Landscape changes that we have made on Earth will still be very visible in a million years. The very absence of landscape change on Earth caused by our Adventurers in the last 100,000 years becomes evidence pointing towards both their technological level and how they may have occupied their time and gained fulfillment.

There may however be a very few sites where they did alter the landscape in ways that we can still see. And if their science focused on living things we have a much better chance of finding evidence, through genetics.

****

Chapter 6 – From new arrivals to residents.

A transitional chapter.

This chapter is a little different from the other chapters, as it marks a transition in the story. So far we have used logical reasoning to speculate about what our Adventurers would have needed to do to establish themselves on Earth. We have based this on thoughts about the Earth and have guessed what our Adventurers' responses might have been to what they found. We have not so far speculated much about what our Adventurers actually did on Earth, except to come to the conclusion that they probably remained a relatively small society and likely had a strong preference for use of renewable resources and modes of transport that did not involve carving highways into the landscape. We have not looked at any specific evidence for them being here. Indeed the most important conclusion as regards evidence is that there isn't likely to be any of the large-scale evidence in the landscape of the kind that humans have created, or detritus from the way their society lived.

Beyond the assumptions I have made, that long-lived aliens came to Earth and that Antarctica was not completely covered by ice when they did, I am endeavouring in this book to provide evidence for my speculations. I want to point you towards the 'uncomfortable facts' that have yet to be explained to my satisfaction by the 'received wisdom' of the different areas of knowledge we are delving into. You can then make your own assessment of which facts are dubious, which are possible but far from proven, and which you think are true beyond reasonable doubt. 'Beyond reasonable doubt' is an interesting phrase as it accepts that things in the past can rarely be proven to be 100% true. It is a matter of the weight of evidence, which is a judgement of the evidence for and against. And weight of evidence can pile up from all sorts of different areas of investigation.

From here on we will be looking at things that might be evidence left behind by our Adventurers, that we can see and investigate. The evidence may be in the ground, in buildings and artefacts, or in the myths and stories that have come down to us. We will have to interpret this in terms of what we think our Adventurers were doing and their purpose, with human viewpoints only as a secondary consideration.

We cannot know how other beings think, we can only try to explain their actions by reference to drives that we understand. We do not really know how other animals on Earth think, let alone alien beings. But we do have some insights. Dogs have been our companions over many years and we work closely with them. We know how dogs behave and we postulate what they might be thinking that makes them behave in this way. We know how they like to eat and relax. We know they like to run around and take joy in their bodies. We know that they can learn to herd sheep in very clever ways and seem to enjoy exercising these skills. When they are active they like to be doing things, exploring, smelling things for clues of other dogs and animals, chasing sticks. We can see how wolves hunt in packs and how they cooperate in making a kill. We can see the hierarchies in packs of dogs and we use their pack instinct to get them to accept us as their master.

In trying to assess how our Adventurers thought we can take some clues from how we see animals behaving, particularly more intelligent animals. We can infer from the fact that a group came to Earth that we have many things in common with them, such as intelligence, technological capability, and sociability. As discussed it is not too great a leap to suggest they also had the animal needs of food, shelter, social position - and sex; species of animals don't survive if they don't have a strong interest in sex when they are in their prime. It really is a mystery how pandas have survived for so long. Social position is often related to sexual urges, when hormones take over from rational behaviour and drive animals to compete with others in their group. The kinds of tensions that might have arisen amongst our Adventurers for these reasons could be a factor in how they behaved, as well as more rational considerations such as their reasons for coming and what their mission was. We should not be surprised if our Adventurers had periods of disharmony in their group, if relationships between individuals changed and rivalries persisted. If stories of such things have come down to us this is only to be expected.

The first decades of our Adventurers' time in Antarctica may well have been taken up by the process of establishing themselves. Initially 100% of their time may have had to be spent creating homes and establishing food supply. But eventually they would get to at least the technological level of organisation that we have managed. Less then 10% of the population of our technologically advanced countries are needed to grow food for the whole population. Or you could think of that as less than 10% of each individual's time. Taking out time for eating, sleeping, leisure and social activities that leaves a fair bit of time for activities with purpose, for following interests.

They would no doubt have explored Antarctica and all the geology, flora and fauna within it. But as we have conjectured Antarctica may not have contained many of the things our Adventurers saw from their spaceship that they would like to look at. In particular it would not have had the most intelligent animals on the planet. I can imagine some anthropologists amongst our Adventurers itching to travel to other parts of the world to start investigating the hominins that they had observed engaging in social and at least semi-intelligent behaviour. While others might have been itching to start traveling around the world to see what additional delights the Earth could provide to make their lives more enjoyable.

The other reason why they might have travelled out from Antarctica to other parts of the world, where they might have left evidence that we can still find, is that they needed or desired things that could only be obtained in other parts of the world. Which is what we will look at next.

****

Chapter 7 – Sugar and spice and all things nice.

It is only if our Adventurers ventured out of Antarctica into the rest of the world that we will be able to find evidence of their existence. So we need to consider what the drivers would have been for this and hence where they may have ventured to. The example we will use is food.

Spaceship food.

They obviously had food production capability in the spacecraft in which they travelled to Earth. Even at the limits of science fiction, with warp-speed and the ability to travel between galaxies this is likely to have taken a long time. The creators of Star Trek opened the episodes describing the Starship Enterprise's five-year mission: to explore strange new worlds, to seek out new life and new civilizations. If you were in a spaceship for 5 years, you would want good and tasty food. We will have to assume the spaceship is equipped to provide this. I doubt that they would exist by re-hydrating dehydrated foods for five years, my guess is that they would have had bacterial cultures and hydroponically grown plants, and some sophisticated food technologies to make these into interesting meals. Spaceship food, if it is going to be eaten for many years, needs to be sufficiently diverse and interesting as this has an effect on the mind; poor food is not conducive to people operating at their best. We are beginning to understand the importance of happiness for our physical well-being and I think our Adventurers would understand this too.

Our food comes from three kinds of organisms, animals, plants and cellular organisms. Animals and plants we have known about for ever but it is only recently that we have started to explore how to grow food in cell cultures. Except of course for our old friend yeast, that has been helping us make tasty food for so long that it is easy to forget that it is so different from plants and animals. When working in Belgium I was told a story about a brewery that modernised their plant and in the process re-roofed the areas where the beer sat in the brewing vats, removing the old and dirty tile roof and replacing it with a much more sanitary and modern roof. There was just one small problem; the beer stopped tasting as it used to, and as the brewery's reputation was built on the fine taste of its beer this was a disaster. They looked at all the possibilities of things they could have inadvertently changed in the refurbishment and eliminated all of them as possible causes of the change in taste, until the only possibility left was that it was something to do with the new roof. Fortunately the old roofing tiles had not been thrown away, They were still in the builder's yard. They brought them back in and all of a sudden the beer started brewing properly again. This may be an apocryphal story but it's a lovely story to illustrate the importance of yeast cultures in giving taste to food, and also the importance of taste in food. There was something in those tiles that was seeding the air in the room in a way that caused the yeast to develop in a slightly different way, which had presumably built up over the years.

All kinds of animals like to have food they consider tasty in their diet. And they will go out of their way to find particularly tasty foods. Our Adventurers will have been no different and would probably have looked forward to exotic new tastes that the Earth might provide.

Animals are fine as a source of food if they can be allowed to roam about and largely look after themselves. All you then have to do is catch them or kill them where they are when they are suitably grown. You may have to follow them around as they move to better pastures, or if they migrate past where you live catch more than you need and dry the meat, as the American Indians used to do with buffalo. Once confined on a farm animals become more problematical. They require large amounts of food to grow and are not very efficient at turning it into protein. They produce large amounts of often noxious waste products. Though you may enjoy a nicely cooked rare steak, if you had to go to all the trouble of growing the cattle to produce the steak, you might eat steak rather less often. Animals such as cattle and pigs need space to exercise. If they are kept in enclosures that are too small they grow less well and there are issues of animal cruelty. Smaller animals such as chickens can be reared in confined spaces, again with the proviso about whether you feel battery farming of chickens is morally acceptable, but still with the waste products to deal with. There is rather a lot of work involved in keeping livestock which would be quite difficult to manage in a spaceship.

We are anyway discovering that a good and balanced diet should probably contain rather less meat than is often eaten by people in the western world. Mainly vegetarian diets are in many ways more healthy and it is certainly possible to be satisfactorily nourished whilst avoiding animal foods. However there are certain things that we can get most easily from animal foods that have beneficial impact on our bodies and minds, such as omega 3 fatty acids from fish oils and B vitamins and iron from red meat. Without animals care would need to be taken to ensure these were included in the diet. We have evolved to be omnivores.

As I am assuming that our Adventurers are technologically advanced, their society will probably have been through the kinds of debates that we are now having about food. We cannot know whether their society came to any moral conclusions about whether or not it is morally right to eat animals. They might even have got as far as refusing to eat plants, as the dividing line between animals and plants is not as clear-cut as many imagine. They could have decided to exist only on food created from cell-cultures. This however is pure speculation, which I am trying to avoid. But we do need to make some guesses about what food production facilities they brought with them and what they expected of the Earth.

I think we can make the assumption that long-lived technologically and medically advanced beings will have had clear insight into what foods their bodies needed to remain in peak condition throughout their long lives. I would be prepared to take a bet that this would be the over-riding concern for such a society. We are beginning to see diet as key to a long life. If it then proved that plants or animals were the most effective sources for things needed in their diet, my guess is that this would over-ride moral concerns about eating them. They would find appropriate ways to grow and kill plants and animals as painlessly as possible, that assuaged their conscience. Nature is based on one thing eating another thing and all beings, no matter how advanced, are part of nature.

Perhaps I am displaying my prejudices here; you can make your own mind up. The key point is that though our Adventurers' spaceship would have contained the facilities to produce a satisfactorily balanced diet, if they did not raise livestock on board there would have been some compromises. If a body needs substances that can be gained either from a nice rare steak, or from a cell culture that produces something of the consistency of tofu, I know that I would prefer the steak, but for the purposes of engaging in an expedition I might be prepared to forgo it and eat the tofu-like substitute. There is however no manufactured substitute for a well-fried egg.

As well as their on-board food production capabilities they might also have brought seeds or cell cultures that were not grown on board, but stored in ways that would leave them still viable after many years travel. According to wikipedia the oldest carbon-14-dated seed found here in Earth, that has grown into a viable plant, was a Judean date palm seed about 2,000 years old. Yeast can be dried and stored and re-activated after 5 years.

This then will have been the starting point for food production by our Adventurers on Earth, a satisfactory if slightly boring diet from food grown in their craft, the opportunity to see if this food or seeds brought with them could grow on Earth, and a wide range of possible foods on Earth that would all need to be checked out for safety, palatability and substances needed in their diet for a long life.

Better food.

Food is one of the delights of life. There are some people who eat to live. I prefer to live to eat. Within the requirements of what is vital for good health there is on Earth a wonderfully wide range of possible good diets. People in different parts of the Earth eat differently, partly because of what is available and partly because different climates cause the body to have different food needs. For example in cold climates a higher calorie diet is needed because of the greater heat loss from the body.

The first step for our Adventurers will have been to explore food sources available in Antarctica. If there had been compromises while traveling such as substituting food from cell-cultures instead of the delights of a steak or an egg, first priority may have been to look to introduce these delights back into their diet. They may also have been lusting for things that grow on plants too big to grow in a spacecraft. If you like walnuts you need a walnut tree that is mature enough, and hence large enough to fruit. Hardly the kind of thing one would take on a spaceship voyage.

With my assumption about the position on the Earth of Antarctica at this time, they will have had available to them a wide variety of climates, all the way from cool climes close to the ice-sheet to mediterranean climes on the Antarctic peninsula. They will not have had the ability to grow foods that need tropical climates. These would have had to be brought to Antarctica.

In the rich western world we have long had access to Bananas, and have sent ships far across the sea to get them. It is worth while looking at what bananas provide as a food, as this illustrates the kind of considerations that our Adventurers might have weighed when looking for useful additions to, or changes in their carefully planned diet.
- Bananas are a high calorie food.

- They contain good amounts of health-benefiting anti-oxidants, minerals, and vitamins.

- They give quick energy with simple sugars like fructose and sucrose which is why athletes use them.

- They have lots of fibre that helps normal bowel movements.

- They contain health antioxidants such as lutein and zea-xanthin that act as protective scavengers against oxygen-derived free radicals, that are involved in aging and various disease processes.

- They are a very good source of vitamin-B6

- They are a moderate source of vitamin-C

- Fresh bananas provide minerals like copper, magnesium, and manganese that the body needs.

- Fresh banana is a very rich source of potassium which is an important component of cell and body fluids that helps control heart rate and blood pressure.

That's quite a list. As I do not have expectations of living hundreds of years I am content to not worry too much about what precise diet will give me longest life. If I die a couple of years earlier than I might I will have lost only say 2% of possible life. If on the other hand a very correct diet could make the difference between living 300 or 400 years, that would be a 25% difference in length of life. I suspect that the fact that we are all living longer is a key driver of the growing concerns about diet for many people. People have a vision of possibly 30 years of life after they reach three-score and ten. To achieve that amount of extra life is worth some extra care about what you eat.

In passing it is worth noting that it is not at all clear how the seedless banana was developed. It appears to have happened around 8000 years ago in South East Asia starting from the heavily seeded wild varieties but it is only now, through genome analysis, that it is becoming clearer what the origins of the various cultivars are. Did mankind get some help in doing this?

I think it would have been a very natural progression for our Adventurers to start looking at the food opportunities that tropical areas provide just as soon as they had explored and started to use useful food sources close to home in Antarctica. They may also have gone to have a look at what was available in northern temperate countries. There is no guarantee that species growing in the northern hemisphere would have been present on Antarctica. Temperate plants growing one side of the Equator have no easy way to migrate through the tropics to the other hemisphere by expanding their range, the only way would have been through seeds carried on migrating birds or floating across the sea. Birds would not carry a walnut and it would be a very long way for a walnut to float and successfully seed. The main temperate land-mass on the Earth is in the northern hemisphere, so there would be every possibility that more tasty plants and animals had developed there than in the southern hemisphere. Walnuts by the way have the reputation of being a really important food for the well-being of the brain, as they contain lots of omega-3. In addition they are reputed to raise melatonin levels promising relief from sleeplessness and insomnia, help the heart by reducing cholesterol and contain important nutrients - manganese, copper, iron, calcium, phosphorus - and more antioxidants, folic acid and vitamin E than any other nut.

Collecting plants and animals.

In our endeavours to get better food we have had some battles and had to be devious and cunning. The British succeeded in stealing tea plants from China and discovered they would happily grow in Ceylon, India and Africa. Though note that they each taste slightly different. The Chinese fully appreciated the trading importance of maintaining a monopoly on silk. It was a capital offense to smuggle silk-worms out of China. However someone took the risk to get both silkworms and their food, mulberry bushes, out of China, so that silk could be produced elsewhere.

As our Adventurers were coming to another planet it is likely that they were very aware of biological contamination. Their first concern would be to ensure that they and their craft were not in danger of being contaminated by anything on the Earth that could cause them problems. As a species we have only fairly recently, in the last few hundred years, discovered the problems that arise from shipping plants, animals, bacteria and viruses around the world. The Europeans carried measles and other diseases to South America, causing most of the population to die as they had no resistance to these diseases. With air flight now common, epidemics such as bird flu and ebola can spread extremely rapidly unless care is taken.

Being aware of these possibilities would very likely have caused our Adventurers to act with caution. They would have taken care not to introduce to Antarctica something that would cause problems in the natural environment of Antarctica. They would probably not have moved plants and animals from where they then existed on the Earth to parts of the world where they did not exist. Introduced species can cause major problems. It would have been better to let the plants continue to grow where they were, and collect the food and other materials they could get from plants, provided they could transport it without it spoiling.

The incentive to get foods from other areas of the world has often been high. Foods and substances that stimulate the human body in various ways can be hugely valuable. A pound of tea in 17th century London cost somewhere between a labourer's weekly wage and that of a journeyman tradesman. Spices were similarly valuable; when Vasco Da Gama brought back the two remaining ships of the five that he had set out with on his two-year voyage, it is said that they brought back a cargo of spices and other exotic products worth 60 times the entire cost of the voyage. The phrase "when my ship comes in" refers to the very risky business of financially backing a ship to go to the far East and bring back spices. Many foundered on the way losing all, but if the ship did make it back the profit on the investment was huge and could provide a fortune for life, such was the demand for spices.

Our Adventurers would also surely have been very careful about introducing to the Earth any plants or creatures that they have brought with them. The only cause they can have had to plant something that did not already grow here would be if they had brought with them seeds of really useful plants of which there were no comparable plants already on the Earth. They might of course also been expert in the genetic modification of plants and if they did this might possibly have used genes from plants they brought with them.

For foods and stimulants that they wanted to add to their diet, that they might have taken to Antarctica or which had to grow elsewhere on Earth, the concern would have been about how to ensure a steady supply over the many years that they wished to continue to have access to these foods. How was the job of cultivation and harvesting to be arranged? And if the foods, stimulants and other resources from plants and animals had to be grown elsewhere and brought back to Antarctica, how was that to be arranged? Our Adventurers probably wished to spend their time in more intellectually engaging ways than time-consuming food and materials production at home or in ferrying these from far away.

****

Chapter 8 – The need for manpower; early development of humans.

In the last chapter I came to the conclusion that our Adventurers, fairly soon after getting themselves established in Antarctica, would want to take advantage of what other parts of the Earth could offer them. We discussed this in terms of food, but there could be other reasons as well. Plants and animals produce materials, some of them in a much better and easier way than any other way we know of to produce comparable things. Musk for example, comes from a gland in the musk deer and is one of the most expensive animal products in the world. It has been used since ancient times as a perfume fixative. One may not agree that perfume is worth more than the life of a musk deer, but some people believe this, just as some people are prepared to pay large amounts of money for elephant ivory and rhinoceros horn.

Perhaps a better example, if we are going to imagine our Adventurers in a rather better light than as mere pleasure seekers, is rubber. Natural rubber can be extracted sustainably from rubber trees, whereas artificial rubber is made from petroleum products that have to be drilled for and refined. Our Adventurers may also have wanted minerals and metals. We do not have any idea what their technology required or what they might have desired for decoration, such as gold or jewels, but it is a fair guess that minerals will have been on their shopping list as well. Gold and jewels of course have uses other than decoration. Industrial diamond is used in drilling and cutting bits, while gold is used extensively in electronics, to coat contacts so that they do not corrode.

Some of their requirements they would have been able to collect themselves, even though I have assumed that there are not many Adventurers in the group. For things they can safely bring back and grow in Antarctica it is just a matter of going out on an expedition and collecting samples of plants or animals. They could have acted similarly to the gentlemen and lady adventurers who in Victorian times went plant hunting in remote parts of the world. Back in Antarctica the whole group of Adventurers could take part in the work of extracting what they want, even if this involved messy or hard work.

If on the other hand what they wanted came from plants and animals that needed to live in the tropics or from minerals that only occur in specific places on Earth, then there would need to have been working parties that spent at least some of their time on extended visits to harvest what they wanted. It is somewhat remarkable that the processes by which the Earth's crust has been created has led to mine-able deposits of key resources occurring only in certain places. Tin for example, which is necessary to make bronze, only occurs as major deposits in four places in Europe. So for the bronze age to happen there must have been trade that transported the tin from these places to the rest of Europe, the Mediterranean and the Middle East. Certain kinds of stone and wood are also only found in certain areas, such as the redwood forests of North America or the cedars of Lebanon. When Stonehenge was built the builders were very fussy about the stone they wanted to use. The bluestones were sourced from the Preseli hills in Wales, a considerable distance away. Though Antarctica, being a very large continent, no doubt had many of the resources our Adventurers wanted the chances are that it did not have everything they wanted. A need or desire to get things from elsewhere is likely.

Such trips to obtain resources might have been hard work and not particularly desirable. Extracting what you want from rocks, plants and animals is a tedious, often repetitive process, that can take hard physical work and be messy. Machines can make the work lighter though they still need to be driven. Automatic machines might be the answer, but our Adventurers would surely be loath to leave valuable machines where they could be damaged by hominins or animals. Machines might be useful to help them get things they only needed to collect occasionally, but this would not work for things they wanted regular supplies of. And some things are better done by hand or cannot easily be mechanised. Going around rubber trees to collect the latex that has slowly dripped into the collectors would be a little hard to mechanise, but it is quite easy for human beings to do once they have been shown how.

Getting what you want takes manpower. And if manpower is plentiful and cheap, as it was for example in the cotton and sugarcane plantations in America and the Caribbean in the 18th and 19th centuries, then there is little incentive or need to create machines. The point at which creation of machines becomes desirable (to the accountants) is when there is a task that can be done in a central location that can be mechanised and hence done very much faster and more reliably than humans can do it. And the drive for the managers who finance and install the machines is profit, rather than the need to secure a sufficiency of products. Our Adventurers, being a small group with no intention of growing the size of their society, would have had no reason to create and use machines if they could find the manpower to reliably gather and process the resources they wanted from rocks, plants and animals.

We must think of 'manpower' as being a very different idea to 'Adventurer power'. It is likely that slaveowners had very little concern about their slaves having to do very hard work, beyond the need to keep them healthy so they could go on doing it. Humans similarly have had little concern about working horses hard or about taking honey produced through the hard work of bees. The mindset is one of considering other creatures to be lesser beings, there to be used if they can be sufficiently domesticated to be useful, with only a duty of welfare being a matter of concern, and that probably only because of the desire to get the maximum from the creatures. Our Adventurers would probably see themselves as superior to all the other animals on the Earth.

'Manpower' however means more than just muscle, it means muscles guided reasonably intelligently. It has to be possible to instruct the creature putting in the effort how their muscles are to be used. The creature exercising the manpower has to be able to understand these instructions and have some understanding of what the task is, if they are to do it without continuous oversight and correction. Human beings have developed all sorts of ways of substituting for manpower and extending it, primarily through horse, dog, bullock or goat power. We have found ways to instruct animals to do our bidding. We do however have to be present to control them. There are only a few examples where animals will do our bidding simply because that is in their nature, such as pigs clearing fields of weeds or geese acting as watchdogs, alerting their owners to intruders. There are a few animals that can be instructed to do things autonomously. Dolphins have been trained by the US Navy to carry out all sorts of tasks on their own. But amongst the land animals the furthest we have got is with chimpanzees, who can do all sorts of clever things. However they can't really be instructed to carry out the tasks that we want doing. They do things either because they want to or to please their trainer. We can't say to a chimpanzee 'chop down those trees and cut the wood into planks' and leave them to it and come back and expect to find the task done.

The sorts of goodies our Adventurers might have wanted to collect from around the Earth needed reasonably intelligent manpower, not chimpanzee power or horse power. They had a straightforward choice. They could either provide that manpower from amongst their number, or they could look for other animals that would do the job. If there were no animals that fitted their requirements, they in all likelihood had an additional choice that we are only just developing – make an animal to fit the requirements. We are now doing this with plants quite openly. We are also doing it with animals in the confines of laboratories that test drugs, genetically modifying laboratory animals for specific tests. Public awareness of genetic manipulation of animals is at the stage of some acceptance of straightforward cloning as with Dolly the sheep, and genetic manipulation within a species, as witnessed by the creation of three-parent human babies that is now being done. Addition of genes from one species into another to create a completely new species is still rather in the realms of science fiction for us, though happening with plants and bacteria. But it may well have been a possibility for our Adventurers to do this with animals.

Once they had decided that creation of manpower was a sensible route to explore, their problem was where this manpower was going to come from. The world they were looking at was inhabited by various sorts of hominin. Homo-habilus existed around 2.3 million years ago, with a brain about the size of that of a chimpanzee. Not that brain size is necessarily indicative of the level of intelligence. It appears homo-habilus used stone tools so they must have had a degree of intelligence. Homo-erectus, using better tools and fire, were around in the period 1.8 to 1.3 million years ago. There then seems to have been somewhat of an explosion of different species, including homo-heidelbergensis, homo-rhodesiensis or homo-antecessor, homo-denisova, homo-floresiensis and homo-neanderthalensis. The period when they were around is estimated to be 100,000 years to 50,000 years ago. Homo-erectus may also have survived alongside these species into this period. Early modern humans were in existence by 200,000 years ago.

We don't know how intelligent such hominins were but we can make some guesses. We think for example that neanderthals buried things with their dead. That is evidence of some higher-level thinking. Tool-making started amongst ancestors of human beings that we would have considered to be more like apes than human beings, but they walked upright and their brains were starting to grow beyond those of the apes. The kinds of stone tools they made became progressively though slowly more sophisticated, which is also evidence of intelligence. It is quite probable that these hominins had some kind of language beyond the kind of calls other animals make.

This is the range of raw material for manpower that would be available to our Adventurers. The first step would have been to see whether it was possible to train any of these species of hominin. We can imagine them experimenting to see how trainable each species was. They would have had the same kinds of frustration that we experience in training chimpanzees though the languages hominins used to communicate between themselves were probably more complex than chimpanzee language. It might have been possible for our Adventurers to learn these languages, but the languages would only have had words or sounds for concepts that were important in the lives of the creatures. They might not have had words for many of the things our Adventurers wanted them to do, which would have had to be communicated by demonstration. Our Adventurers would have considered whether they could teach these beings new words to describe the things they wanted them to get or do. They would also have had to work out how to incentivise these creatures to do their bidding. Food rewards are a very short-term incentive and as soon as hunger is satisfied the rewards become much less powerful. Amongst the creatures we see in the world it is only humans that can be easily incentivised by delayed rewards that only appear some time into the future, after several days or weeks of work has been done.

As long-lived beings our Adventurers would also have experimented with selective breeding to see if they could improve the intelligence and usefulness of a specific species. Mankind has created many different kinds of horse, including the cart horse for heavy work and the race horse for speed. It takes quite a lot of generations of animals to do this and some luck in what natural mutations happen, but our Adventurers had the time if they had the patience. Once they discovered the limits of the natural intelligence of the creatures available as possible manpower, they would have been able to recognise whether they could selectively breed the required intelligence and language capabilities. And if not, then they could turn to genetic modification.

The question for us then is whether or not we can find any evidence to point to changes in mankind that might be the result of training, breeding or genetic modification by our Adventurers.

Cro Magnon man.

There is much debate about the various hominins on the Earth 100,000 years ago and how they interacted with each other, and interbred. The genomes of many present-day humans appear to contain elements contributed by other hominins. For example most current human beings have genes that come from homo-neanderthalensis – neanderthal man. There is also a lot of debate about the movements of the various species that existed at the time.

In this field it is necessary to understand that until recently all the identification of different species of hominin has been based on their skeletal features. It is the shape of the skull and the build of the rest of the skeleton that distinguishes neanderthals from early modern humans. The same applies to differentiating homo-floriensis and homo-naledi from humans. Now however we have the added tool of DNA analysis of ancient bones, which is enabling the genomes of the different species to be investigated. This is a much more secure way of being sure that the different species really are different, and not just extremes of the differences within species. They are however closely related species as witnessed by the fact that they could interbreed.

New studies are being done all the time now that we have much greater expertise in exploring genetics, so views are changing. It is a rather exciting time as differences in the DNA of humans around the world still exist, because we have only had cross-racial breeding to a very small extent in many areas, up to the last fifty years or so. This ability to study modern racial DNA differences is now being combined with the ability to extract DNA from fossil bones, allowing identification of the genetic markers that indicate humans are derived from a variety of other species to some extent. It is also allowing us to construct a family tree of how humans moved around Europe and the world, taking mutations that originated in one area into other populations.

The papers on the genomes of hominins and early mankind are complicated but often the summaries that are published give the highlights that will enable you to follow this. The challenge is to see what we can deduce from well-based facts that could help inform the theory we are exploring, the possible existence of our Adventurers. There are two very well established facts that strike me as important. The first is that it is undeniable that a significant change to early modern humans happened fairly recently, 50 or 60 thousand years ago, creating the humans that are sometimes described as

Cro-Magnon man, also known as the Aurignacian culture. In both cases these names refer to the places their remains were first found. The second key point is that this evolution of early modern humans produced a rapid change in the evidence that they left behind, which shows a lot of evidence of higher-level thinking.

Though I shall refer to these humans that had evolved higher-level thinking as cro-magnon man, do not take that to mean that they actually evolved in Cro-Magnon. They are so named because the first bones found that were associated with artefacts showing higher-level thinking were found in the Cro-Magnon rock shelter. They could have first evolved anywhere across Europe, Western Asia and the Arabian peninsula, as there is growing evidence of them right across this area. They then spread from here right around the world, reaching Australia some 40,000 years ago.

Archeologists can tell us about the bone structure and hence physical shape of the various hominins. But the bones don't tell us anything much about their intelligence. No difference has been detected in the brain size of early modern humans before the emergence of cro-magnon man and and after, the change must have been in how their brains worked. Brain size may be an indicator of intelligence, but homo-floriensis had only a small brain but made and used stone tools and may have used fire. Homo-neanderthalis had a larger brain than homo-sapiens, but we survived and they apparently did not, with some people theorising that we may have been instrumental in their decline. We have to look for evidence other than bones to indicate intelligence.

It is intelligence that would have been the deciding factor in whether or not hominins could be used by our Adventurers as self-directed manpower. The very earliest evidence we have found of hominins expressing their thoughts are engraved v-shaped marks on the shell of a fossilised freshwater clam, found at Trinil in Indonesia. This has been dated to between 430,000 and 540,000 years ago. It is believed that this must have been done by a homo-erectus, as homo-erectus remains have been found in the area. This is a very long time before early modern humans appeared perhaps 200,000 years ago, and indeed before we believe other hominins developed, so we will have to imagine very slowly developing intelligence and creative urges in hominins generally. Much closer to us in time are the flowers found in neanderthal graves mentioned earlier that indicate some kind of abstract thought. But at this stage, prior to 60,000 years ago, we don't have evidence of greater development in the making of marks by any hominins, that could indicate a higher level of intelligence. The slow development of intelligence is best seen in the slowly growing sophistication of the stone tools they made.

In this long history from homo-erectus, through the development of other hominins to the development of very intelligent humans, the change 60,000 years ago is rather abrupt. What makes the humans in this period interesting and remarkable is that in addition to leaving behind very well worked stone tools, that are much more sophisticated than tools found with earlier hominins, they also left behind them cave art in France and Spain. The El Castillo cave art, such as the images of hands created by blowing paint at a hand held on the rock, are estimated to have been created 40,000 years ago (see http://news.nationalgeographic.com/news/2012/06/120614-neanderthal-cave-paintings-spain-science-pike/). These artworks show a level of sophistication that suggests that they were first attempts, with art estimated to be of later date becoming more sophisticated. By 30,000 years ago they were creating sophisticated pictures of animals, as seen in the caves at Chauvet in France (see http://www.bradshawfoundation.com/chauvet/). This amounts to very rapid development compared with the hundreds of thousands of years from the first hominin-made marks. With stone tools first appearing a few million years ago, improvements in tool making also took hundreds of thousands of years. From the evidence cro magnon people left we can see art appearing and then becoming more sophisticated in just ten thousand years. The ways that animals and humans were represented in the Chauvet artwork suggests that cro magnon man may have had an intellect not far removed from our own. There is also evidence of jewelry and body ornamentation with beads such as the ostrich-egg beads found in the Denisova cave, and of the start of musical instruments. There are even hints that humans were making much more sophisticated clothes than neanderthals, using fur from small mammals, probably around the ends of sleeves and around hoods, that enabled them to work in colder temperatures.

Once cro-magnon man appears in the fossil record, we start getting increasing evidence of abstract thought. And the progressive development of the artwork, jewelry and clothes implies not just a more intelligent hominin, but one with an innate desire to improve on what they did. If there had been this kind of curiosity and desire to improve in earlier hominins, it would surely not have taken the immense length of time that it did to go from initial mark-making to cave art. The stone tools would show a more even development as well, rather than the sudden increase in their sophistication that appears alongside the development of cro-magnon man.

How evolution works - as far as we know.

We do not actually know how the evolution of new species works. We do know that random mutations happen in our genes. We have some idea of how often these genetic mutations are likely to happen. These then get embedded in our genome if the individuals that have those changes survive and reproduce well. These are small random changes when genes are copied as new cells are made. They make small changes to animals and then through Darwin's survival of the fittest process sub-species slowly develop. This is how the Galapagos island sub-species of finch came to have different beak shapes that allowed them to occupy specialised niches in the ecosystem, able to access different kinds of seeds.

We don't know whether it is possible for a small random change in a gene to create a big change in the capabilities of an animal. We haven't seen this happening over recorded history. In mankind we haven't seen another development of brainpower that has enabled the tribe where the genetic change happened to become pre-eminent over neighbouring tribes. Or at least we don't think we have seen this. This starts to bear on all the discussions that have been promoted by various people on eugenics. As it is generally frowned upon to promote ideas of one race of human beings having greater intelligence than others, there hasn't in recent years been much research into this. However just through common-sense observation of different races of humans around the world, we can't see any differences in intelligence over the last 10,000 years of recorded history that put a particular human race onto a much faster development path, in the way that cro-magnon man started to develop so much faster than the other hominins around at the time. If it had happened, then that race of mankind would probably have displaced the rest of us, in the same way that cro-magnon man spread into other areas of the world and appear to have displaced homo-neanderthalis, homo-erectus, homo-florienses and any other earlier hominins. We can see that homo-sapiens has developed into the pygmy tribes of Africa as well as humans of 'normal' size, into caucasian, negro, Australian aborigine, Chinese and other human racial types. But these are minor evolutionary changes comparable to changes in finch beak shape, not major changes that conferred major advantages over pre-cursor species and created a new species. Humans all over the world have brains that are constructed and work in the same ways.

As to how cro-magnon man arose, it may be that some small random genetic mutation in an individual did confer hugely superior thinking capabilities and that this then got embedded in the genome of the tribe and became dominant. Or maybe this wasn't just a small genetic change caused by random mutation. I read somewhere a few years ago that there is some evidence that new genes appeared in the human genome around this period, but haven't re-found the reference yet (this book wasn't even a pipe-dream at that stage of my reading and researching). If so, where did the genes come from? Chance mutation? Interbreeding with another species we haven't found yet? Or could it be genetic modification?

The early movements of humans.

In this complex and developing field new insights are being gained almost every week it seems. I follow these developments through subscribing to New Scientist, from where the following information came.

Interesting evidence is being found from analysis of the Y chromosome in men from Africa, Eurasia and Central America. The Y chromosome mutates over time and hence can be used to create a family tree of men. Mutations that are in more of the chromosomes analysed are considered to have occurred earlier and those that are in fewer chromosomes to have occurred later. David Poznik and Carlos Bustamante at Stanford University have revealed from their analysis a couple of crucial population splits (see http://med.stanford.edu/ism/2013/august/bustamante.html). These probably occurred around 50,000 years ago when modern human beings were concentrated mainly in the area of the Arabian peninsula, the top of Africa and the area that is now Iran, Turkey and the Caucasus. It appears that the human population at this time split into three distinct groups, with just a single genetic mutation differentiating each of the groups. The fact of there being just a single genetic mutation differentiating them would, if this were a natural mutation, indicate a timescale of the order of just 150 years between those mutations. The three population groups that have descended from the males in which these mutations happened can still be identified today, and they are centred on different areas of the world. One group is centred on the Caucasus and Western Asia, the second group is centred on India, and the third group is spread far and wide but did give rise to the early inhabitants of North America.

Mutations to Y chromosomes happen in individual men. Then as their male children interbreed with the daughters of other men in the tribe, the mutation is mixed into the chromosomes of their descendants. Over enough generations in a relatively small group of people, nearly all of the tribe will come to possess the mutation. It is the absence of the mutation in the other groups of humans that is the interesting point. This has to point to a separation of the groups so that they don't interbreed, otherwise it would not be possible today to still to be able to identify where these groups with different mutations were and are centred.

So we have to imagine that the more intelligent (cro-magnon) humans that had apparently evolved somewhere in the Arabian Peninsula / Caucasus / Europe area, split into tribes that migrated, one into areas south of the Himalayas and the other probably into the area north of the Himalayas and Siberia, eventually making it over to America much later, with the third group remaining in the Caucasus/Western Asia/Europe area. Now is it sheer chance that these mutations happened and never re-mixed back into the other populations? And why have they become so widely geographically separated?

This could be explained if two tribes started moving in these directions and kept on moving, putting sufficient distance between the two moving tribes and the tribe remaining in the Caucasus area, to reduce inter-marrying of men into these other tribes to a negligible level. This is a perfectly reasonable explanation given how tribes in neighbouring territories tend to fight each other rather than socialise. The mutations must have happened once the tribes had split out of the original group and were in the process of migrating. Once they got hundreds of miles away from the original group it is easy to see how the populations remain distinct and apart. The distance is important. Though tribes living next to each other fight, they also steal women and rape, so genomes get mixed over a reasonably long period of time. It is only a large distance separating the tribes that could stop this mixing.

But 150 years is quite a small time for a tribe to travel a large distance. An article in Scientific American (see http://blogs.scientificamerican.com/guest-blog/2011/08/16/hunter-gatherers-show-human-populations-are-hardwired-for-density/) informs me that the size of hunter-gatherer territories doesn't vary in a linear way. It suggests a hunter-gatherer group of 10 people would have a territory of 5.6 sq km, 50 people an area of 10.8 sq km and a group of 100 people an area of 31.6 sq km. Heavens knows how they calculated such accurate figures but that's not important, we just need to look at the orders of magnitude of these territories. A group of 100 people would be quite a large tribe to keep together in a long migration, but let's use their size of territory as the example as it is the biggest territory. A 30 sq km territory, if round would be about 6 km across. If the group then split into two and 50 people moved off to a new territory, they would only need to travel 5 or 6 km to be well clear of their old territory and to have a territory of their own that did not impinge on the hunting area of the tribe remaining behind.

Why would they go any further? We could imagine that the reason for splitting off from their original tribe was perhaps changes in climate or animal movements that were making the original territory inhospitable, and that this was the courageous group prepared to split off on their own. Though a more likely reason is that the tribe had become too big to be supported well by their existing territory. It's not really likely that they were following an animal migration that had changed. Groups that live off animals with seasonal migrations, such as reindeer, follow where they go. The whole tribe would have moved. The moving tribe must have had reasons to keep on going, otherwise we would not now have the distinct groups identified. If they were moving because the climate in their old territory had seriously deteriorated, how would they know in which direction to move to find a climate that supported more fauna and flora? They weren't moving south to be nearer the sun, which would be an understandable reaction to climate becoming colder, the tribes that moved to India and over towards Eastern Asia were both traveling East (even if the poles were 2000km from where they now are). I could imagine the tribe heading for India following the Tigris or Euphrates all the way to the sea and then carrying on round the coast to India. And it would have been possible for the other tribe to have followed rivers going north into Siberia. If the poles were in different positions, the climate in Siberia could at that time have been temperate rather than cold steppe land. But the distance of separation to allow groups to remain distinct until now does not to me feel like just an expansion of a growing tribe into new territory. There must have been something to keep them moving.

The essence of being a successful hunter-gatherer is to know how animals move around the territory and to know what their habits are, and to know where there are good areas of plants to forage. There is incentive to explore as far as it is a reasonable walk from the various home bases used in the territory, which could open up new territory and cause a gradual movement if the food possibilities of the new territory in the direction of movement continue to improve. If not they would return to their old haunts. We are talking here of separations between the groups of two or three thousand miles. That need not have all happened in the 150 years between mutations, as long as there was continuing incentive to migrate rather than return. The question is what distance we might expect a hunter-gatherer tribe to move in a generation. The older people in the tribe would carry the memory of the food provided by the territories they occupied in their youth. I find it hard to imagine that the elders of the tribe would allow the tribe's territory to move more than a few days walk from the territory of their youth, say 100 miles? 150 years amounts to probably 4 or 5 generations, if we imagine the elders of the tribe to be 30 or 40 years old. So we could imagine the tribe moving 500 miles or so in 150 years, which would be enough initial separation to keep the groups distinct. But as stated above, this depends upon new territory being more productive than their existing territory. Any barren area a few miles across would cause a stop to the migration until some pressure such as population growth became strong enough to force some intrepid members of the tribe to go exploring, at some considerable risk to themselves.

From these considerations one would expect modern humans to have a more mixed genome, except for situations where the geography of the Earth creates natural 'pinch-points' that hinder migration, so that only a small group got through the pinch-point. The best example of this is the difficulty of getting from Eurasia into the Americas, with only a narrow land bridge at quite high and rather cold latitudes. I can't see in the atlas any comparable pinch-points between the Middle East and the distinct groups that ended up in India/S.E. Asia and Siberia.

So could there be another reason why groups of early humans split from the original group, started moving and carried on moving until they were more than 2000 miles away? Could it be that our Adventurers decided that this was the time to split their herd of manpower and to establish some of them in some different areas of the world?

There are some other puzzles in our development as well. Homo-sapiens is the hairless ape. If we have come originally from a common ancestor from which apes are also descended, when did we lose our hair. And given that losing hair is counter-intuitive from a survival point of view, how did we develop the adaptions that allow us to be hairless? Hair protected early hominins from both cold and heat, just as well as it does for other animals. In hot climates did losing our hair come first and force the adaption of colored pigmentation to protect our skin from the sun? And how did we manage to migrate into areas where the much hairier neanderthal lived? And did we then adopt clothing to protect from cold nights, as hair had protected the creatures early humans evolved from? Or did both loss of hair and adoption of clothing happen together in some way.

We can't answer these questions yet. They are just that, intriguing questions. The answers when we do discover them might support our story, or they may prove to have an explanation that does not require any involvement of our Adventurers.

While keeping a watch on the scientific developments that are shedding more light on this period in our history, it is time to get back to our story. Let us consider how our Adventurers might have been involved and whether a scenario in which they were involved makes any better sense of these and other puzzling issues.

****

Chapter 9 - Creating manpower.

Genetically modifying hominins.

Imagine yourself setting out to genetically engineer some more useful animals, capable of taking instructions and working autonomously. You need two things, an animal to start with and some genes to add. We are currently far from clear how this all works. We do know that DNA in genes provides the capability to encode and make proteins and those proteins enable the organism to do things it could not do before. But we don't know at all precisely how or why genes are 'turned on' and become active in changing the organism. And it is not a straightforward matter of having genes 'for' something; genes are not individually responsible for specific diseases or capabilities, even though there are some genes that appear to pre-dispose people to certain conditions and illnesses. There is even evidence that genes are affected by the environment an organism is living in. The great hope that being able to sequence the human genome would provide a great leap forward in medicine has not yet materialised. It has helped but nothing like as much as many hoped. Scientists are now studying what they term 'epigenetics' which is about how genes inter-relate with each other and how the environment they exist in affects whether they are active or not.

Though we don't yet know the science properly our Adventurers may well have known it much better. They may for example have had knowledge of how to engineer the bodily capability for complex vocalisations. This is the capability we have that has enabled us to develop language and speech to a high level, which our nearest current neighbours in our genetic tree, the chimpanzees, have only to a very limited extent. Other hominins too may have had much more limited language through inability to vocalise a sufficient range of sounds, but we just don't know. Our Adventurers might also have known how to engineer better thinking capability. I think we can assume that they had at least the capability in genetic manipulation that we have and probably more, how much more is just a guess.

But let's go step by step. For the animal to start with our adventurers probably had a fair degree of choice. We should not jump straight to the conclusion that a hominin would be first choice. As discussed, we train dogs to herd sheep because they have better capabilities for this job. Which is also why we train pigs to find truffles and horses to pull carts. If the job to be done was fruit or nut picking perhaps it might be better to train monkeys as they can climb better. But if you are going to go to the trouble of genetically engineering a new species there is some advantage in creating one multi-purpose creature rather than several specialised creatures. The success of hominins in spreading around the world will have been clear. They had shown themselves able to exist in different environments and to protect themselves against different threats.

However the main consideration in creating 'manpower' is how that manpower is going to be instructed to do tasks. And how they will be able to work independently without continuous control by an Adventurer, such as is needed to control horses. This makes language and intelligence the two most important features to be added to the chosen animal. That would have biased the decision towards starting with a hominin. Hominins probably already had some amount of language, given what we know about their ability to hunt and kill large animals, so it would be a matter of improving what they had rather than adding an entirely new capability. And their stone tools and use of fire indicated a level of intelligence beyond most other animals, though we should not underestimate the intelligence other animals have. We are now discovering that many animals use tools with some, such as crows, being very adept and displaying considerable intelligence.

I think we can also assume that our Adventurers would have been able to sequence the genomes of the various hominins and compare them. Though it cost millions of pounds to sequence the human genome the first time it was done, the cost to sequence an individual's genome is now down to a couple of thousand pounds. No doubt in the future it will be cheaper still. In sequencing the genomes of humans and other animals we have come across a few surprises. Probably the main surprise is how much of our DNA we share with other animals. Human and chimpanzee DNA is somewhere around 95%-98% the same. Not many differences in our DNA are responsible for the fairly considerable differences between us and chimpanzees. Our Adventurers would have been able to identify where the differences in hominin genomes were and to at least make some guesses as to what needed to be done to their genome to create the changes they wanted to make.

While talking about chimpanzee DNA compared to that of humans, it is worth noting in passing that there is another difference. Chimpanzee DNA has considerably more diversity than the DNA of humans. I see from the Smithsonian National Museum of Natural History website, as an example of this, that the subspecies of the chimpanzee that lives just in central Africa, pan troglodytes troglodytes, has higher levels of DNA diversity than do humans globally. A New Scientist article (Aug 2015) refers to this with the statement "human genetic diversity is abysmally low".

It is interesting when scientists and scientific writers use words like 'abysmally' because it clearly expresses how surprising they find this fact. They are saying that the low diversity in human DNA is so very different to the DNA diversity found in other species that it is remarkable. Thinking about this logically, we know that most of the diversity in DNA is small differences that cause the minor things that differentiate one animal from another of the same species, rather than the bigger differences between different species. We also know that these minor differences occur through random mutations in different individuals, over long periods of time. So for an animal to have high diversity of DNA across the species, we can either imagine that the species arose many hundreds of thousands of years ago, to give time for the high diversity to develop. Or we can imagine that evolution of one species from another does not happen just through one individual, but happens multiple times through mutations in a number of animals that are mutually supportive, so that the DNA diversity possessed by all these individual members of the pre-cursor species is passed down into the genome of the new species. In contrast, very low diversity in DNA suggests that there was a pinch-point in development of the new species, with very few individuals of the pre-cursor species contributing the diversity of their DNA to the new species. This might well be a point that is relevant to the idea we are developing here. If humans globally are all descended from a very few individuals who rapidly became a new species and ceased inter-breeding with the pre-cursor hominin species they developed from, low diversity in our DNA is what we should expect.

As to where the genes that conferred higher intelligence came from, these presumably were not present in any of the hominins available, otherwise they would surely have displayed this intelligence in the artefacts they produced. It is of course also possible that our Adventurers' bodies used DNA in the same way that animals on Earth do. DNA does seem to be the universal basis of life on Earth. It might just be the universal basis of life everywhere across the universe. Did it arrive on Earth in bacteria carried across interstellar space? This is the theory of panspermia which scientists are considering as a possible way life originated on Earth. There is a growing amount of evidence that organic molecules arrive on Earth from space. Numerous meteorites have been found to contain structures that may be fossilised bacteria, as they are hard to explain any other way, and the red rain that fell in Kerala, India just after a sonic boom, that may have been a meteorite breaking, up contained unusual cell-like structures. Add to this that during the Perseid meteor shower a scientific balloon returned samples of micro-organisms from 27 km above the Earth, which is considered too high for them to have originated on Earth. Attempts are now being made to assess whether light that reaches us from distant stars contains signatures that would indicate that life exists there. If panspermia has happened and our Adventurers' bodies were based on DNA, they would have been able to identify the differences between hominin DNA and their own. Just as with us and chimpanzees, they might have found there was not a lot of difference between their DNA and hominin DNA, just a few critical differences.

When we genetically modify plants, we identify parts of the DNA of one plant that we think are responsible for enabling that plant to have certain desirable qualities. We then endeavour to get those bits of DNA into the DNA of another plant. We can then assess if our target plant gains the desired qualities. The problem for our Adventurers would have been where to find the sections of DNA that they wished to add to the hominin they had decided was the best starting point. If hominins were the most intelligent species on Earth at the time would this have been a trial and error process of mixing DNA from different hominins? Or could they use sections of their own DNA? At the start of the book I decided to assume that our Adventurers were carbon-based lifeforms because they could survive on a watery planet. I am now going to assume that they did indeed have DNA just like all Earth animals. And that it was sections of their own DNA that were used to add intelligence into early modern humans.

This might be considered by some of our Adventurers to be a very contentious act. They were setting out to create a species that would always be a sub-species in their view. One can imagine some of them worrying that there would be trouble ahead, just as many of us would worry if someone decides to try to add some of our DNA into chimpanzee DNA. I am sure you can imagine what discussions would be likely to happen, were we to create a species half-way between ourselves and chimpanzees. It would probably be identifiably different to us humans, but as we have even got to the point of discussing whether intelligent robots might need to have rights analogous to human rights, the line could become very blurred. Hold this thought in your mind until later in the story.

Creating the first manpower.

Having chosen a hominin to work on, presumably the early modern humans, and having modified the genes in fertilised eggs, and re-implanted the eggs back into the mothers, the mothers chosen would need to have been carefully cared for. As the genetically modified progeny would need to learn the hunter-gatherer skills that would enable them to survive, the mothers would no doubt be left amongst their tribe. If they had the language to do so they would no doubt tell the rest of their tribe a story not unsimilar to the alien abduction stories that are reported now and again by humans. So our Adventurers would really be working with a chosen tribe rather than just individual female hominins.

When the genetically modified offspring were born they would have needed to be taught things their actual mother could not teach them, such as much more sophisticated language. This needs teaching early while the language areas of the brain are still forming. There are some languages on Earth that it is impossible to speak properly if the capability to produce certain sounds has not been developed in the first few years of life. Our Adventurers would have needed to establish some kind of relationship with the tribe of hominins in order to be able to gain sufficient access to the offspring. This is not quite like a zoo, because the whole point was to develop a self-sustaining animal that would look after itself and proliferate. The youngsters would need to learn the life skills of their parents, hunting and gathering, as well as new skills their parents could not teach them. They would have been very precocious children, not only thinking they know better than their parents as human children often do, but probably quite able to see how things their parents did could be done better.

There would then probably have been the need to do some selective breeding over several generations, for which our newly created more intelligent humans would need to be carefully managed in a closed community where their capabilities could be developed and tested. As the first offspring would have had quite a lot of contact with some of our Adventurers, in order to develop their language skills, once they became adults and led the tribe the relationship they had with the Adventurers would become a part of their life expectations. Our Adventurers would need to take care that the relationship developed was the right kind of super-species to sub-species relationship, that would enable our Adventurers to use their new manpower in the ways that they wanted to. And that did not enable the humans to feel that they were the same as our Adventurers.

Our Adventurers would want to keep their genetically engineered humans separated from the non-engineered varieties, in case they interbred and diluted or destroyed the effects of the genetic modification. They would need to keep them separated until the new species had diverged sufficiently to make breeding with the root stock unlikely. We know that some modern humans have DNA containing some bits of neanderthal DNA, showing that inter-breeding was indeed possible. If they came into contact with early modern humans that had not been genetically altered inter-breeding would be very likely. They would need to develop in the tribe a sense that they were special and different to the early modern humans, the sense of being a 'chosen tribe', to inhibit them from inter-breeding. And our Adventurers would need to build up a sufficient number of these new beings to guarantee their continued survival and growth of their numbers 'in the wild'. If the new intelligent humans were not already by nature highly social, this would need to be developed so that they became a strong tribe, supportive of each other and able to defend themselves against other creatures. However sociability is probably a trait inherent in all hominins.

As our Adventurers were few in number it would not really have been an option to build fences around a wide enough area of several square kilometres, to give their new creatures a hunting area. But with the very effective weapons our Adventurers must have had, and their ability to easily move around presumably by air, it would be possible to select an area and to clear it of major predators and those non-engineered hominins to stop interbreeding. This could be policed with occasional forays to discourage other hominins and dangerous animals. A good place to choose would be a valley with a relatively narrow open end, that goes up into high, preferably snow-covered mountains at the other end and on its sides.

Once cleared of the predators and hominins that might attack the new community of intelligent humans, they would no doubt look after the first few generations very carefully, until they had bred into a small tribe capable of rearing new infants and teaching them advanced language and survival skills themselves. If a side-effect of genetic engineering to increase intelligence and speech capabilities had been them becoming hairless, one of the skills they would need to learn and pass on would be creation of better clothing to protect themselves from cold.

It would probably not have been be too difficult to keep them in the valley, by making it an easy and pleasant place to live. Our Adventurers will have helped them to plant trees and other plants for easy foraging and quite possibly make sure they also planted the food crops of animals that they wanted to live in the valley, for them to hunt. In a hundred years or so they could have had perhaps 6 generations of intelligent humans. If each pair managed to produce 6 offspring that survive – which as they would be looking after them pretty closely is not unlikely – after 6 generations the tribe could be as many as 1500 - much larger than hunter-gatherer societies normally are now. The valley would also by then have fully mature fruit and nut trees and bushes self-seeding in this garden valley. It would be a special place where the living was easy compared to un-improved territory.

Let's call this place the Garden of Eden.

Where was the Garden of Eden?

If I was in charge of genetically engineering the most competent animals on a planet, to make them even more competent, I would want this work to happen in a safe place. Safe for me that is. Genetically engineered organisms can escape. If some fool ever decides to genetically engineer a food plant so that it produces chemicals that can be made into potent drugs, who is to say that pollen from this engineered version of the plant will not cross-contaminate the food plants, and that this might become dominant, rapidly making that food plant inedible. Yet just such a thing was proposed by one of the companies involved with genetic engineering, and for all I know may be happening right now. Our Adventurers were setting out to genetically engineer a dangerous animal. They may have thought they had containment worked out but things can always go wrong. Our Adventurers might not have had over-much concern for the impact of intelligent humans on other hominins and animals, but they would surely have wanted to make sure there was no threat to themselves.

If the genetic experimentation had been carried out in Antarctica, there would have been an issue of containment. Big animals are somewhat easier to contain than genetically modified seeds and pollen, but even so there would have been a risk they might have escaped. They would have had to be given a territory big enough to hunt in, as we discussed in the last section, that would be hard to guard. My guess is that until our Adventurers had seen what they had created and had assessed the danger, they would have wanted to keep this work away from their main home in Antarctica.

Given what we know about the spread of early modern humans, the best guess is that the garden of Eden was probably somewhere in Asia, around the Middle East or the top of Africa. The mountains of the Caucasus might have provided an appropriate valley. If we decided to take more seriously the stories in the bible and other ancient religious works about the garden of Eden, there are very clear indications where it was believed to be. The book of Genesis talks about it being where the four rivers rise. Two of these are undoubtedly the Tigris and the Euphrates, and though there is debate about which are the other two rivers the location must be close to where the Tigris and Euphrates rise. They rise close to each other in Armenian Kurdistan, which is now part of Eastern Turkey. Andrew Collins in his book about Gobekli Tepe has theorised at some length on precisely where the garden of Eden was. He came to a fairly precise conclusion as to where in Armenian Kurdistan it actually was.

From the point of view of our developing story all we need to note is that these ideas fit well with our current understanding of where intelligent humans emerged.

As the ability of scientists to extract DNA from ancient fossil bones is increasing, as is the speed with which they can sequence the DNA in modern humans, we may one day get even more light shed on how intelligent humans came into existence. Watch this space!

****

Chapter 10 – Developing manpower.

Human intellectual development.

The main difference between human beings and previous hominins is our brains. Humans out-competed other hominins and it is with humans that we see the major development of culture and eventually written language. If we are to conjure with whether evidence for the existence of the gods has come down to us in any ways, we need to gain a bit of insight into how early human beings thought, because that will dictate what kinds of memories and ideas might have been transmitted down the generations.

Scholars have to speculate about how human beings developed intellectually as until we get to recorded history, that we can find evidence of in written language, we have to rely on the archeological record and the stories that have come down to us. We have to infer development from the things we can find that mankind has left behind. We have mentioned the cave-art as some of the first evidence. Most historians and archeologists think that writing first arose in Sumeria around 7000 years ago, but there are 10,000 year old engraved bones, and beautiful carvings from this time and earlier. Richard Rudgley in his book Lost Civilisations of the Stone Age quotes archeologists who thought that ice-age peoples, prior to 20,000 years ago, had at least come very close to creating an alphabet. There are all sorts of inscribed symbols from this period that may amount to as much. In my mind it is quite possible that Sumerian writing was not the first writing, just the first that has come down to us in sufficient quantity for us to make sense of it. If the first city civilisations were drowned by rising sea level any libraries or record stores will have been lost with them.

We should also not under-estimate the level of civilisation that it is possible to develop around a purely oral culture. There are many human beings who exhibit extraordinary memory, and if you have no concept of keeping written records you get into the habit of keeping detailed memories of your contacts, transactions with others and stories you have heard. Socrates objected to the rise of writing because he considered that using writing eroded memory. It is generally thought that trade and collection of taxes was a main stimulus for the creation of writing in quantity. If trade is extensive and the numbers in a large town have exceeded what can be remembered even by those with exceptional memory, there has to be another way. And if taxes on trade are to be levied, there has to be a record of that trade. This problem of course does not arise until groups become bigger than tribes where everyone knows everyone else, and where trade is more complicated than exchange and barter.

From the moment human beings became 'modern man' in both physical form and in brain, they could have started to develop along the route that has led to us and the way we think. Though we can assess the sizes of the brains of humans relative to homo-neanderthalis or homo-floriensis. we have no idea how comparable their brains were in operation; we cannot tell how they were connected internally. There is currently a lot of neuroscience research into the nature of the human brain. One relatively recent discovery is that the human brain has considerable plasticity. That is, it continues to develop through life by being used. However in the early development of children there are certain stages of development as a child grows, that it is critical to capitalise on. John Abbot on the ChangeLearning website talks about windows of opportunity, when areas of the brain are ready to enable certain skills to be developed. If these skills are not developed the brain will re-wire those neurons for other skills. For example, as mentioned earlier, language development is easier when children are young and speech development needs to happen by a certain age. If you do not develop the ability to sound 'th' by around age 3 or 4, it is very much harder to learn to do it in later life, as Japanese people have discovered. Similarly there are sounds in Japanese that Japanese babies learn easily, but which Europeans find difficult to master when they learn the language at a later age.

This kind of forming of childrens' brains obviously depends on their parents and society providing the examples for the children to learn from, so we can imagine this being a fairly slow process in mankind's development. There is still brain plasticity and opportunity for brain growth during adult life, but nothing like as much as in the early years. Continued use of the brain in certain ways will reinforce the capabilities you regularly practice. If you could look at the brain of a London taxi-cab driver you would find the sections needed for direction-finding and route-planning very considerably enhanced, from their initial long study doing 'the knowledge' in order to become a cab driver, and their continued use of these skills throughout their working life. Einstein's brain, which has been preserved, was much more developed than most brains. He had spent his whole life exercising it, so this should not really be surprising.

The key point I am driving at here, is that though cro-magnon man may have been very similar to us physically and in brain capability, their thinking may have been quite different, at least initially. It is pretty hard to imagine how peoples' minds worked even a hundred years ago. For example they accepted death in a way that people in the western world now find hard to imagine. Many children died very young and men were expected to go to wars in which many died. That is almost unthinkable today when even a few soldiers dying has become almost unacceptable in western societies. To many of us now, in our information age, it is inconceivable that we would allow ourselves to be corralled into huge armies to fight to the death in trenches, over a family feud between 3 cousins who wanted to be the rulers of bigger territories. Yet that episode was only 100 years ago! That is perhaps a slightly unfair characterisation of the first world war, which was really a clash between empires, at a time when the populations of the countries involved enjoyed the benefits of empire and felt those benefits worth fighting for, but it is nevertheless an illustration of how our thinking has moved on.

You also probably cannot get your mind around how it felt to be a peasant, tied to the land and unable to move somewhere else, or to escape the lord of the manor's demands for labour and taxes. But set against that the fact that we do still have in the world the society of North Korea, where there is almost worship of their Leader, at least by some. Go back in history even to medieval times and very many people were tied peasants. If the majority had been as acutely uncomfortable with this as we would be now, they would have revolted. But they didn't. It is possible that the early tribes of humans conceived of themselves quite differently to how you conceive of yourself. The concept of individuality, that drives a lot of the way we behave now, may not have been available to them as an idea to conjure with in the same way as it is for us. They may have thought of their identity much more as a member of the tribe, working for the good of the tribe, than as an individual striving for themselves. We of course don't know, but I want to make the point that the ideas that have driven people to do what we know they have done are different when you go back in time. And hence their memories of these things and the stories they tell will be different.

The nature of early humans; nature versus nurture.

Human beings, even today, have patterns of thought that are so in-grained that we take them for granted. For example we are inquisitive, social and interested in technology in the sense of being tool-makers. It is only when we come across an individual who does not automatically think like this, such as an autistic person, that we realise how inherently social we are. Inquisitiveness too just seems natural. We are prone to wonder about things that we do not have an explanation for, such as what makes the sky and stars, where we came from and why we are here. However once human beings accept an explanation for unexplained phenomena, they can become really quite fanatical in refusing to accept any alternative explanation, even if there is considerable evidence that the new explanation is scientifically better. We have over the centuries seen this happening with ideas such as the Earth-centric universe, the existence of spirits and magic, and with the various ways that religions have persuaded people that they need to worship the religion's conception of God.

It is not at all clear whether we think these ways because of the way our brains are constructed or whether as babies we rapidly learn to think like this, because the people around us think in these ways. If this kind of discussion interests you, I strongly recommend Rupert Sheldrake's ideas on this. I will leave in-depth discussion of his ideas for another book, but his overall idea is very relevant to whether human behaviour now might still be influenced by things that happened a long time ago, over the thousands of years we are discussing. The essence of his somewhat controversial theory is that we all exist in contact with a 'morphic field' that guides the way we grow, develop and act, individually and as a species. But this morphic field is also itself informed and developed by what we all do in the present. The idea has some similarities with the ideas of a 'collective unconscious' and suggests that ingrained habits of our species have a tendency to persist down the generations. This is in essence saying that it is a great deal easier to continue with behaviours that have been widely adopted by humans in the past, than to create new behaviours guided only by the needs of the present.

An example of persistence of habits that is closer to everyone's experience and which has a broader base of research is gender typing. There has been a long-running debate about whether men and women think differently, which illustrates how actual physical differences, cultural expectations and learned behaviours are muddled together. Over the past ten years the consensus has been swinging away from the idea that mens' and womens' brains are 'wired' differently, towards the apparent differences in the way males and females think and act being created by gender stereotyping from an early age. The idea that boys and girls should perhaps be taught a little differently has been rubbished by many commentators because of this feeling that perceived differences are all down to learned behaviours rather than differences in the ways boys and girls think. But now some real differences in how womens' and mens' brains are connected are being discovered. Some researchers are now feeling that what has been recently discovered could very well provide a physical basis, for example, for men being better at spatial tasks and women being better at verbal and social tasks. Whatever the true cause is, around age 7 boys and girls start behaving differently, even if great care has been taken to avoid gender stereotyping in the way that they have been brought up. They start to gather in groups that are exclusively boys or girls, instead of playing together as they did when they were younger. The girl groups develop very verbal inter-relationships whereas the boys groups develop a hierarchy around activity. If boys and girls are tapping in to some kind of collective unconscious about how men and women should behave this could be an explanation for this. However, whether innate or learned, many of our behaviours are extremely deeply embedded in our consciousness, to the point that they may be unconscious.

The point I want to explore is how strongly our behaviour and thoughts might be conditioned by the ways that our ancestors behaved and thought. And how strongly our Adventurers might have been able to lead the development of certain behaviours, to the point that they became innate behaviours that passed down through the generations, completely unquestioned. What is undoubtedly true is that whole groups of people can be brainwashed to profoundly believe in things that are most unlikely to be true. People can be persuaded to adopt a religious viewpoint that makes them happy to blow themselves and lots of other people to pieces. Without going to these extremes there are many religious sects where followers are persuaded to fervently believe certain things that people outside those sects consider to be ridiculous. Imagine the power of a behaviour that absolutely everyone in the society unquestioningly believes, in conditioning the young to similarly unquestioningly believe and transmit to their children. In the times we are talking of there were no global communications to bring in other ideas, and only occasional visitors come to trade, who would have little incentive to promote ideas different to the convictions of the tribe.

Of most interest to me are the deepest and most embedded and unquestioned thoughts, religious ideas. The Jesuits are reputed to have said "Give us the child before the age of seven and we will have the man for life", implying that ideas and habits learnt at that impressionable age are extremely difficult to break out of. When we look at the world history of the major civilisations, religious ideas have been central to a lot of the ways that societies have behaved. In many cases they still are.

There is of course a huge range of religions, which require worship to be performed in numerous different ways, but if we look to the core of religious sentiment there are essentially two types of thinking. Larger societies and civilisations tend to have religions involving the worship of a God or Gods. Small and remote tribes that have not been influenced by missionaries tend instead to have a shamanistic kind of worship that involves helping individuals to connect with and experience the spirit world, rather than to pray to individual Gods. Sometimes this is focused on ancestor spirits, sometimes on spirits related to the sky, animals or nature, but whatever kind of spirits they focus on this way of thinking is rather different to worshiping the kind of Gods that Sumerian, Greek and Roman people believed in and the one-God ideas of faiths such as Christianity and Islam, that focus worship on an identified being.

It is a very broad generalisation that I have just made which can of course be challenged. However you must surely admit that worship of a god or gods through rituals led by priests is very different to activities such as imbibing psychotic drugs or frenetic dancing, designed to get your brain into an altered state of reality so that you can appreciate the spirit world. The book to read to explore this area of belief in spirit worlds is Graham Hancock's book Supernatural.

Bearing all these thoughts in mind, let us return to the practicalities of what happened to the newly genetically engineered human tribe.

Controlling the tribe of intelligent humans.

We must think of our tribe as being as intelligent as we are. But as discussed that does not mean that they could necessarily think of the same things we can think of. Some people consider that you cannot think about something unless you have invented language to talk about it. This is going a bit far as it is possible to think in images or musically, but they have a point. Observing that something is different to something similar, that you already have a word to describe, is the first step to inventing the word that helps you think about this new thing. In your own head you can notice and think about these differences without necessarily labelling them with a word. The need for precise words comes to the fore when you want to discuss these things with another person.

The eskimos have 16 words to describe snow. They need 16 words because different kinds of snow behave differently and they need to discuss different approaches to dealing with different kinds of snow so that they can collaborate in their snowy environment. You can't easily do that unless you use different words for the different kinds of snow, because otherwise it gets very long-winded. Our train companies in the UK could no doubt use a word for "the kind of snow that is very light but which drifts into the electrics of our trains and causes breakdown even when the amount of snow that has actually fallen is so puny that no-one can understand why the trains have broken down due to snow". Perhaps we should invent a word for this, maybe "puny-amount-train-stop snow", or maybe just "train-stop snow", that we all appreciate is snow that does little to stop any other kind of transport but which causes havoc on the rail network (or at least used to).

Words do have a life of their own in that they allow us to build a consensual understanding in our society about the thing the word describes. You can see this happening in science where a word like 'energy' has allowed us to build a whole network of understandings around an idea, that at its root is really very nebulous. Energy can manifest itself through the vibrations of atoms and molecules, or through a speeding car, or in radio and light waves, but nobody is really sure what it is. Even though Einstein created the energy-mass equation and showed that even mass is a form of energy, the physicists prefer to frame their ideas through mass rather than energy. They talk about the particles in the 'standard model' of nuclear physics, even though each particle is in reality just a bundle of energy. Though 'energy' is a nebulous idea we all have some kind of understanding of what it is. When we use words for ideas that have even less tangible reality, the consensus understanding of what the word really means is even harder to describe. For example the word 'culture' will probably be described differently by everyone, but we all have some idea of what the culture of our society is and what it means to be a cultured person.

The only way that we know anything of how people thought in human societies thousands of years ago is through words, that have come down to us through repeated practices and rituals, and in myths. Though the various rituals and myths may express ideas differently, there are likely to be some core ideas on which we can agree. For example, we know there was almost certainly a very big and nasty worldwide flood; the myths are too widespread right across the world to deny this. And though the myths may relate to different episodes that have been combined into one folk memory, a significant flooding episode that brought communities to the brink of extinction almost certainly happened.

The Garden of Eden may be an invention by the writers of ancient religious texts or it may be a folk memory, we don't know. But let's conjure with what our adventurers would do to maintain control over the tribe and to develop mankind, and what they would do once the capacity of their chosen valley was being stretched by the number of human beings in it. And let us consider whether the approaches they took might have left behind ingrained memories and behaviours, and maybe words to describe big ideas.

Leaving the Garden of Eden.

When sheep over-graze their field, the farmer moves them to another field. Hill farmers kick their sheep out of the lush lowland fields every Spring, onto the harsh moorlands and mountains, in order to let the fields grow for hay and then next winter's grass, to be eaten when they bring the sheep down. At some point the growing tribe of early humans would outgrow that valley where they were living. Some would have to be chosen to be moved to new territory. Or maybe the whole tribe, would be kicked out of their lovely lush, well provisioned and productive valley and forced to move to less well managed areas, where they would themselves have to find the nut and fruit trees and work out where animals could be best hunted. They would need to be able to survive wherever in the world our Adventurers wanted to use manpower. What our Adventurers would not want to happen would be for groups of these more intelligent humans to compete with each other for the territory, to fight and kill each other. They were after all endeavouring to create manpower they could use.

Let us think about what memories the tribes would take with them as they spread around the world. As they will have been closely observed and managed by our Adventurers, our human tribe will be well aware of them. They might be rather schizophrenic about them, worshiping them on the one hand as bringers of food and help, while fearing them on the other hand. They may have observed our Adventurers exercising forceful management if one or several of their number had stepped out of line or even maybe threatened an Adventurer. Our Adventurers might have looked quite similar to humans in some ways, because the human/ape structure of arms and legs and a mobile head with forward facing eyes is a good adaption for animals that need to be capable of many things. So our Adventurers may have appeared to the humans as human-like, but all knowing and all powerful creatures, who must be served, revered and feared. For our Adventurers developing unquestioning obedience would have been essential.

In talking to each other about their time in their Garden of Eden and these beings that directed them in various ways, and in discussing the apparently capricious reasons for their ejection to other parts of the world, the humans will of course have needed a word to describe our Adventurers. I wonder if they talked of them as 'the gods'?

It is surprisingly easy to get human beings to think as you want them to, if you have total control over their lives. When I worked for Yorkshire Television we filmed young people who had been persuaded to enter a sect in California. It was a classic case of the use of standard brainwashing techniques. The leader of the sect demanded daily rituals and the requirement to give up all their worldly goods to the sect. The leader developed a culture of unquestioning obedience. Those who had been in the sect for a while were engaged as 'trusties' who had the job of instilling the sect's culture and beliefs into new recruits. But in fact the sect was run (for profit!) by a pretty ordinary though very manipulative human couple. They lived away from where the sect workers lived, in considerably greater luxury. They surrounded themselves with a small group of male sect recruits who were given special privileges and acted as their guards and sect police, in case of any revolt by recruits to the sect. The man and his wife were extremely controlling in the ways they interacted with the members of the sect. They developed an extremely strong dependence culture where the sect members looked up to them and revered them as their leaders. We also interviewed some desperate parents who could not understand how their children had come to believe in such an outrageous con. Many of the young people in the sect were highly intelligent and had studied at university, which made it all the more surprising to us that they could be led to believe so strongly in the words of their leader. The leader and his wife were pretty obviously just out to get whatever they could from their followers with main aims of luxury and wealth, not any higher purpose. They had no doubt agreed to the filming with the hope of promoting their sect, but I am glad to say that Alan Whicker the reporter did a rather good hatchet-job on them, enabling all viewers of the programme to realise what kind of people they were.

Our Adventurers, no doubt being different in some ways from humans, and certainly possessing technology that would make them seem like wizards, would have been in an immeasurably stronger position to brainwash early humans into a belief that our Adventurers were gods from the heavens. They may even have given us humans the word god! They will no doubt have told the first generations of humans how they were to behave towards the gods and made sure that they understood that the gods had created mankind. Note the small 'g' please, I will offer a few words later as to whether or not I believe in a real God. And I certainly would not want you to read this book as a polemic against the possible existence of a God. We can't avoid using the word god because civilisations through history have used it to describe the God or pantheons of Gods that they worshiped.

I want us to explore whether there is any muddled thinking that confuses gods and God, that still survives in our consensual societal understanding of what the word did mean when used in ancient scriptures and what it means now. The idea that there is some higher power is a pretty natural thought once you begin to wonder about the nature of the universe and why we are here, and to look at the beautiful complexities of nature. If there were tangible beings with apparently miraculous powers who manipulated you to believe that they had created humans and the world in which you lived, the Garden of Eden, and who convinced you that they knew all the secrets of the universe that you don't know, it would be pretty easy to be confused about this. And maybe our Adventurers very actively reinforced that confusion, a matter we will keep returning to.

From this point in the book I am turning the perspective around. Instead of trying to work out logically what our Adventurers might do, and then considering their possible impact on human beings, I will now start looking at it the other way. What do we know about the history of human beings and what might that tell us to confirm or deny our speculations?

And to understand what human sources might be telling us, we need to be thinking about how human beings thought and talked about our Adventurers.

So we had better use the words they probably did, or we will get very confused. We must start talking about the alien group, our Adventurers, as 'the gods'.

****

Chapter 11 - Using manpower.

How would the gods set about using their manpower?

So now our Adventurers, the gods, have some potential manpower. How would they want to use it, for what, and what would this entail? We are now starting to put some real dates into our story. The cave paintings in Southern France and Spain were created from around 40,000 years ago, so intelligent humans had come into existence by this time and had spread from the initial place where this happened. We know that the civilisations archeologists have investigated in the Middle East started growing and developing around 12,000 years ago (10,000 BC). We have some 30,000 years between these dates. What could have been happening in this period?

We can imagine tribes of humans being established in various places around the world from which the gods wished to gain produce and resources. The issue would have been how to manage these tribes and how to get them to perform the activities needed. One option would be to establish master-slave relationships as western colonialists did. This needs people to work as gang-masters ensuring, in a very hands-on way, that the slaves do what they are told. A more effective, easier and overall cheaper approach would be to find a way of getting the tribes to produce what was required and to give it to the gods because they had an internal motivation to do so. This would mean the gods only having to turn up occasionally to collect the goods and maybe to re-assert whatever was motivating the humans to behave in this way.

In the process of growing a tribe of humans through several generations, it is likely that the gods would have interacted with this tribe through tribal leaders. The early individual humans might have been cared for personally by gods and taught by them. Once numbers grew to several hundred the gods would surely have wanted to keep rather more distance between themselves and the human beings. A crowd of a hundred human beings is a lot more dangerous than a few individuals. If you want to approach a herd of cows when there is a bull in the field, it is wise to talk to the bull first and make sure it's friendly. Humans are rather more social animals and perhaps a better analogy would be a wolf-pack. The subservient dogs follow the leader of the pack and do as the leader tells them.

In human societies now we have plenty of examples of the willingness of the majority of humans to follow leaders, even if they are self-selected rather than democratically elected. The gods are likely to have seen this tendency for leaders to emerge developing quite naturally amongst the group of humans. It seems to be a very natural feature of human societies that a few people will take leadership, whether by age, temperament, authority from higher intelligence or greater social awareness, or by greed and force. It could be said that a good leader is a bully with empathy!

It is quite easy to imagine that the gods would have developed controlling relationships with the natural leaders of the tribes of humans. The leaders would have been born into a society that already revered the gods absolutely and had some established rituals and times when the gods appeared. The gods would essentially have been running a giant confidence trick, but we don't bother to think in this way when we train dogs and horses, we just do what is necessary to gain obedience. They would probably have developed ways to make serving the gods' needs a high cost for the humans, with expensive sacrifices and offerings and regular rituals that were seen by the humans as essential to their welfare and life. Humans who are sold art fakes at huge cost by confidence tricksters often enter a state of complete denial that what they have purchased at such high cost might be a fake. With a confidence trick such as the gods probably established, running across several generations, its power would be immense. If your parents and everyone else in your society sincerely believes that what they do to worship and make offerings to the gods is essential, and can tell you stories from several generations ago about godly retribution that happened when the group failed to do as the god demanded, it would be very hard to gainsay this. Anyone who tried would raise great fear amongst the mass of believers and would be considered a dangerous heretic who might cause the gods displeasure.

The gods would have been able to work on potential leaders from birth, to develop the kind of power relationship they felt best served their needs. This would not have been the same as one set of human beings developing power over other human beings. The newly created humans would have had no reason to think of their 'gods' as being the same as them. The gods may have made men 'in their own image' but they would seem to the human beings to be miraculous, with clothes, tools, vehicles and powers that the humans would not be able to explain in any way. Arthur C Clarke is quoted as saying that any technology sufficiently beyond the technology you possess is indistinguishable from magic. Our Adventurers would have looked very magical to human beings. If the gods did look pretty much the same as human beings they could have worn costumes that were so far beyond any kind of clothes humans could imagine that they would have been seen as different beings. If this was done, then we might expect to see this reflected in ancient carvings depicting gods.

There would need to be interactions with the leaders. The gods might 'speak to them from on high', and through doing this help develop and guide their development. Language would have to be developed so that humans could receive instructions from the Gods. It would of course have been a common language for all humans. It would not be until mankind started developing independently around the world that languages of different tribes would diverge. In this context the stories around the tower of Babel are rather interesting.

The gods would be able to watch and listen from distances that humans could not comprehend them seeing and hearing, so could appear all-knowing without difficulty. We can see what is possible from the way we put webcams in bird-boxes and how we film wildlife. A nice tall 'magical' totem pole in the middle of the humans' settlements could host video cameras. As well as interacting with the leaders the gods might quite early on have developed mass rituals that the whole tribe engaged in. This would reinforce the power of the leaders to demand what the gods wanted, through providing a bit of 'awe and wonder' when the gods appeared, riding their 'flaming chariots'. It's quite an interesting thought exercise to imagine how one would set about creating absolute allegiance and huge reverence amongst a tribe of early humans, if you were a 'god', with even just the technology we have today.

However, while frightening the mass of the populace and using their reverence of a god to secure offerings might work well with the majority, there is a rather different problem-set with leaders. It would be necessary at some point to change the instructions for what the leaders should get their tribe to do, which would involve close contact. And leaders might need support to stop them being challenged. There would need to be a closer relationship with leaders than with the mass of the people, with the consequent danger that familiarity breeds contempt.

The problem with intelligent manpower.

There is a pretty big problem in using manpower. Talk to any manager of a business and they will tell you that staff can be a major headache. Any creature intelligent enough to be instructed to carry out a task will also be thinking for themselves to some extent; they have their own agendas and issues which can get in the way of them doing what you want them to do. The more intelligent they are the more devious they can be in progressing their own agenda rather than yours. Leaders particularly can be troublesome. They are often strongly motivated to climb to the top of the heap and ruthless in the way that they use any opportunity to their own advantage.

It's a rather imprecise science to work out what is the best balance between workers thinking for themselves and just doing what they are told to do. For mundane and repetitive jobs managers have often felt that it is a bad thing to have workers educated too much. This was an issue that was discussed as recently as the 19th century, with some arguing against universal education. Other industrial leaders saw education as important. Some such as Sir Titus Salt promoted learning and were very concerned to ensure their workers developed the right culture. The approach Titus Salt took was to incentivise his workers to obey and slave for him by making their life just sufficiently more comfortable than other mill owners did, and more comfortable than the life his workers would experience back as farm labourers. But he had to continually battle against the desire of some workers to avoid the hard labour in the mill and to seek out other pleasures instead. There are no public houses selling alcohol in Saltaire, the model village that he built around the mill to house the workers, Titus Salt made sure of that. Instead he provided alternative 'cultural' opportunities for the small amount of leisure time his workers had. Workers who did not toe the line and who were at all rebellious were likely to find themselves out of not only a job but a home as well.

Intelligence needed depends on the tasks you want people to do. The more complex the tasks you want them to do, and hence the easier they make your life, the more you need them to think for themselves. And as they do this, there is greater opportunity for them to put their hand in the till, so to speak. The gods were probably well aware of this and they would have had the choice of deciding, if they felt that the humans they had created were too intelligent, of destroying the first batch and having another go. If on the other hand an aim was to develop mankind or the gods had complex tasks they wanted humans to do, reasonably high intelligence in their newly created humans would have been useful. In any event it is unlikely that something as complex as intelligence can be easily controlled in genetic manipulation. It may be possible to insert a bit of genetic code into a plant to get it to produce a specific protein and hence gain some desirable quality, but increasing intelligence must be hugely more complex. And hence much more likely to be variable.

There would also have been the issue that if the gods wanted groups of humans to provide them with something that was not necessary to the survival of the humans, for example natural rubber or metal ore from exposed veins of rock, this would be an additional task for the humans. They would have had to have been persuaded to allocate time to this task, extra to the time they spent on survival tasks. This needs rather stronger leadership than just persuading people to forgo a 10% tithe on what they are producing for their own needs. Which makes it a good idea to build some kind of support around a leader, to bolster their power with their people in any time of weakness.

Throughout history we have seen whole populations subservient to the church or the state, behaving in very controlled ways. A key part of this is the way that leaders have managed to get 'middle managers' to adopt and propagate the processes of control down to the lowest levels. The middle managers are persuaded that the required rules and rituals are the 'right thing to do' and they then instill this into the populace as a whole. A leader will look to appoint people into these roles who are reliable people who are not rebellious, people who are happy to maintain routine procedures and whose ambition is satisfied by the relatively small advantage they have over the rest of the workers.

But in all populations there will be some individuals who think more than others, who have ambitions beyond those of others and who are prepared to be rebellious and clever to achieve what they want. As rulers have discovered over many years, people who think for themselves like this can be a nuisance if they start thinking things that you don't want them to. It may be an apocryphal story but it is said that the German army at around the time of the first world war classified people into four categories. Those not very intelligent and lazy became the privates, those not very intelligent and energetic became the sergeants, those intelligent and energetic became the junior officers, but the top jobs in the command were reserved for those who were intelligent and lazy. That does mean that the commanders would be naturally inclined to delegate, which is a good thing, but it also means that the dangerous intelligent, energetic and possibly rebellious people remain at junior officer level, kept under control by the commanding officers, who are too lazy and content to want to challenge the system as a whole.

With intelligent and rebellious people it is not enough to control them by fear or reward, for some will respond in devious ways to this. They may persuade colleagues to be disruptive or maybe even to run away and form their own tribe, if sufficient food can be found without the help of the society they belong to. For control extending over many generations a method must be found that works with these people. It is said of politics "You can control all of the people some of the time and some of the people all of the time but you can't control all of the people all of the time." The gods will have needed to control all of their manpower all of the time, if they were not to become at least a nuisance and possibly dangerous.

Human civilisations have developed ways to deal with intelligent and disruptive individuals. The usual approach is to establish institutions that enlist intelligent individuals at an early age and which then control them through a mixture of brainwashing, promise of advancement, policing and punishment of some kind, and finally excommunication and effective banishment from the society. Physically active individuals were enlisted in the army and made officers, who enjoyed a privileged lifestyle somewhat comparable to, if not quite at the level of that of the leaders. Intellectually active individuals were recruited into the priesthood or church, which then included academia. Disobeying rules in the army leads immediately to court-martial and severe punishment or even death. Heretical thinking in the church leads to excommunication and loss of any influence and probably loss of livelihood. Heretical thinking by people in the church could also lead to death in times past. Considerable thought control is still exerted in academia, through preferment of those who think the 'right' things and disbursement of research grants only to those who research the 'right' things (with a few honourable exceptions). All of the sanctions these institutions use, and the conferring of a social stigma on individuals prepared to challenge the rules of these groups, warns other members of the society that consorting with individuals who think differently is dangerous, both socially and for one's career, or even maybe one's life.

While these may have been mechanisms that the gods would approve of for leaders to use to control tribes of humans, and which they may have helped leaders develop by dictating what the religion of worshiping the gods should involve, this is really too low level to be the main concern of the gods. Their need would be to exercise thought control over the top leaders, so that it became inconceivable for them to think of disobeying the Gods and not doing their bidding. And they would need to ensure that successive leaders would take over where the last leader left off, continuing to ensure the tribe did what the gods required of it.

Intrinsic versus extrinsic control.

The ways that we train and control animals are predominantly extrinsic. We put animals in fields, we herd them with dogs and round them up into pens. We grab hold of them and sheer them. But good farmers develop quite a lot of intrinsic control as well, with the animals behaving as the farmer wants them to because they themselves want to behave in that way. Cows gather at the gate when it is time to come down for milking and farmers have experimented with drop-in milking where cows can decide for themselves when to come to an automatic milking shed, to get themselves milked. Even our family cat got into the habit of joining as at the end of the garden when we relaxed in the evening Summer sun. It was a time to come and get a stroke from us, which she presumably liked; we did nothing other than give her a stroke when she appeared running across the grass. Perhaps it is possible to develop intrinsic control mechanisms in any intelligent animal if fear is sufficiently distant.

So what are the ways that intrinsic control could have been developed in human tribes and particularly in leaders? Human motives vary. Some people nowadays are driven by wealth, some by power and some by the desire to do good. Some people may be driven by a desire to be evil, or maybe that is just a side-effect of an overwhelming desire for power. Power and wealth tend to go hand-in-hand, as power provides the opportunity to gain wealth and wealth is a powerful tool to gain power over others. We are discussing how the gods might have controlled the leaders of the tribes, so desire or willingness in the leaders to exercise power will need to be assumed. The concept of good and evil probably did not enter into the gods' considerations much, though they might have had a preference, as leaders who control their tribes in evil ways tend to get deposed eventually in a bloody coup, with a rebellious leader taking over. Being able to predict who would become the next leader would be a better process to guarantee as far as possible that the tribe continued to behave in the ways that the gods wanted them to.

The ideal would be to grow and develop new leaders before the old leader became too weak and infirm to lead. Some societies manage this by having most leadership control exercised by a group of priests or elders, who then select a new leader when necessary. But the most common way throughout history is for leadership to pass through family dynasties, with younger members of the family effectively being trained from birth to assume leadership. Even in the USA, which is meant to be a democracy, the Bush dynasty has managed to gain significant power through several generations, as indeed did the Kennedys.

Where there is a well established dynasty, with the mass of people believing in the (divine?) right of the children to succeed their fathers as leaders, it is often a more sensible strategy for ambitious people to support the assumed successor. Attempts to replace them might not go down well with the populace. There are however always upsets such as a lack of heirs and people dying unexpectedly, so the methods for ensuring smooth succession ideally need to be vested in a group that is sufficiently large, while still being exclusive, to ensure an appropriate leader can be found and securely put in post whenever necessary.

The role of religion in maintaining intrinsic control and power.

We are assuming that the gods' medium to long range intention is to get humans to do things for them, such as mine, gather or construct. Before they could be instructed in this, the idea would have had to be developed that what the gods said was entirely non-negotiable, gods would command and humans would comply. And we have discussed that an obvious way to do this is through a combination of fear and reward. This builds the intrinsic desire in people to do what is expected of them. It is best if the perceived reward element is stronger than the perceived fear element, as people don't work well under stress. But the reward may be operating deep down at the level of people feeling good about doing things 'the right way' or feelings about 'living a good life'. Whether these ideas stem from the social wiring in the brain and self-interest, from God or a spirit world, or from the fact that we, our parents and grandparents have all been brain-washed into unquestioningly accepting them, these are all intrinsic drives.

Religions are very good at developing these intrinsic drives. Because of this leaders often align themselves with a religion because this helps them maintain power and influence over the people. The Catholic Church is a good example. The Roman emperor Constantine started to link the Roman state with the Catholic Church in 313AD, leading to Christianity becoming the state religion of the Roman Empire under Emperor Theodosius I in 380AD. The kind of power that a religion exerts is complementary to the power of the state. The state essentially controls people extrinsically, punishing people who do wrong, but with some rewards of help in times of famine and disaster. Religions develop intrinsic control with people behaving in certain ways because they believe it is right. This can help the religion to become so powerful that it too is able to exercise massive extrinsic power, with the agreement of the state and acceptance of the majority of the populace – as witnessed by how the Catholic Church developed in the middle ages.

This particular period in the history of the Catholic Church could be viewed as a time when the intrinsic control mechanisms were breaking down. The Cathars had 'escaped' and developed a different belief system and there was a danger that other groups might follow them and leave the Catholic Church. As the Cathars had fully transferred their intrinsic control thoughts to a different religion, probably the only way of dealing with them was to frighten them back into the Catholic Church or if that could not be achieved to kill them. Which the Catholic church did, killing the Cathars in their hundreds. Though the Catholic Church's power has now waned from its height the phrase 'Spanish Inquisition' still causes an involuntary shudder. The various sects of Islam are also a good example of intrinsic control, succeeding in getting adherents to pray several times a day and to adopt a life-view that is defined by the religion. Note that this is a matter of adherence to the religion just as much as adherence to a belief in a God. The different Islamic sects are prepared to be at war with other sects, that at root draw their power from the same God and the words of the same prophet. The Catholic and Protestant variants of Christianity did likewise, and killed each other, not that many hundreds of years ago.

Reward in the afterlife and the rewards of being in the social group who are adherents of the religion may be the starting point for developing control over people, but then the idea of eternal damnation if you are not saved can be introduced. This allowed the Catholic Church for example to introduce a whole new set of rewards to save you from your sins, through confession. As everyone pretty regularly does things that are not as good or as caring as they could be, everyone has something they can regularly confess to, so the reward of absolution from sins works really rather well. But in reality the religion has created and propagated an insecurity, which the religion then feeds on to develop stronger intrinsic control. It's a very neat trick, quite independently of whether there is, or is not, any truth in what the religion is saying about an omnipotent God and the realities of afterlife, reincarnation or whatever the belief system is in the religion.

There is a debate to be had about whether the authorities that dictate how a religion operates and what its adherents must do are actually fulfilling the words and desires of the prophet who originally gathered adherents, or whether they have used the spiritual intentions of the prophet to develop an entirely human organisation that can exert power over people. You might wish to conjure whether there are some parallels here with what the gods might have done. And hence whether any of the prophets we read about in ancient times were in reality false prophets, transmitting the word of the gods rather than the word of God.

Once people get into a religious mindset we know it is possible for them to be led into doing things they would not normally think of doing. I am not in any way trying to deny that there may be a truly spiritual element at the heart of religions, or that some people find their religions of great help personally. I am just asking you to think about the control methods used to keep those who might not naturally obey in line with the demands of the religion. I feel we need to think separately about the ideas of God, belief and religion. I found it interesting that the last UK population census form had a question as to whether I adhere to a religion. Answering no to this would obviously classify me as a non-believer in the analysis of the census. And it required me to specify the religion I adhere to. There was no question that would have allowed me to state a strong belief in a God but to not be an adherent of a religion. This is illustrative of the deep confusion that exists around these matters. Whoever designed that form could not conceive of people who might wish to define themselves as believers but not want to link that belief to any religion and that religion's vision of God.

The question I am posing, to which I do not have an answer, is whether the whole idea of worshiping gods rather than the shamanistic idea of trying to connect with the spirit world, might be a learned behaviour that has become so embedded that it has persisted through the ages down to the present day. The idea of making tangible offerings to the gods must have arisen somewhere, as must the idea that leaders are divine, or at least have a divine right to be leaders. Has all this become part of the 'collective unconscious' of human beings, a habit that has become so ingrained that it has appeared to be natural and right and hence unquestioned until relatively recently?

Controlling leaders.

The danger for the gods in getting close to the leaders of tribes of humans would have been that it might enable the leader to think the un-thinkable, that the gods were not real gods but merely more advanced people. It would have been necessary to keep a considerable degree of fear and awe. It would also be desirable that what happened between the gods and the leader was not visible to, or heard by, all of the rest of the population, so as to build up the mystery. Far better to command the leader to climb a mountain or sacred hill, or to enter an inner sanctum in a temple, where the gods might reveal themselves to a greater degree than they did in public. There would be strong incentives for the leader to use this to their advantage and keep secret much of what transpired between the gods and themselves. Helpful hints from the gods in how the tribe could do things better, such as grow food more successfully, could then be presented as ideas the leader had themselves thought of, as well as being things that would find favour with the gods.

Individuals are unpredictable and can mis-hear or misunderstand commandments. Individuals can also be ill and of course die, so having some kind of small group that is involved with hearing the pronouncements from god along with the leader, and in working out how they are to be implemented, is a good idea. To create a small group you could start with a couple of people who are chosen to accompany the leader, to help take the offerings to the gods. This would no doubt be done in great fear and trepidation, at least for the first time, and would be accompanied by some special reward. It is quite easy to imagine how this could have led to the formation of a priesthood. The priesthood would take responsibility for looking after the place where the gods occasionally appeared. They would ensure that the whole tribe gathered at appropriate times. The priesthood could then also be a mechanism to control what the leader did in the presence of the gods, to stop them over-stepping themselves and becoming too familiar. Once rituals were established as to how a king should approach a god and how a dialogue would be conducted, the priesthood would exert very strong pressure on a newly appointed leader or king to follow the accepted ritual.

And the priesthood would help to bridge those awkward times when a leader has to be replaced. Within a few generations of development of a priesthood, a new leader would be introduced to their role relative to the gods by an old and wise member of the priesthood. This would be someone who long ago had given up any idea of ambitions to be leader themselves, and who would have cast their own ideas about fame and being remembered into their role as a leader of the priesthood. As a Head Priest they would of course have completely internalised the notion that gods who appeared to them were indeed real gods. The job of the Head Priest would be to recruit a few selected young individuals who could be brought up as 'special' people and groomed for a life in the priesthood. They would be inducted into various secrets as they gained in seniority and their reliability grew. This group would then be able to instruct the new leader into how to behave in front of the gods. Even if the new leader was not too concerned about incurring the displeasure of the god, the priests would be. And the priests could also make it clear to the populace if the king had over-stepped the mark and hence some benefit expected from the god had not materialised.

The existence of a priesthood would have further reinforced the separation of the leader from the rest of the tribe and enhanced the leader's special status, as well as increasing the separation of the gods from the ordinary people. One wonders if at some point the status of the leader could have moved up, from tribal leader who is seen as just the most senior person in the tribe, to a divinely appointed king, selected by the gods. The leader might see themselves as divine in some way because they really have been chosen by the gods, who the people sincerely believe to be divine. Such an approach would surely also suit the priesthood as it would reinforce their role as the intermediaries with the gods. The idea of the divine status of kings has to have originated somewhere.

At this point we should also mention buildings. There is a long tradition of religions using buildings to instill awe into people. If you drive along the Isle of Ely in Cambridgeshire, from West to East, the road is heading directly towards Ely cathedral. The top of the Isle of Ely is flat so you can see the cathedral from two or three miles away, and as you get closer and closer it gets bigger and bigger. The tower of the cathedral is immense. If the weather is slightly misty and you can't clearly see the detail of the stonework, it looks like a rocket pointing up to space. It was built in medieval times, when the people living on the Isle of Ely lived in huts built of mud-brick or wattle and daub. Can you imagine how the Cathedral appeared to them? And in those times the ordinary people would not have been allowed into the inner sanctum; that was reserved for the clergy who led a privileged life funded by tithes on the ordinary people.

It is possible of course for kings to build fine buildings for themselves but everyone knows what these are for. They are built to impress the ordinary people with their wealth and power and probably also to impress neighbouring kings and their peoples. Religions however can relate the building of cathedrals to the necessity to glorify god. There doesn't have to be a rational earth-bound reason to make religious buildings impressive, it is something that some priesthoods have told us is necessary to glorify God. And there is no common-sense limit to what needs to be spent on religious buildings, because there is no way of assessing what is necessary to glorify god, except for what the priests says is necessary. They after all are the group that hears the word of god. The building is built in the way it is simply because the priesthood says that god demands it and the people naturally want to stay on the right side of god. Medieval cathedrals follow in a very long tradition of the building of massive temples, that goes right back into antiquity. It is small wonder that there have been numerous back-lashes against this idea by prophets and preachers who have eschewed all the splendour of cathedrals and ecclesiastical vestments, in favour of very simplistic worship.

I do sincerely wonder what Jesus Christ would have thought of the Catholic Church at its height in the middle ages, or what Mohamed might think about the clashes between the different islamic sects that are happening now. However the historical fact is that the combination of state and religion has proved so effective at generating compliance amongst human populations, that it has been used time and again by leaders.

An interesting question is when this magic mix of state power and religious power first developed. What would the local populace have thought about the Sphinx Temple or Osirion in Egypt. Not only are these buildings huge, but they are built of massive megalithic stones. If we go back to around 8000 BC there are the enigmatic constructions at Gobekli Tepe in Turkish Kurdistan, that must have been at the centre of gatherings of the populace from a considerable area. Go even further back and we probably need to look under the sea. Read Graham Hancock's book Underworld to explore what buildings we might find there. (You will find more on buildings to explore in the appendix.)

It is of course perfectly possible to imagine that clever and devious humans have devised the hierarchies and the control mechanisms that we have seen operating throughout history, inventing gods, and rituals to appease them, and developing priesthoods to create separation between the ordinary people and those 'in the know' to greater or lesser degrees. I just have that nagging feeling that the more natural development of spiritual feelings would lead to the kind of observances that we see in shamanistic activities to gain revelation, that are far more personal and are mediated through an individual shaman not though a religion or priesthood. People engage in these activities in order to achieve personal revelations about the spirit world. The shamanistic leader is a guide rather than being the deliverer of the word of god.

And I have a feeling that the whole idea of gods that can be conceived of as tangible beings of some kind and that can be represented as graven images, that require worship in set rituals and offerings, is not necessarily linked to any true God at all.

Could this, and the idea that gods have direct positive and negative impacts on human beings, be just be an idea that is so ingrained in our past that it is taking us thousands of years to break out of the habit of this way of thinking, to a more enlightened view? An idea that was established by our Adventurers, the gods, specifically to exert control over humans?

****

Chapter 12 – Humans in Antarctica?

When the gods came to consider use of their newly created manpower, they would have had two main options, to use their new manpower only outside Antarctica, or to introduce manpower to Antarctica as well. All the work for the gods in the Garden of Eden in creating manpower would have been like a posting to a colony or a scientific station, much as we now have scientific stations in Antarctica. Home, home comforts and the main society of the gods we have assumed were in Antarctica. Just as we now send scientists to Antarctica for periods to study, one can imagine some of the gods happily spending months or years at a time managing the process of creating human beings on an extended posting. It would have been fascinating to see what the new humans got up to and to direct their development towards those capacities that would be most useful to the gods. The majority of the gods, certainly those engaged on other projects and those not particularly interested in creating humans, would have remained in Antarctica.

Home would be the most important place for the gods' society, so one main use of the new manpower could be to help back at home. During the many human generations involved in increasing the size of the human population to satisfactory numbers, the gods would have discovered that humans can be manipulated and controlled to a considerable extent, managing the potential danger they posed. The initial decision to keep themselves well separated from dangerous hominins could have been reversed once they were sure they could satisfactorily control humans.

At home you need food, shelter, energy and whatever other resources are needed for your lifestyle. If you want an easy life and lots of time to pursue interests you need slaves or servants to grow and process food, dig or cut materials to make and service your shelter and to find renewable fuel to heat it. And servants to bring things to you and to wash and clean things. If I was taking over a whole new world I would want to live in reasonably palatial surroundings. To create and run this I would need a sizable workforce, working the surrounding area and servicing my household needs. I would have a few particular 'trusties' trained as palace guards and personal servants and with high technology available I'm sure it would not be too hard to create a weapon-free zone of safety. This could perhaps be aided by having my personal accommodation at the top of a hill or pyramid to give me time to reach for my personal finger-print controlled weapons should there be an uprising - carved images of gods quite often show them carrying what looks a bit like a handbag. Then there would be some humans trained as controllers of the mass of workers, who would manage the larger number of people actually needed to service my needs. Of course all these humans would be required to revere me as a god through religious rituals and observances that would make it socially unthinkable to contemplate harming their god.

To progress the story we need to make a decision as to whether we think human beings were taken to Antarctica. I think they would have been, but only a selected few.

In Antarctica these humans would have been exposed to many more of the gods and to much more of their technology and way of life. Those engaged in producing what the gods needed would probably only see them occasionally as the gods would live in enclosed surroundings similar to the Forbidden City in Beijing, where the Chinese Emperors lived. But the gods would be real tangible beings and humans would have known clearly where they lived. For those that had access to the gods' enclosures or were required to come into the presence of the god, their closeness to the gods would have required very strict rules to ensure the safety of the gods. Perhaps rules that they should prostrate themselves flat on the ground whenever a god appeared. That would be a good start to protect against a sudden attack. The gods would only actually converse with a very few people such as their high-priest and maybe one or two personal servants.

The relationship the gods would have with humans would no doubt have been a bit different to how humans experienced the gods in the rest of the world. The gods would still keep sufficient distance and reverence to ensure they were not challenged. Being perceived as gods would still be a very valuable tool for control, even with the gods living alongside humans. But instead of the gods speaking to men "from on high", it would have been more likely that in Antarctica, "in those days the gods walked among men".

The humans in Antarctica would probably have been developed more intensively than tribes of human beings elsewhere. The main danger to the gods would be that humans would escape and live wild in Antarctica, and over time breed to sufficient numbers that they could threaten the tame humans and maybe even our Adventurers themselves. That would need to have been prohibited. An infra-red night-sight in a helicopter, with a taser to bring them down and god-like retribution exhibited to the others would probably have done the job. Combined with making life so good that escaping to live in the wild was actually unthinkable. Population size of the human tribe in Antarctica could have been controlled, probably by persuading the humans themselves to implement control so that it was not necessary to kill some of them off every now and again. Though that would of course have been an option for the gods.

Over a few generations one can see this leading to quite different populations of humans in Antarctica and elsewhere in the world. They would have had the same initial genetic make-up, so they would be the same creature, but their intellectual development might have proceeded considerably faster in Antarctica. Over time the DNA of the humans in Antarctica would have diverged a bit from the DNA of humans elsewhere in the world. Humans taken back home to Antarctica would have lived in a most privileged society and should they travel to other parts of the world and meet humans there, they would probably have considered them to be uncivilised savages, much as early explorers from Europe considered the tribes they found in Africa.

This group of humans would have been the world's first large human civilisation, a society of many hundreds or maybe thousands, living in close proximity in the Earth's first city, in which there were palaces for the gods. They would have well developed social rules for the operation of their society and they would have a religion. They would worship their gods. They would have had no way to conceive of the word God meaning anything other than the gods that they occasionally saw and to whom they offered prayer and offerings. This would have been a pantheon of gods similar to the pantheons that the Greeks and Romans believed in. Only the pantheon would include real identifiable individual gods, who were related to each other. Which is what we find in the Greek and Roman stories about their gods. With real tangible gods to whom they prayed there would have been no room in their minds for any other conception about a God, nor any word to describe such a concept. Any strange physical or spiritual phenomena they encountered would have been explained away as some mysterious purpose of the gods and the worship the gods required would no doubt contain a narrative to help the humans conceive of life and death in a way that maintained their allegiance to, and subservience to, the gods. The gods would ensure that the priests and the temples were central to the processes of mediating death and to dealing with the necessary processes around death, so that there was no temptation to develop other rituals which might lead to other conceptions of the meaning of life and God. Instead of simple burial one can imagine a whole culture being built up around death, in the way such a culture existed around the Egyptian pharaohs and high functionaries in Egyptian dynastic times. This would all have been part of the control mechanism that the gods used to ensure their absolute dominance over humans.

The tasks that the gods would have got the humans to do would be similar to those elsewhere in the world with one key difference. The things that the gods were acquiring through the labours of their manpower elsewhere in the world would need to be brought to Antarctica. It would probably pretty soon occur to the gods that they could use humans to do this task too. They would need to train them how to build ships and how to be seafarers. Soon, over a few generations, the civilisation in Antarctica would become a maritime nation sending ships all over the world, of which more later.

Leaders of mankind in Antarctica.

The gods might have had a different approach to managing the leaders of this civilisation, compared to how they managed leaders of tribes elsewhere in the world. If they found a very wise leader it would be rather annoying if this leader died when they were only 50 years old. Leaders have to learn their job and once they become experienced they are usually considerably better leaders. If this took them until they were 25 or 30 yrs old, the gods would only have been getting say 20 years of service out of a leader. If you yourself have a lifetime of hundreds of years that would appear to be a very rapid turnover of leaders and a lot of work to prepare new leaders to take their place.

Would it not therefore be a good idea to keep the leaders alive for longer so they did not have to replace them so often? If the gods were able to use medical approaches that worked at the genetic level, they might have been able to overcome the leaders' genetic pre-dispositions to disease and to get those parts of the body that wear out to re-generate. Our scientists are already looking closely at the ability of salamanders to re-grow whole body parts. The leader, and probably his whole family, could have been turned into a long-lived family with immense privileges. With the help of the gods leaders could have become venerated leaders protected from any challenges. The process of passing the leadership from one generation to the next could be prepared for over perhaps a hundred years instead of a decade.

I am introducing this thought because there is a rather unbelievable assertion in the bible. Namely that there was a succession of patriarchs descended from Adam and it is claimed they lived very long lives, typically around 900 years for the early patriarchs but reducing to 175 years by the time of Abraham. It is difficult to interpret this. If the length of life of the early patriarchs was exaggerated to make them seem more impressive, why was the lifetime of Abraham not exaggerated so much? We are unlikely to find answers to this but will have to decide, when we get to that part of the story, whether we believe Noah lived for 950 years or not. If we decide we do believe this, then our developing theory will have to accommodate that fact.

****

Chapter 13 – From myths and legends to written history.

Changing our perspective; looking for evidence.

Our hunt for physical artefacts that the gods left behind will of course be thwarted in Antarctica. But if the picture I have painted is right there will be places elsewhere in the world from which the gods were receiving things they wanted, it is possible these places might have started to support city civilisations as well. There is just one small problem. As the route by which these things made their way to Antarctica was by sea, the ports from which goods were collected will have been at sea level. Which in this period was 300 feet lower that today. So these civilisations too will be inaccessible, under the sea.

So what can we find to help us understand this period, after intelligent humans appeared but before we start to get archeological evidence. Let us look at the overall shape of the evidence available.

First we have geological evidence. This can tell us about the environment in which mankind lived. If we can read the evidence properly it may also tell us about difficult and disastrous periods which mankind had to survive which would have given rise to stories and legends. We will however need to be aware that most geologists don't seem to like the idea of there having been cataclysmic changes. They do accept that there was a cataclysmic event that caused the demise of the dinosaurs some 60 million years ago, which the iridium layer found all over the Earth clearly indicates was a comet impact. Graham Hancock in Magicians of the Gods chronicles the fight the geological establishment have put up to try to deny the likely cause of the cataclysm that started the younger dryas period 12,800 years ago, which he identifies as a comet breaking up over and then hitting the North American ice sheet. Geologists know that the younger dryas period started very suddenly but still largely refuse to consider sudden (and hence cataclysmic) happenings which could have caused it.

Then we have the archeological evidence of things we can find on or in the ground and in caves. This is a pretty good source of evidence provided things found can be reliably dated. This works for excavations in ground that has not been disturbed, where the stratification can be relied upon, and particularly where material that can be carbon-dated can be found. The archeologists are also quite good at producing evidence that informs or supports things found in written history when we start getting this, as archeology and written histories can support each other. But for evidence that cannot be reliably dated or related to written history, which includes structure built of stone, the archeological community is very conservative, particularly in regard to any thought that these might date to times before written history appears.

Next there is historical evidence. This really starts with writing that we can decipher, so this kind of evidence doesn't come into play until around 7,000 years ago when the Sumerians started to inscribe clay blocks and to carve writing into stone. Where these written records relate to kings and civilisations that existed at the time, they can be used to construct reasonably reliable histories of nations, and contacts and conflicts between nations. Though there can be considerable confusion from the different names used in different nations for the same real people.

The written evidence of stories is analysed differently. These of course did not appear from thin air, they are written versions of stories that are much older, which were passed down orally. If the preceding chapters are anything like a true representation of what actually happened in the early days of mankind, you can imagine how powerful and rich the stories will have been, and how relevant they would have been to the current experience of people still living with a tangible, if occasional presence of gods. Where these kinds of stories appear as written histories, historians treat them rather differently to how they treat king lists and stories of battles and conquests. They consider them to be myths and legends. They are prepared to acknowledge that there may have been ancient individuals whose lives and actions have provided a basis for the stories, but they tend not to believe much of what is in these stories as actual fact. I will suggest some ways later through which you might judge what degree of truth there may be in myths and legends.

Through the early chapters of this book I have had a lot to say about DNA evidence. The science looks to me to be pretty good. It is horrendously complicated but the researchers go to great lengths to discuss how they have validated their findings and these studies are peer-reviewed before publication. So the facts are pretty solid. What is in question is what happened to create these genetic facts that we are discovering about ancient (and indeed modern) populations, which the scientists tend not to speculate about.

And finally in this review of the kinds of evidence available I must include the study of how languages have evolved, having mentioned the issue of where the Basque language in Northern Spain came from.

All of this amounts to a huge amount of evidence from widely different kinds of sources. Hence juggling with it all and trying to make it all fit together is rather difficult. But this is the task I have set myself which I hope you are enjoying following. So let us look first at the indisputable geological evidence, which defines the geographical and environmental context in which our history happened.

The shape of history from 50,000 years ago to the present.

In this story we are still in the period between 50,000 years ago and about 20,000 years ago, which was the last glacial maximum. That period then leads into the period from 20,000 years ago to the present during which there was melting of ice and sea-level rise.

We have a lot of information from geology and a lot of what we have is very reliable. Thanks to the work of geologists we have good dates for when the ice cover of the most recent ice period melted, though there is still work to be done here to get a clear picture. Dr Glenn Milne, the geologist that Graham Hancock consulted when writing Underworld concludes that ice cover was fairly stable up to the last glacial maximum approximately 22,000 years ago. There were then several phases of melting and hence several periods of flooding. He reckons there was some melting from 19,000 years ago but with little impact on the coastlines of the time, with the major melting starting around 16,500 years ago (14,500BC). He dates the submergence of huge areas of land around Malaysia and the East coast of China to somewhere between 14,000 and 11,000 years ago (12,000BC – 9,000BC). The three main islands of Japan were a continuous landmass until about 12,000 years ago. Hancock also quotes work by Professor John Shaw identifying three major episodes of rise of sea level from melting ice, 15,000 to 14,000 years ago, 12,000 to 11,000 years ago and 8000 to 7000 years ago.

Hapgood in his book, The Path of the Pole, concludes that there was a shift of the pole due to Earth crust displacement in the period 17,000 – 12,000 years ago which, if we believe the theory, provides a key part of the explanation for the melting, if not the whole reason. All of these dates have of course some degree of error so we should treat them as guides rather than fixed dates, but they definitely agree that sea-level rise happened in this period.

We also have information about the younger dryas period from a variety of sources of evidence such as ice and ocean-floor cores. This was a 1,200 year period of cold climatic conditions and drought, with increasing glaciation, which occurred between approximately 12,800 and 11,600 years ago (between 10,800BC and 9600BC). Different authorities read the dates in their evidence slightly differently, so we can't tie the precise dates down absolutely, but all agree that it was a 1200 year period and it appears to have started and ended very suddenly.

So while there does not yet seem to be complete agreement between geologists, there is a pretty good consensus that there was melting of ice from 20,000 years ago, starting slowly and then accelerating and raising sea level, with a re-glaciation for a 1200 year period 12,800 to 11,600, after which there was continued melting of the ice caps down to the size they were before our 20th century global warming started, with sea level reaching current levels by around 8000 years ago.

Myths, legends and history.

History is the story of the world and human beings, as told by the victors and survivors. People who get killed don't get a chance to write history. Those who lose battles or who are displaced by others may get a chance to leave something behind but it is not likely to be as visible as what is left by the victors. There is an imbalance that we must take into account. People also do not always write or draw the truth. 'Truth' is a perception, it is how we think about the things we know of. What is an undeniable truth to one person may be completely wrong according to another.

Myths and legends that survive down the ages are those stories which are told by survivors that people like to hear being re-told. This might be because the stories make them feel good, or because they give them a sense of their past and where they have come from which the adults feel it important to transmit to their children, or because the stories are exciting and make good entertainment.

The problem of knowing what to believe from histories and legends, what is and is not true, would be bad enough if it were simply the matter of unpicking the perceptions of different people, but we have to add to this the devious ways that people have of perverting actual history and turning it to their political ends. Examples abound. The Bayeux Tapestry was created by the French and hence is a French view of the battle of Hastings. In the middle ages the crusades were perpetrated as holy wars, which is almost equivalent to writing your own history before it happens. The crusades were seen very differently from the Arab side, who saw then as invasions to grab territory.

History as recorded in the bible is a selection from a wide range of available sources. The bible as we know it was put together around AD325, and it was decided not to include various old scriptures. These excluded scriptures, such as the book of Enoch (see http://book-ofenoch.com), may have said things that the church and politicians in AD325 thought would be unhelpful messages to expose their people to. The reasons for excluding them may have been much more to do with the political acceptability at that time of what they said, rather than their truth. The first book of Enoch for example describes activities of the 'watchers', angels who fathered the Nephilim. This is one of those things that has been speculated about, religiously and non-religiously, that you will have to make up your own mind about. I will only encourage you to consider the detail in Enoch's descriptions of what happened, with an open mind about what he may be describing. I will say some more about levels of detail in stories later.

Even in ancient writings that have been studied at great length, there are matters which are presented by the current 'authorities' as the truth but which may not be. One source of these errors is translation. Scribes translating from one language to another may have mis-read words, or may have misinterpreted words that can have dual meanings. There are enough of these to keep scholars busy for many years.

And finally, we have some things recorded in ancient texts, about which there is a consensus that they are so impossible to believe that they must be wrong. When scholars get to this point, to maintain the reputation, integrity and apparent truthfulness of the rest of these written works, they resort to the idea that what has been written is not fact but spiritual myth. They suggest the works were written in that way to make it easier for the people of the time to grasp the central ideas, without intention that what is written should be considered literally true. The Book of Genesis falls into this category, as do many other stories in the Bible and in the texts of other religions. And of course the book of Enoch just mentioned.

When we get to oral traditions we do not even have the written text to guide us in trying to assess what is true, may be true or is not true. Before the easy availability of writing materials, or perhaps through an understanding that things that are written have a habit of decaying or going missing, transmitting knowledge orally was an art. For example, some who have studied epic poems have come to the conclusion that the verses of epic poems would be invented by the poet relaying them to their current audience, and hence would be different as relayed by different poets. As this makes them unreliable in that the detail of the story changes, scholars of these epic poems therefore feel that what was critically important was not the details or even the characters in the story, but the shape of the underlying story that was being told, and the numbers that appeared in the stories in various ways. Hence it is these things that may carry the truth rather than the location of the story or personalities in the stories.

All of the above make interpreting written history, myths and legends very difficult. To overcome this I try to concentrate not on what they actually say or on what different scholars reckon they mean, but on a deeper level that may be a more reliable indicator of their truth.

Should we believe sources literally?

The point to be clear on about all these sources is that real people have made decisions about whether or not things written down are true, when they decided to make copies or to incorporate stories into their scriptures. They may have been right but they could be wrong. Where the transmitter of the story who made the copy believed the things in the text were impossible and therefore must be myth, and categorised the story as myth, others might have thought otherwise. Alice, in Alice in Wonderland said "There's no use trying, One can't believe impossible things." To which the Red Queen replied "I dare say you haven't had much practice. When I was your age, I always did it for half an hour a day. Why, sometimes I've believed as many as six impossible things before breakfast.". People who dare to suspend their belief for a while and ask "what if it were true….." can sometimes hit on important truths that create great insight. It is worth challenging those who would have us believe that 'unbelievable' and 'impossible' things in ancient texts must be inventions.

The structure of DNA came to Francis Crick in a dream, but he took the trouble to check if his dream could be true. Analysis of DNA is now beginning to point to a single 'Mitochondrial Eve' and a most recent common male ancestor (MRCA) 'Adam' that all currently living modern humans would be able to trace their descent from. Given this discovery, should we be completely sure that the book of Genesis is fable and contains no truth? Did Eve and Adam actually exist or did whoever created the story understand enough about how DNA is passed down the generations to be able to assert that there would be such individual ancestors of all humans? Getting into the science that appears to behind folklore or myths is rather a good way to explore what truth there may be in them. The book Spaceships of Ezekiel is an example of this, of which more later.

A second way to validate myths and folklore that are not accepted as fact is to do a 'meta-study' of many different sources. Some things appear in myths and legends so widely around the world that the weight of evidence starts to become overwhelming. The key legend in this category is the story of the Flood. The sheer amount of evidence from around the world makes such myths or legends worthy of serious investigation, but it is best if this is focused on the core of the story rather than on one element. The various attempts to find Noah's ark have come to nought, whereas Graham Hancock's serious search for flooded civilisations all over the Earth has borne considerable fruit.

In any investigation there will be some pieces of potential evidence that will come to carry more weight than others. You may have noticed that I have dropped into the story a few phrases from the bible that resonate rather well with the theory we are exploring. These however are just useful snippets, providing only small amounts of support to the theory relative to what we may come to believe are the main planks of evidence. The known ice-cover in the northern hemisphere during the last ice age that was discussed in the section on Earth crust displacement I consider to be strong evidence. Any theory of the history of the last 100,000 years must take it into account and explain it, whereas a line from the bible can be dismissed relatively easily if it does not fit the theory. The quantity of physical evidence of ice cover makes it undeniable, even if some of the detail is wrong. Similarly the quantity of evidence of a major extinction-level flood to me makes it undeniable that some very unusual flooding event happened. This evidence may be in myths and stories rather than as tangible evidence in the ground, but the volume of evidence gives comparable weight to the stories.

The stories of an extinction-level flood exist just as the evidence of ice-cover exists. They must have come from somewhere. So if you judge that the weight of evidence is on the side of there being some truth behind the stories, then this truth must have a place in our story of the last 100,000 years just as much as the changes in ice cover must be included.

It is also worth questioning words that are used in stories. When the stories that had been passed down orally came to be committed to texts such as the bible and the epic of Gilgamesh, words that had complex meaning at the time were used, words that we no longer understand. For example, words such as Nephilim, Annunaki and Angel. All that we can definitely know is that the writers expected the readers to know the difference between these words and other words that might have been used. These words refer to beings that were in some important way different to ordinary humans, but who were amongst humans. And they do not refer to gods or God, otherwise the writers would have used these words and not bothered to differentiate.

This is quite an important point. If you are transmitting an oral tradition, and you use a word that your audience does not understand, such as Nephilim, they will ask you to explain what the word refers to. Dictionaries didn't exist but the dictionary definition did. Those who had asked the question before would be able to remember how the word was defined last time, so there would have been a common consensual understanding of what it meant. When the oral tradition came to be written down, the original scribes must have considered that their readers would also know what the word meant.

We are pretty sure we know when people started to commit stories into writing, in Sumeria, around 3500BC. If this was the first time 'nephilim' was written down, and if the nephilim really are different kinds of being this means that the people alive at that time fully accepted that the existence of nephilim was part of their history. They knew what the differences to humans were that the word nephilim contains. After the original committing of the word from the oral tradition to the written word, the word may have started to take on a meaning somewhat different to the original truth. Books don't come with a built-in dictionary in the same way that an epic poem or ballad comes with a balladeer to provide extra detail and explanations. Nephilim is an historical word not a mythological word – unless you believe that the whole story was invented as a fairy-tale with mythological creatures. But in this case it surely would not have ended up in religious scriptures?

****

Chapter 14 - The period 40,000 to 20,000 years ago.

The period from 40,000 to 20,000 years ago must surely be about steadily growing social organisation and complexity of human societies. The assumption of archeologists is that this period was continuance of the hunter-gatherer lifestyles of small groups of people. We have no evidence of agriculture from this period and no evidence of stone structures that can be dated to this time. Evidence of agriculture can last a long time, for example the field systems of the medieval period, traces of which can still be seen today, as can ancient terraces in South East Asia. This belief that agriculture did not happen in this period, and only appeared after 12,000 years ago, could be an example of researchers denying something exists just because they can't find the evidence. Maybe agriculture was started in this period by some groups of humans, alongside other groups that maintained a hunter-gatherer lifestyle, but the evidence has not been found yet.

It is hard to imagine intelligent humans not taking some advantage of the fact that if you sow seeds they grow into plants. The Arabs in the empty quarter of Saudi Arabia have a tradition that a date stone must never be thrown into the fire. If it is thrown in the sand it will have almost no chance of growing into a date palm, but it might. Humans must have noticed that discarded seeds sometimes grew into useful plants. If they were nomadic this may not have been much use to them, unless they came back to the same places on a yearly cycle following animal migrations. Nomads anyway tend to operate on marginal land and hence probably don't have any great attraction to one area over another. Where the living is good and an area is producing plentiful food, people tend to be rather more territorial. Might those living in a stable hunting/gathering area not have thrown their date stones and other seeds into a sensible place and occasionally thrown water on them?

If we wish to look for signs of agriculture in this period, I think we should first ask where the good and plentiful land was in pre-Flood times before our current inter-glacial period started. If you live on land that can be easily stirred up with a stick when is it damp, in order to get seeds into the ground where they have more chance of evading birds and small mammals, it is much more likely that people will have started doing this. It must have been possible for people to observe that if crab-apple seeds were dumped in a damp corner and some got covered with soil, that they then grew. I feed the birds with grain and of course some seeds get trapped in cracks between the paving stones, where in damp weather they pretty quickly shoot and start growing. Humans preparing gathered seeds to eat outside their cave will surely also have seen this.

The easily cultivatable land is alluvial flood plains created by rivers. All the places on Earth where there were extensive flat lands close to the sea in this period have been flooded. The coastlines that are now still similar to what they were 20,000 years ago, where the sea has not encroached for miles, are coastlines that shelve at a steep angle into the sea. Humans living in such places who might have wished to practice agriculture would have had to create fields progressively higher up in order to use more land. If any evidence of their agriculture survives today it will have to be from farmers who were prepared to climb at least 300 feet above sea level in order to get to their fields. It seems very illogical to me to place your home next to the sea where you can take advantage of seafood, and then to insist on climbing 300 feet to any plants you may wish to use for food. There were plenty of places where the land was flat and close to the sea

I think we just have to accept that the most interesting archeological sites from this period can only be investigated by archeologists who are also good divers.

We do however have one site from this period that gives us a lot of insight into what life was like, Dolni Vestonice in the Czech Republic. Wikipedia states that there is evidence in Dolni Vestonice of a structure with a roof supported by wood that dates from 23,000 BC. We should not imagine human beings just living in caves or tents created from animal hides in this period. There will have been at least villages and there may well have been much larger civilisations that we have not yet found the evidence for (read Underworld!).

The Dolni Vestonice site is described as 'unique' because of the large number of clay figurines found there. 'Unique' tends to imply that it is the only one, but what is actually meant is that this is the only such site from this period that has so far been found. It is a reasonable bet that the technology indicated by this site would be far more widespread. This was a settled community producing cultural artefacts. There is lots of other archeological evidence there as well, such as evidence that nets were used to capture and kill mammoths and other large animals, that baskets and woven materials were made and there are 'enigmatic engravings'.

Even more fascinating, there is evidence of shellfish in their diet which originated in the Mediterranean. This indicates travel or trade over considerable distances and difficult terrain. Dolni Vestonice is over 200 miles from the sea. As hunter-gatherers they will have been very used to walking, so would probably think little about walking 30 miles in a day. But 200 miles still amounts to a couple of weeks for a round trip. This one fact, once you start to un-pick what it means, has many implications. There is no evidence of the use of pack animals such as mules or donkeys in this period, so the shellfish must have been carried by people. To justify spending six days carrying a load, the shellfish must have been considered high value.

This also implies that there was a group on the Mediterranean coast collecting the shellfish. And presumably whoever carried the shellfish returned carrying something else, perhaps clay figurines and sculptures?

The picture that I get is of a society that was quite large, well organised, quite technologically advanced and in communication with other such societies elsewhere. And if this kind of society existed more than 20,000 years ago, it makes the lack of pre-cursors to the civilisations of the last 10,000 years even more puzzling, unless there was a really big set-back to human development between the two.

The gods in the period 40,000 to 20,000 years ago.

We should also spend a little time wondering what the gods were doing during the period from 40,000 years to 20,000 years ago. Once the gods had been through the process of creating manpower and had got tribes growing successfully, they would not need to remain 'hands on' in control of their manpower if they could find a better way of sourcing what they wanted. They might however have undertaken scientific activities to watch and guide the development of mankind. They could have kept themselves largely to Antarctica with only occasional visits to collect offerings or to observe, and to reinforce their power as gods.

The idea that the Gods were observing the development of mankind is an interesting idea to conjure with, because another word for observer is watcher. This makes the suggestion in the book of Enoch that there were 'Watchers' who got rather more heavily involved with mankind than they perhaps should have done a rather intriguing idea. If we were watching development of indigenous beings on another planet we had gone to, the older and more experienced members of the group might well leave the task of regular watching of the developing native inhabitants of the planet to the younger members, who were more able to withstand the relative privations of being at locations amongst the natives rather than in the comforts back at base. That however is a speculative diversion, only possibly a small piece of the jigsaw based on rather thin evidence.

To get back to the gods, we have assumed they created mankind to be the manpower they needed to supply them with the things they wanted, and have suggested that they could have trained humans to be seafarers. It has been proved by the Kon Tiki expedition that a craft can be made without metal technologies that is capable of crossing oceans. There is also possibly evidence of a 6500 year old wooden boat, obviously made without use of metal as this was before copper started to be used, that has been found off the south coast of England.

Antarctica is well placed for sailing to other parts of the world. It sits in 'the middle of the one-world ocean' so they could easily sail in any direction. The initial journey is quite a long way, more than 2000 miles to the tip of Africa, or maybe the route to Europe would have been the 1000 or so miles to the tip of South America and then across the Atlantic at the shortest point between South America and Africa; there are some interesting possibly prehistoric remains being investigated on the Azores, which could have been a stopping-off point two-thirds of the way across the Atlantic. However these journeys are less than half the distance the Kon Tiki sailed, from South America to Polynesia, so it is quite feasible to suggest they were crossed in stone-age boats.

All the rest of the journeys would have been along the coasts so that ships could seek refuge if there were really bad storms, and so that they could access provisions such as water, wood for cooking fires and fruits. The humans in other areas of the world would likely have developed their main civilisations in easily accessible places on rivers, so they would have been easy to access. For those who like the sea, seafaring is a way of life. Families would live on board and would do some hunting and gathering as they went. It is possible to imagine our small number of gods comfortably ensconced in Antarctica, with a large human workforce most of whom spent their days at sea getting to and from the sources of what the gods wanted.

We have a recent example of how to get what you want from the various parts of the Earth – the British Empire. The British went out and conquered and took what they wanted by force, but pretty soon another approach developed, trade. Most human beings seem to want things that they don't have. These may be necessary things that they find difficult to source locally, such as salt. Or they may be luxuries such as beads and ornaments, or weapons to fight neighbours. Or drugs such as Opium. The British used all these to buy what they wanted, which were spices and flavourings that would not grow in England, stimulants that also would not grow (tea and coffee), materials that would not grow in England such as hardwoods like mahogany, and other materials that would support their manufacturing and power, such as cotton. They could often acquire a commodity in one place that would enable them to buy things they wanted in another. Opium could be grown in Afghanistan and exported to China to buy silk.

By having lots of boats trading around the world the gods could arrange regular shipments of what they wanted. Humans in other parts of the world would have had regular visits by boats to buy their produce in exchange for exotic goods brought from elsewhere. A single obsidian knife might buy a great deal from tribes with no source of obsidian locally - it is found only in specific places that have experienced rhyolitic eruptions (look it up!).

I put it to you that we may now be talking about the Atlanteans.

It is quite easy to imagine our Adventurers establishing an Atlantean civilisation for this purpose. Whilst they might have started to extract what they wanted from humans by exercising godly power, to continue with this they would have needed to make occasional appearances at all the places from which they required things. Far better to teach the humans they sent out round the world to trade. The gods could then have returned to an easy life in Antarctica, making only such forays into the rest of the world as they wished to, to study mankind or for whatever other purposes they had. Trade would have been a more reliable means of getting what they wanted as it would not rely on having to instruct leaders to produce offerings. The leaders of tribes in different parts of the world would have had their own internal reasons for engaging in trade, to get the things their people wanted and luxuries for themselves.

It is quite possible however that the leaders and priests of tribes would have kept the system of gods and offerings going in their own interests. And the gods might have supported this by occasionally letting mankind observe their presence and their power. Throughout the ages we can see religions demanding what were effectively taxes all the way up to the tithes demanded by the English church in the middle ages. These often enabled the priesthoods to live in some style. The monasteries of England in the 1500s controlled huge swathes of the best land in the country and were fabulously wealthy. The Abbots and Bishops of the Church in England were extremely powerful. Which is of course a key reason why Henry the Eighth went after their wealth and lands.

Outside Antarctica I am painting a picture where there is little or no activity by the gods unless their involvement and equipment is necessary, perhaps say for mining. So there will be little or no evidence of the gods from this period that is available in the world and that we can now access, except for impact they may have had on traditions like religion and for mentions of them in legends.

Atlanteans before the flood.

There has been a great deal written about Atlantis, with many speculations that the story was based on happenings such as the volcanic explosion that destroyed the island of Thera and caused the end of the Minoan civilisation on Crete. All these speculations tend to obscure where the story originated and what this original source actually says.

If we are to assess whether there is evidence in this for the existence of the Atlanteans and the gods it is worth reading in full the relevant part of Plato's Timaeus, where the story appears. Plato reports a conversation between Solon, one of his ancestors, and an Egyptian priest. However be aware that there is good evidence that Solon did not just invent the story out of thin air. Graham Hancock in Magicians of the Gods reports that the Horus temple at Edfu in Egypt has hieroglyphics telling a very similar story. You might decide that what is carved in the Horus temple was also just a myth, but even this would put the Atlantis story on a par with stories like the epic of Gilgamesh, that are reckoned by most to have some kind of truth behind them. However the Egyptians tended to only commit things they felt important to the walls of their temples. It takes rather a lot of effort to carve hieroglyphics and there is limited space on temple walls, so those with the power to decide will naturally only do this for stories considered a key part of their history or major political statements to promote the power and glory of the pharaoh.

Plato reports Solon's conversation with the priests as follows. The sections I have italicised we will then consider in detail. The bold italics are my addition.

> "Tell us, said the other, the whole story, and how and from whom Solon heard this veritable tradition."
>
> "He replied:—In the Egyptian Delta, at the head of which the river Nile divides, there is a certain district which is called the district of Sais, and the great city of the district is also called Sais, and is the city from which King Amasis came. The citizens have a deity for their foundress; she is called in the Egyptian tongue Neith, and is asserted by them to be the same whom the Hellenes call Athene; they are great lovers of the Athenians, and say that they are in some way related to them.
>
> To this city came Solon, and was received there with great honour; he asked the priests who were most skillful in such matters, about antiquity, and made the discovery that neither he nor any other Hellene knew anything worth mentioning about the times of old. On one occasion, wishing to draw them on to speak of antiquity, he began to tell about the most ancient things in our part of the world — about Phoroneus, who is called 'the first man,' and about Niobe; and after the Deluge, of the survival of Deucalion and Pyrrha; and he traced the genealogy of their descendants, and reckoning up the dates, tried to compute how many years ago the events of which he was speaking happened.
>
> Thereupon one of the priests, who was of a very great age, said: O Solon, Solon, you Hellenes are never anything but children, and there is not an old man among you. Solon in return asked him what he meant. I

mean to say, he replied, that in mind you are all young; there is no old opinion handed down among you by ancient tradition, nor any science which is hoary with age.

And I will tell you why. There have been, and will be again, many destructions of mankind arising out of many causes; the greatest have been brought about by the agencies of fire and water, and other lesser ones by innumerable other causes. There is a story, which even you have preserved, that once upon a time Phaëthon, the son of Helios, having yoked the steeds in his father's chariot, because he was not able to drive them in the path of his father, burnt up all that was upon the earth, and was himself destroyed by a thunderbolt.

Now this has the form of a myth, but really signifies a declination of the bodies moving in the heavens around the earth, and a great conflagration of things upon the earth, which recurs after long intervals; at such times those who live upon the mountains and in dry and lofty places are more liable to destruction than those who dwell by rivers or on the seashore. And from this calamity the Nile, who is our never failing saviour, delivers and preserves us. When, on the other hand, the gods purge the earth with a deluge of water, the survivors in your country are herdsmen and shepherds who dwell on the mountains, but those who, like you, live in cities are carried by the rivers into the sea. Whereas in this land, neither then nor at any other time, does the water come down from above on the fields, having always a tendency to come up from below; for which reason the traditions preserved here are the most ancient.

The fact is, that wherever the extremity of winter frost or of summer sun does not prevent, mankind exist, sometimes in greater, sometimes in lesser numbers. And whatever happened either in your country or in ours, or in any other region of which we are informed — if there were any actions noble or great or in any other way remarkable, they have all been written down by us of old, and are preserved in our temples. Whereas just when you and other nations are beginning to be provided with letters and the other requisites of civilized life, after the usual interval, the stream from heaven, like a pestilence, comes pouring down, and leaves only those of you who are destitute of letters and education; and so you have to begin all over again like children, and know nothing of what happened in ancient times, either among us or among yourselves.

As for those genealogies of yours which you just now recounted to us, Solon, they are no better than the tales of children. In the first place you remember a single deluge only, but there were many previous ones; in the next place, you do not know that there formerly dwelt in your land the fairest and noblest race of men which ever lived, and that you and your whole city are descended from a small seed or remnant of them which survived. And this was unknown to you, because, for many generations, the survivors of that destruction died, leaving no written word. For there was a time, Solon, before the great deluge of all, when the city which now is Athens was first in war and in every way the best governed of all cities, and is said to have performed the noblest deeds and to have had the fairest constitution of any of which tradition tells, under the face of heaven.

Solon marveled at his words, and earnestly requested the priests to inform him exactly and in order about these former citizens.

You are welcome to hear about them, Solon, said the priest, both for your own sake and for that of your city, and above all, for the sake of the goddess who is the common patron and parent and educator of both our cities. She founded your city a thousand years before ours, receiving from the Earth and Hephaestus the seed of your race, and afterwards she founded ours, of which the constitution is recorded in our sacred registers to be 8000 years old.

As touching your citizens of 9000 years ago, I will briefly inform you of their laws and of their most famous action; the exact particulars of the whole we will hereafter go through at our leisure in the sacred registers themselves. If you compare these very laws with ours you will find that many of ours are the counterpart of yours as they were in the olden time. In the first place, there is the caste of priests, which is separated from all the others; next, there are the artificers, who ply their several crafts by themselves and do not intermix; and also there is the class of shepherds and of hunters, as well as that of husbandmen; and you will observe, too, that the warriors in Egypt are distinct from all the other classes, and are commanded by the law to devote themselves solely to military pursuits; moreover, the weapons which they carry are shields and spears, a style of equipment which the goddess taught of Asiatics first to us, as in your part of the world first to you.

Then as to wisdom, do you observe how our law from the very first made a study of the whole order of things, extending even to prophecy and medicine which gives health; out of these divine elements deriving what was needful for human life, and adding every sort of knowledge which was akin to them. All this order and arrangement the goddess first imparted to you when establishing your city; and she chose the spot of earth in which you were born, because she saw that the happy temperament of the seasons in that land would produce the wisest of men. Wherefore the goddess, who was a lover both of war and of wisdom, selected and first of all settled that spot which was the most likely to produce men likest herself. And there you dwelt, having such laws as these and still better ones, and excelled all mankind in all virtue, as became the children and disciples of the gods.

The most glorious act of ancient Athens was the deliverance of Europe and Libya from the power of Atlantis. Soon afterwards both empires disappeared.

Many great and wonderful deeds are recorded of your state in our histories. But one of them exceeds all the rest in greatness and valour. For **these histories tell of a mighty power which unprovoked made an expedition against the whole of Europe and Asia**, and to which your city put an end.

This power came forth out of the Atlantic Ocean, for in those days the Atlantic was navigable. And there was an island situated in front of the straits which are by you called the pillars of Heracles; the island was larger than Libya and Asia put together, and was the way to other islands, and from these you might pass to the whole of the opposite continent which surrounded the true ocean; for this sea which is within the Straits of Heracles is only a harbour, having a narrow entrance, but that other is a real sea, and the surrounding land may be most truly called a boundless continent.

> Now in this island of Atlantis there was a great and wonderful empire **which had rule over the whole island and several others, and over parts of the continent**, and, furthermore, the men of Atlantis had subjected the parts of Libya within the columns of Heracles as far as Egypt, and of Europe as far as Tyrrhenia. This vast power, gathered into one, endeavoured to subdue at a blow our country and yours and the whole of the region within the straits; and then, Solon, your country shone forth, in the excellence of her virtue and strength, among all mankind. She was preeminent in courage and military skill, and was the leader of the Hellenes. And when the rest fell off from her, being compelled to stand alone, after having undergone the very extremity of danger, she defeated and triumphed over the invaders, and preserved from slavery those who were not yet subjugated, and generously liberated all the rest of us who dwell within the pillars.
>
> But afterwards there occurred violent earthquakes and floods; and **in a single day and night of misfortune all your warlike men in a body sank into the earth, and the island of Atlantis in like manner disappeared in the depths of the sea.** For which reason the sea in those parts is impassable and impenetrable, because there is a shoal of mud in the way; and this was caused by the subsidence of the island.

If we take this at face value, what are the key elements? Let's work backwards:

- *"But afterwards there occurred violent earthquakes and floods; and in a single day and night of misfortune all your warlike men in a body sank into the earth, and the island of Atlantis in like manner disappeared in the depths of the sea."*

The story of the Hellenes (Greeks) defeating the Atlanteans is a story of something that happened just before a major Earth cataclysm. Despite the cataclysm the story had somehow been transmitted down to the Egyptian priests of 600BC, presumably initially by survivors and then because Egyptian civilisation had become established and maintained some stability and records from then. In an earlier part of Solon's story he is told by the priests why Egypt is less susceptible to the kinds of disasters that would devastate countries like Greece. The story that is being told is of something that happened in the Mediterranean, but at the same time as "all your (Athenian) warlike men in a body sank into the earth", "Atlantis in like manner disappeared in the depths of the sea." So Atlantis was also overwhelmed. Wherever it was, this was a catastrophe that engulfed at least the Atlantic ocean and the Mediterranean. This could well be describing a global catastrophe. The phrase about Atlantis "sinking into the sea" does not necessarily mean that the land sank, it could mean that the island of Atlantis was completely covered by a vast tsunami. Given that Antarctica is completely surrounded by the Pacific, Atlantic and Indian oceans, if they swirled around sufficiently one can imagine this happening to at least the islands around Antarctica and the Antarctic peninsula.

- ***"these histories tell of a mighty power which unprovoked made an expedition against the whole of Europe and Asia."*** This was an invasion attempting to take control of the whole Mediterranean and what we now call the Middle East, 'at a blow'. It was stated that the Atlanteans already had conquered 'Libya' which in those days meant the whole North African coast up to present-day Libya, and 'Europe as far as Tyrrhenia' which means Spain France and Italy, the Tyrrhenian Sea being the sea to the west of Italy with Tyrrhenia itself being west and central Italy. The Atlanteans were already well known in the Mediterranean so this was not an empire suddenly appearing, it was an attack 'unprovoked' which implies that contact between Greek and Egyptian people and the Atlanteans had been relatively good before this event, and they therefore could not see any kind of provocation that would give cause for the attack. Whoever recorded the story did not understand why a people who they had co-existed peacefully with should suddenly rise up and attempt to conquer the rest of the Mediterranean and 'Asia' which in those days will have meant Turkey, Iran and Iraq. Was this because an influx of Atlanteans had arrived from elsewhere, maybe Antarctica? Even if countries such as Egypt and Greece had relatively small populations at that time, this must have still been a large invasion force if it was spread so as to attack all the countries with civilisations around the Eastern Mediterranean coast, at the same time. If the need to conquer and subjugate more of the Mediterranean was driven by an influx of Atlanteans, you could imagine the towns and cities that were already subjugated becoming overcrowded with immigrants, creating pressure to move further along the Mediterranean and a decision to mount a major attack.

- *"This power came forth out of the Atlantic Ocean, for in those days the Atlantic was navigable."* It doesn't really make sense to describe an ocean as 'not navigable' in the sense this term would be used of a river, that of there being insufficient water or too many rocks to allow ships to pass. Navigable must surely mean that the Atlanteans had the ship technology to be able to cross it, rather than that it was for some reason impossible for ships to cross it. At the time of Solon Greek and Egyptian ship technology may still not have reached a level where they were confident to cross oceans. Ships designed for coast-hugging sailing in the Mediterranean will have existed at the time the story was told, but probably would not have been able to cope with Atlantic storms and waves.

- *"there was an island situated in front of the straits which are by you called the Pillars of Heracles; the island was larger than Libya and Asia put together,"* The phrase 'in front of' is a little confusing, because it implies that if you sailed through the straits of Gibraltar you would bump into this island. But if you were sailing from the Mediterranean into "the one great ocean" of the world, then as you turned into the Atlantic to head to the Southern oceans the Antarctic continent would indeed have been in front of you all the way. 'Island' makes us think of small islands, but what it really means is 'fully surrounded by sea', rather than connected to other continents as Europe, Asia and Africa are, and the Americas nearly are (and may have been then). Australia is an island. And so is Antarctica. The size the story quotes for the island is immense. Lybia and Asia together means all of North Africa and all of Asia across to the east of Iran. If you have your atlas to hand and can put a tracing of Antarctica first over 'Libya and Asia' and then over the Atlantic ocean (using maps at the same scale of course) you will see that Antarctica is comparable in size to, though a bit smaller than 'Lybia and Asia combined'. An island the size of Lybia and Asia would completely fill the Atlantic Ocean. It is rather unlikely that an island of this size has disappeared in the middle of the Atlantic, we have far too much evidence about the nature of the Atlantic floor to suppose this. And to think that the story might be referring to an island chain such as the Azores just does not agree with the story.

And finally we have the statement:

- *"and in a single day and night of misfortune all your warlike men in a body sank into the earth"*. This rather sounds to me as describing ALL warlike men being destroyed, in other words not only the Greeks who had been fighting the invaders and had stopped their further advance, but the invading armies as well. And the story confirms the empires were destroyed.

And the date:

- *"as touching your citizens of 9000 years ago"*, which as Solon lived around 2600 years ago (636BC to 558BC) puts the story of this time just before the final flood and the flood itself back to 11600 years ago. This date is a bit of a problem to this story, as you will see shortly that I date the Flood to the start of the younger dryas period, 12,800 years ago. It is however possible to construe the words in the story slightly differently. When the priest talks of "your citizens of 9000 years ago" it is in the context of the then Greek civilisation having been founded by the goddess 1000 years before the Egyptian civilisation. These are both post-Flood happenings, dating the start of the Greek civilisation to 11,600 BP and the Egyptian civilisation to 10,600 BP. The priest goes on to talk about the laws of this post-flood civilisation. The introduction to the story of the defeat of the Atlanteans starts "the most glorious act of ancient Athens....", which might well be referring not to the then current Athenian civilisation, but to the previous civilisation that was destroyed by the Flood. We think of ancient Athens as the time Solon and the Egyptian priest were living in, their understanding of ancient Athens would relate to a previous Athenian civilisation back in the mists of time. This reading of the words would allow us to date the destruction of the Atlanteans to a time earlier than 11,600 BP, and make my dating of the Flood to 12,800 BP possible.

Let us describe this story a little differently.

It states "Now in this island of Atlantis there was a great and wonderful empire which had rule over the whole island and several others, and over parts of the continent"

There is a wonderful empire, so wonderful that it is beyond comparison with the Mediterranean and Middle Eastern civilisations that created this story and passed it down to the Egyptian priest. And it was still considered to be wonderful by the Egyptian priests of Solon's time, when Egypt was itself a great civilisation. For these civilisations to know of it and how wonderful it was there must have must have been some links in order for the stories to be heard about it's wonder. My guess is that these were trading links, with ships moving around the Mediterranean between areas 'subjugated by Atlantis' and Greece, the Lebanon and Egypt.

The Atlanteans are stated to have had complete control of Atlantis and some other islands. And they had outposts in various places on 'the continent', which refers to the continent surrounding the one great ocean. This paints a picture of the Atlantean empire being global. We should expect from this that there were Atlantean cities in places such as South East Asia and South America, which may have left traces behind that we can find today. But remember the time we are at in the story. Though there will have been flooding of coastlines happening since 19,000 years ago, at this time before the major flood sea level would still have been at least 100 or 200 feet below where it is now, so these cities might well have been on land that is now submerged, such as the South China sea. But there is hope that some remains from this period may still be above sea level. Gunung Padang in Indonesia may prove to be one such site.

The 'wonderful empire' not only was wonderful at home, but presumably had wonderful ships way beyond the capabilities of those living around the Mediterranean at the time. This was very much a maritime empire, one that might have originated the 'Maps of the Ancient Sea Kings' to use the title of another book by Hapgood that is worth a look.

In thinking about what such an empire was like perhaps the best model to compare it with is the British Empire. This started as a series of trading posts around the world, such as Hong Kong and Shanghai, were goods desired back home were bought. To ensure the safety of the British citizens who ran these trading posts and assembled the goods the ships would come to pick up, sufficient areas of land were seized and cities were built. There is however a difference between how the British empire developed and how the Atlantean empire probably developed. The trigger for the major expansion of the British empire and the conquering of the whole of India and huge swathes of Africa and the Caribbean was population explosion at home and the industrial revolution driven by capitalism and greed. Prior to this in the 18th century there was no need to conquer massive areas. A lot of the trade was carried out through barter rather than with money and the drive was more to do with goods desired by those in England than by markets to sell manufactured goods. The time of the Atlanteans was before metals came into use and energy was harnessed to drive machines. There can not have been the manufacturing and markets drive to expand their empire. And we don't have any evidence of any kind of globally acceptable currencies from this period. Currency through the ages has needed to be durable so it lasts in the archeological record. So the Atlantean empire may well have been much more stable, serving much smaller populations than existed at the time of the British empire, and hence able to last for hundreds or thousands of years without great change.

Without the drive for building empires, where the English, Dutch, Spanish, Portuguese and French were competing for global dominance, and without the greed and capitalism, it makes no sense at all for the Atlanteans to have launched a major attack to gain dominance over Greece, Egypt and Asia. Their model of development had been to progressively subjugate towns and cities, and though the Egyptians referred to this as the people being subjugated into slavery by the Atlanteans, it may well have been driven as much by the populace wanting the advantages of the higher technology and societal organisation the Atlanteans had.

The Atlanteans were not seen as a current threat, they co-existed with the other civilisations in the Mediterranean. Then, for some reason, this stable situation is upset by "a mighty power which unprovoked made an expedition against the whole of Europe and Asia". For some reason the Atlanteans decided they needed a rapid expansion of the territory they controlled.

Now what on Earth made them think that?

The role of the gods in Atlantean civilisation.

The story in Timaeus also has some interesting things to say about what the gods were doing at this time. We can try to infer how involved they were from the way this story has developed.

The Egyptian priest was happy to tell Solon the histories "......for the sake of the goddess who is the common patron and parent and educator of both our cities. She founded your city a thousand years before ours, receiving from the Earth and Hephaestus the seed of your race, and afterwards she founded ours, of which the constitution is recorded in our sacred registers to be 8000 years old.". The priest then makes further statements about the god who founded Athens and Sais, "All this order and arrangement the goddess first imparted to you when establishing your city; and she chose the spot of earth in which you were born, because she saw that the happy temperament of the seasons in that land would produce the wisest of men. Wherefore the goddess, who was a lover both of war and of wisdom, selected and first of all settled that spot which was the most likely to produce men likest herself.". This is all talking about the goddess in very matter of fact terms. This is not describing some remote deity but a god making practical decisions, helping to establish Athens and to educate and develop its populace and to define how the society should operate and its laws.

If this is a true report of what the Egyptian priest said, we will have to believe that this is how they viewed the gods in their times.

So what this story is telling us does not give us any information about what the gods were doing before the Flood, but is helpful to a later chapter where I consider what happens after the Flood. We will have to infer or guess how active the gods might have been around the world before the Flood from how we have speculated they developed and controlled mankind.

If the gods were controlling mankind in Antarctica through the thought control of a religion that required them to worship the gods and to serve them in defined ways, this will have been a very deeply embedded part of Atlantean life. Wherever Atlanteans went in the world they will have carried this absolute conviction of the importance and power of their gods with them. One can imagine the gods themselves perhaps giving Atlanteans a little support in setting up trading outposts around the world, with a few shock and awe tactics and occasional appearances in the area to frighten the natives. But once they had trained the Atlanteans in seafaring and war they would have been a pretty unstoppable force in their own right. And once trading was established the natives in different parts of the world would probably have welcomed the Atlanteans for what they could bring, particularly if they did not try to displace local rulers and leaders.

As this developed Atlantean trading posts around the world might have grown into substantial cities. The Atlanteans would want to develop these cities to have at least some of the sophistication and facilities that could be found in the home base of their empire, which would no doubt include fine buildings and temples. This might have been a reason for the gods to visit those cities and to have greater involvement in their development, perhaps bringing their technology to make them more splendid.

The logic of our story therefore suggests that stories from many parts of the world might contain stories about the gods, and the religions ancient civilisations developed might reflect the same kind of confusions between the gods and God that I discussed relative to the Middle Eastern and Mediterranean religions. This is an area that I will be looking into, to add to future versions of this book.

****

Chapter 15 – Floods and The Flood.

We now come to the critical moment in the story. All the indicators appear to point to something momentous happening at the start of the younger dryas period 12,800 years ago, which to remind you was a 1200 year period when the geological record clearly shows that the Earth suddenly cooled, glaciers stopped melting and there was re-glaciation, until the period very suddenly ended 11.600 BP.

We know there was some melting of ice in the 4000 years before this critical juncture in the history of mankind. We are told that this is because the Earth was warming but if Earth crust displacement happens, this may have been the major cause. As the scientists who assess Earth temperature in past time don't take this into account it is not easy to see whether it was one or the other or both factors causing melting of ice. I am going to assume that Earth crust displacement was happening in this period

It is my belief that a major worldwide flood was part of what happened to start the younger dryas period. So it is time to explore what might have caused a flood that nearly exterminated mankind. This is what those who wrote the flood stories believed. Though they were no doubt describing what happened in their part of the world, and other parts may have escaped more lightly, they definitely saw this flood as an exceptional event. Not just a once-in-a-lifetime event, but something for which there was no precedent. And people all over the world have legends of an extermination-level flood, so this was a global event.

For a flood to happen the water has to come from somewhere. The two possibilities are much more rain than can be removed to the sea by the rivers, or the sea washing over the land - or both. The evidence suggests that ice is involved in this in some way, so let's look at ice first.

Ice and sea level.

We have speculated that when our Adventurers, the gods, arrived at Earth that Antarctica at least in parts was in warmer climes, because the South Pole was at a different place around 2000 miles from where it is now. The ice cap at the South Pole would have been half over Antarctica and half over the sea. At the North Pole there was a big ice cap centred over the Hudson

Bay, covering Canada, the top of the USA and Greenland. This is the Laurentide ice sheet that was known to exist up to around 20,000 years ago. There were also the ice sheets over the western edge of Europe. That there was more ice than now in the northern hemisphere is not in debate, there is good scientific evidence that there was. There may have been a bit less ice in the southern hemisphere if half the Antarctic ice sheet was over the sea, but overall there was much more ice in the world. It would be good to understand why.

There is a set amount of water in the world, the majority being either in the sea, or in glaciers and ice-caps several thousands of feet thick, with a little in the rocks of the Earth's crust. We know from our current problems with global warming that a warmer climate causes melting of ice and rises in sea level, with islands in the Pacific that are only a few metres above sea level now being in dire peril. The critical issue with regard to the impact on mankind of the balance between water in seas or in ice is by how much sea level has changed. And how fast. Slow rise in sea level does not cause a disastrous rapid flood, you can see the problem developing and move home, unless you are living on a low-lying island that will soon be completely covered by the sea. For the sea to be involved in causing an extinction-level flood something else must have happened.

Before we go more precisely into how the Flood might have happened, and hence how it could have affected the gods, the Atlanteans, and mankind elsewhere on the Earth, consider first the difference between ice on sea and ice on land. The Arctic ice cap is floating whereas the current Antarctic ice cap is on land. Ice has a density pretty close to that of water. Frozen water is slightly less dense than liquid water, with the greatest density of water occurring at 4 degrees Centigrade. Most substances contract when they freeze and the fact that water does not is very strange and wonderful. Water is really quite amazing. If ice was more dense than liquid water as soon as ice formed on the surface of a pond it would sink to the bottom and the pond would freeze totally, from the bottom up. There would be no life left in the pond. The same would happen to the sea when it froze if ice was denser than water. This is a slight diversion from our story but considering the physics can help us reach conclusions about what might have happened.

Because ice is pretty much the same density as water, it floats with only a small part of the ice above water level. It is common knowledge, known by school children since the Titanic went down, that 90% of an iceberg is under water. So when an ice sheet is floating, only 10% or so of the water that has frozen is lifted above sea level. However it is not a straightforward calculation that the ice above sea level equals water removed from the sea, because following the Archimedes principal the weight of water the iceberg displaces is equal to the weight of the iceberg. It has been calculated that the melting of all floating ice and ice shelves could add 2.6% to the volume of the sea and raise sea level by around 4 centimetres. The 'bottom line' as far as this story is concerned is that we can see that floating ice does not make much of a contribution to raising sea level when it melts.

Contrast that with an ice cap forming on land. In this case all the water is removed from the sea. When it melts and flows back into the sea all of the water adds to the volume of the sea. And ice on land can be very thick. The Antarctic ice sheet is in places around 4000m (around 12,000 feet) thick. You can find various estimates of how much sea level would rise if all the Antarctic ice melted, and they are of the order of 50m - 70m rise in sea level. As we know sea level has risen much more than this since 20,000 years ago, there must then have been a lot more ice on land than there is now.

The overall temperature of the Earth, primarily due to our distance from the sun, is such that the poles will be freezing (as long as we don't fully turn the Earth into a greenhouse by burning more fossil fuels!). That is, the air at the poles will be freezing. A US submarine has been to the North Pole under the ice. Sea and ice can co-exist next to each other because salt water freezes at a lower temperature than fresh water, typically minus 2 degrees but with some variation due to variations in salinity. The ice in the sea is fresh-water ice either from rain and snow falling on existing sea ice or because it is icebergs that have calved from glaciers. The fact that sea water currents move around provides a mechanism for the floating ice to melt more easily than that on land, if warmer currents displace the minus 2 degrees sea that is keeping the sea ice frozen. The sea ice at the North Pole advances every Winter and retreats every Summer, whereas the ice cap on Greenland is static by comparison, the advance and retreat is far less.

It is in fact not clear how the hugely thick ice caps on Greenland and Antarctica came about. To build a thick ice cap you need snow, rain or hail, 'precipitation' to use the word to encompass all water coming from the atmosphere onto the Earth's surface. There is currently very little precipitation each year in Greenland and Antarctica, so the scientists are puzzled as to how the several kilometre thick ice sheets developed. It is possible that they may have developed over a much longer timescale than has been thought so far, and simply have never in that long time moved out of the polar zones. But as Greenland has an ice sheet from inside the Arctic Circle all the way to 60 degrees north of the Equator, why isn't the whole of Norway covered in ice too? Bergen and Oslo are both further north than 60 degrees. The top of Scotland is at about 58 degrees north but there is no all-year-round ice in Scotland. This is another bit of evidence to suggest that the poles have moved, with Greenland always being in sufficiently cold air to stop the ice melting much, but Europe having alternated between polar regions and sufficiently far out of polar regions for all ice except mountain glaciers to melt.

The point we are working towards is that if there was land at the North Pole sea level would be much lower than it is today. An ice sheet as thick as that on Antarctica could be sitting on that land and all that water would be removed from the sea. If you have a globe of the Earth you can now do a little practical experiment. You can also do it with an atlas but it's a bit harder. Try holding the globe between two fingers, top and bottom. And see where you have to place your fingers to get land at both the North and South Poles. At the southern end you have only one continent to play with so your finger will have to be somewhere on Antarctica. To get most land at the opposite end of the Earth's axis you will then find your other finger somewhere over the north of Canada. This then dictates that your southern finger needs to be on the edge of Antarctica towards Australia and India. Get someone to mark these points for you and then draw yourself some new Arctic and Antarctic circles.

Your new Arctic circle will encompass Greenland, some of Alaska and all those islands that lie north of Canada. The other side of this new Arctic circle will cover all of Canada and a large part of the USA. There is still some sea inside this new Arctic circle but it is surrounded by land. In Antarctica currently, where there is sea nearly surrounded by land there are ice shelves, the Ross, Ronne and Filchner shelves. Here the ice is only partially floating as it bridges across between the land, sufficiently to hold up a much greater thickness of ice above sea level than there would be if that ice was floating. Ice shelves typically support ice to a height of between 100m and 1000m. In your new Arctic circle the same would likely happen. The Hudson Bay and the Baffin basin would likely be ice shelves.

This would mean that most of the area inside your new Arctic circle was supporting an ice cap of comparable thickness to today's Greenland and Antarctic ice caps. And there would be a thick ice sheet over half of Antarctica, which would also spread out as sea ice. It is possible that the south of Australia and Tasmania may also have had ice sheets. The impact on sea level would be considerable. If melting all of Antarctica's ice now would add 50m - 70m to sea level, then having a comparable ice sheet in the northern hemisphere as well as at least half the southern hemisphere ice on land in Antarctica, would mean a sea level more than 100m (around 300 feet) below where it is now. Which is where the sea level was estimated to have been 20,000 years ago.

Was it an ice age?

When we think of ice ages most people think of a world much colder than it is today. In fact we are currently living in an ice-age. To be fully correct we are living in an interglacial period in an ice age. In other words the ice has retreated a bit from where it has been through most of the current ice age. World temperature has been considerably higher in the past, going back millions of years. Don't let this distract you from the current problems of global warming; the Earth may be quite happy operating at a much higher temperature with only small ice caps but we humans would find the transition just as difficult as our current global warming will soon be to the Maldives, that have an average height above sea level of just 1.5m. The 'last glacial maximum' that started to decline some 20,000 years ago was only really of concern to those countries covered by ice or sufficiently close to the edge of the ice cap that they were unproductive tundra. The concept of 'ice age' as most people think about it is much more to do with where there was ice than what the temperature of the Earth was. Even in the depths of an ice age there is still a considerable part of the Earth that is ice free.

The temperature in Antarctica going back many thousands of years has been measured from ice cores (from where the ice is thickest). These show that the 'normal' state of the Earth is colder than our current temperature, with temperatures in that part of Antarctica being around minus 85 degrees during ice ages and minus 65 degrees during interglacial periods such as the period we are in now. This 20 degree rise has happened during the last 20,000 years ago. The average Earth temperature as a whole only varies by a few degrees.

We don't know the mechanisms which in times past caused overall Earth temperature to change and ice cover to extend or reduce. One theory for the cause of ice ages is the 'Milankovitch wobble' theory. The Earth's axis is tilted relative to the plane of the Earth's orbit round the sun. However this tilt of the axis very slowly rotates, taking around 26,000 years to precess around a complete rotation. The Earth's orbit around the sun is also not quite circular, it is slightly elliptical, and this too rotates over an even longer timescale. Combining precession and our elliptical orbit round the sun creates a 21,000 year cycle of 'astronomical seasons'. On top of this the Earth's axis of rotation changes slightly on a 41,000 year cycle. It's mind-bogglingly hard to work out how all these cycles interact, but by changing slightly how far the Earth is from the sun and how much the poles are tilted towards the sun, the amount of sunlight falling on high latitudes changes. The Milankovitch theory basically says that around 20,000 years ago the amount of sunlight falling on the big ice sheets at that time increased causing temperature to rise and the ice to start melting. This may be true, but to me Earth crust displacement is a much more convincing reason for the Laurentide ice sheet starting to melt. Shifting polar ice to latitudes much closer to the Equator would cause relatively rapid melting, dependent on how fast the shift happened.

It could be that the changes in ice cover in 'ice ages' are much more to do with displacement of the crust and how much land is at the poles, than they are to do with temperature of the Earth.

Melting ice – the effect on sea level.

Whatever the cause of the melting of ice, this was probably a gradual process over some hundreds of years. Sea level would rise but relatively gradually. However there could have been some more sudden sea-level rises. This is pure speculation, but suppose the Baffin Basin had become an ice shelf on top of which was a thousand metres of ice. The sea water underneath the ice shelf could possibly melt the ice shelf where it met the edges of the land. Melting of the ice on top of the ice shelf caused by the sun would create melt-water that would find it's way into the ice, melting the ice as it flows down cracks in the ice. It is not inconceivable that the ice could fracture along the coasts of Greenland and Baffin Island. If the whole of this ice shelf broke away from the ice on land and slid into the sea and became floating ice and hence no longer above sea level, sea level would rise considerably and pretty suddenly. Close to where the ice slid into the sea there would be a tsunami-like wave that would inundate coasts quickly. Elsewhere round the world, within a few days or maybe weeks, people would see that the tides were now coming somewhat higher. But this is nowhere near comparable to all of the Antarctica ice melting, so the rise would be a small fraction of the 50m-70m estimates of sea level rise from that.

A second possibility is that whole glaciers could slide. Beneath the Greenland ice cap there is a deep canyon twice the length of the Grand Canyon. It starts out some 200m deep and deepens to 800m. It is 10 kilometres wide for much of its length. There has been some discussion as to whether this whole mass of ice could slide into the sea. Scientists currently believe that this canyon is actually making the base of the Greenland ice sheet less slippy by allowing water to drain away, however our knowledge of how ice sheets react to rising temperature is poor.

A further possibility for relatively sudden sea-level rise could be that the topography of North America and the ice sheet might have trapped a very large volume of water from melted ice. On the East of North America there is the Appalachian mountain chain and on the West there are the Rocky mountains and together they form a sort of V shape. If this whole area was covered by a thick ice sheet that started to melt at it's western side, could that have caused very large volumes of water to escape out to the Pacific round the southern end of the Rocky Mountains? I have no basis for this thought, except that there is in this area a geological feature with considerable mystery about how it was formed – the Grand Canyon. Just how much water did it take to cut the Grand Canyon? There is an area in the USA called the scabland where there is evidence of major floods. Most geologists who study this consider the flooding was cause by continued blocking of meltwater lakes by ice, with continual melting of the blocks and release of floods. Graham Hancock and an increasing number of geologists think the flooding had a different cause - of which more below.

There is another area of the world where a large channel was cut by water probably very quickly – the Bosphorous. There is good evidence that the Black Sea was formerly a fresh water lake some hundreds of feet below the sea level of the Mediterranean, until one day the sea overflowed at the lowest point of the land between it and the depression that now holds the Black Sea, and rapidly cut the Bosphorus. Could a similarly massive outpouring of water the other side of the world have cut the Grand Canyon and hence caused a rather sudden rise in sea level as huge volumes of melted ice were released from a massive lake over North America? The Bosphorous is however only around 100 metres deep. The Grand Canyon is in places 1200 metres deep. I would be interested to find estimates of how much water it takes to cut a canyon to a depth of 1200 metres. The geologists believe it was cut by steady flows of water over immense periods of time, but cataclysmic flows would considerably speed-up erosion.

So we have plenty of evidence that melting of ice could have caused floods of a severity to be remembered in folk tales, but mainly these would be localised and not global. That the ice melted we know conclusively, and sea level did rise, so any humans living close to the sea will have been badly affected, and those living on low-lying land will have had to move. Those people living in the Black Sea area lost their homes just as those in lands now under the major seas, that were considerably more extensive. There will also in the past have been earthquakes that produced tsunamis, of the kind we saw in the Indonesian tsunami that happened in 2004. These are catastrophic happenings for the people affected, but they don't come into the same category as the flood proposed by the flood legends around the world, that are supposed to have brought mankind and animals to the brink of extinction.

So what could cause such a disastrous worldwide flood, if none of the above ideas would do this?

The cause of the Flood of the legends.

I have yet to find any scientific discussion of possible causes of a global flood of the severity described in the myths and legends, so what follows is speculation on my part.

If there was a flood that nearly killed off mankind, there would also have been major impact on wildlife. But we do know that sufficient wildlife survived the flood to be able to re-populate areas where animals were killed. If this happened as we suggest 12,800 years ago, it was not a major extinction event for most animals, or we would see this in the fossil record. It could have been this that finally killed off the mega-fauna such as the mammoths in Siberia, but most species survived. If it was a fairly major near-extinction event for mankind, but not for animals, are there differences between mankind and animals?

Let's think about what would happen today. If huge waves suddenly sloshed all around the Earth covering coastal land up to a height of 300 feet, the majority of cities on the Earth would be flooded and everyone in them would be killed. The coastal cities would go first but even cities quite a long way inland would be destroyed if there was enough volume of water involved. Here in England even Birmingham, right in the middle of the country and at an elevation of 334 feet might be lost. This would certainly count in the eyes of many people as humankind being brought to the edge of extinction. But I would survive if I was at home at the time, as my house is at an elevation of a bit over 600 feet. And most kinds of livestock and wild animals that live in England would survive somewhere, as 300 feet is not sufficiently high to stop the large majority of animals from living there. They would be able to re-populate areas once the floods subsided. The difference between mankind and animals is that we tend to create settlements that house the majority of the population. And these tend to be near to rivers and on lower ground (at least until human populations grew to the point where we started fighting each other, and started to live in hill-forts for protection).

You will have to decide for yourself whether the flood was caused by water that came down as rain or water that came from the sea. I don't believe it was just rain. Too many people would have realised what was happening and run for the hills. It takes time for the volume of water to build from rain. I think this has to be water from the sea. Flooding from the sea arrives very fast and unpredictably, as we see with tsunamis. In the middle of the sea a tsunami wave would be almost unnoticeable. But when it reachers the shelving land close to the shore this causes the wave to rise to huge heights. And if the swell of water in the sea extended over a great distance, there would be an immense volume of water available to keep the wave at this great height and to push it a long way inland. Very fast.

For floods of the level described in the flood legends, which also mention rain thereafter for 40 days and 40 nights, we have to consider a worldwide event. So we should look for a worldwide event that made the sea slosh over ALL the low-lying land in the world, rather than tsunamis that are relatively local to the individual earthquake that causes them. Now what physical happening could cause a worldwide sloshing around of the seas? Hurricanes don't get close to doing this, their effect is local to the few-miles wide swathe where they hit land. Earthquake and volcanic activity is also too localised. One can imagine a major displacement of the San Andreas fault causing California to slip below sea level, but even that would be localised rather than a whole-world event.

And if we place the Flood at 12,800 years ago, the start of the younger dryas period, we should enquire how they are linked. To create considerable re-glaciation during the younger dryas it is necessary to have temperature falling to a considerable extent and much increased precipitation – it needs to rain for forty days and forty nights, or quite possibly for longer, with less heat from the sun reaching the ground. We can postulate that the necessary colder temperatures could have been caused by world-wide volcanic activity of a scale that did not occur any other time in the last 100,000 years. Volcanic ash can stay in the atmosphere for a long time, blocking out the sun. If volcanoes erupted worldwide we need a cause for this. And we are still left with the problem of how to get sufficient water into the atmosphere for rain to fall for forty days and forty nights. The usual way water gets into the atmosphere is through evaporation from oceans caused by the sun, with a little help from evaporation from vegetation. That would not be easy if volcanic clouds were cutting down the amount of sun reaching the sea.

So how else could water get into the atmosphere? It is time to think about how water behaves.

What could make the oceans move?

The source of water for the Flood has to be the seas and oceans of Earth. For the oceans to well up and drown the land in many places on the Earth, to a sufficient distance inland to kill a high percentage of the people living within many tens of miles of the sea, there has to be a cause beyond waves, wind and tsunamis. So let's think a bit about the physics of the oceans of the Earth.

The oceans are rotating around the Earth's axis of rotation with the land masses, the rotation being maintained by the very heavy core of the Earth. The only force that can act to slow down the rotation of the core is gravity from other bodies in space, such as the moon and the sun. The moon has most effect and it is slowing down the Earth's rate of rotation, making the moon orbit the Earth a little bit quicker and a bit further away. But it is a very small effect. A day will be 2 milliseconds longer in 100 years time. The oceans rotate at the same speed as the Earth's crust because over millennia the ocean bottoms and sides have accelerated the water up to this speed. Every day the tidal forces cause the oceans to move slightly differently to the core of the Earth, bulging out towards the moon, but this doesn't change the rotational speed of the water in the oceans. It would take a moon-sized planetoid passing very close to the Earth to cause disturbance to rotation of the Earth and upset the oceans, but this would likely cause massive disturbance to the tectonic plates. There just isn't any evidence for disruption of the Earth on this scale.

But think what would happen if the crust of the Earth, including the ocean basins, slipped suddenly over the core of the Earth. If the crust displaced in the way we have supposed, the north of Canada moving from being over the North Pole to it's current position, with a similar movement of the South Pole, the crust would be rotating around a couple of points on the Equator 90 degrees longitude from the longitude that slipped most. These points would be somewhere in Africa and somewhere in the Pacific. These points would stay almost still relative to the rotation of the crust, they would carry on rotating at the same speed as the Earth revolves. It is the places in the longitudes that move the most that would shift relative to the axis of rotation. The water in the north of the Atlantic and the North Pacific would be moved towards the Equator. Water in the Indian ocean, South Atlantic and South Pacific would all be moved towards the poles. What does this cause?

At the Equator the circumference of the Earth is approximately 40,075 km. A point on the Equator goes around the Earth in 24hrs so all the water at the Equator is traveling at 1669km/hr. The distance round the Earth at the Arctic circle is around 17,662 km, so water at this latitude is going 736km/hr. At the Tropic of Cancer between the two the distance round the Earth is 36,787km, so the water here is going at 1532km/hr. You can see that the speed difference per degree of latitude is greater as you get towards the poles but even between the Equator and the Tropics of Cancer or Capricorn there is a 137km/hr difference in the speed of water in the oceans.

At one period in my life I occasionally drove a minibus for groups, and the guy who checked out my driving asked me to drive as though there was a bucketful of water on the floor next to me. I am sure you will appreciate how hard it would be to drive without the water slopping over the edge of the bucket. Every speed change would cause the water to slop around. The point was that if I could drive without making the water fall over the edge of the (imaginary) bucket I would know how to drive to stop passengers falling over!

Now imagine the Earth's crust, carrying the oceans, slipping maybe 2000km over the core of the Earth. If it went slowly and steadily the water might be speeded up or slowed down without flooding the shores. It all depends on how fast the movement was. Water is very heavy and hence it has a lot of kinetic energy and a strong tendency to carry on moving in the same direction and at the same speed. You have to move a very full bucket of water pretty slowly to move it without the water sloshing over the edge.

To get a feel for what we are talking about here, try swinging a bucket full of water around in a circle rather fast. You can build up the speed slowly so it doesn't spill. Then both pull it up and at the same time slow down how fast you are swinging it round. Or drop it down and speed up the swinging around the circle. I suggest you wear waterproof shoes or do this in bare feet because the water will very likely splash all over the place. Now imagine the water in the bucket as ocean and the bit of exposed side at the top of the bucket being the coastal hills around the edge of the ocean.

Hapgood's theory of Earth crust displacement envisages an imbalance of the weight of the crust being driven towards the Equator by centrifugal force. I can't do full justice to the detail in his theory in a short section here, but in essence he envisages the crust slowing starting to move due to the centrifugal force. As the force is constant the speed of the displacement will slowly increase. The point of the slippage is at the bottom of the crust where it meets the mantle. However it is believed that the bottom of the Earth's crust is not smooth and that there will be considerable friction between the crust and the mantle. This will heat the mantle up and make it more liquid. This in turn will reduce the friction, enabling the centrifugal force to make the crust slip faster.

Creation of a major world-wide flood through crust displacement all depends on how fast this process happens. Hapgood suggests these displacements happen over many years, with the speed of movement being maybe some metres per year. If the poles moved 2000 Km but took 20,000 years to do so, that is only 10 metres a year which is about 2 or 3 cm a day. My guess is that this may be enough to cause some unusually high tides in a few places where the shape of the coast funnels the water, but not fast enough to cause a major flood.

But the other bit of evidence in the frame is the younger dryas period. To account for the younger dryas period there needs to be something else happening as well as these processes that Hapgood describes as the drivers of crust displacement. Hapgood makes a good argument for there having been three crust displacements in the last 100,000 years, but there has only been one younger-dryas type event. Suppose that an Earth crust displacement was under way, and had reached the point where the mantle had been heated and made more fluid. At this point there would be almost no friction between the crust and the underlying mantle. Suppose that at this inauspicious moment a large comet crashed into the Earth at a low angle, applying a large force in the same direction as the crust was slipping. The result would be a sudden transfer of energy from the comet to the Earth. Some of this might be dissipated by melting the impact crater and by ejecting material into the air, but the majority of the energy might go to a sudden acceleration in the speed the crust was moving.

It is possible to do a back-of-the-envelope calculation on how much such an asteroid impact would accelerate the movement of the crust - see the appendix for more details. With a bit of help from the Internet you can find the necessary formulae to set up a spreadsheet to calculate this. It's pretty simple maths and using a spreadsheet means you don't have to juggle with the huge numbers, once you have put the formulae into the spreadsheet it does that for you. Calculate the volume of the crust by subtracting the volume of the core of the Earth from the whole volume. Work out the crust mass from the known density of oceanic and continental crust. Make some guesses about the size and speed of the asteroid, lets say a 10km wide asteroid traveling at 35 km/s (an average speed for meteorites). Then all you need to know is that the force the asteroid will exert on the crust is the rate of change of its momentum - mass x velocity divided by the time it takes to stop. The acceleration imparted to the crust is the force divided by the mass of the crust. My calculation indicates that such an asteroid impact like this could cause the crust to accelerate to a speed of forty metres a day, which would be a great deal faster than the slow crust displacement of a few metres a year.

Moving the crust forty metres in a day may not sound a lot, but when you consider the huge mass of the water in the oceans, and the inertia and resistance to movement that it has, my guess is that this would be more than enough to cause vast waves. If you look at the shape of the North Atlantic and North Pacific, they narrow with Siberia and Alaska coming closer to each other as you go north in the Pacific, and Canada and Europe doing like wise. The amount of water in the Atlantic between Miami and the Canary Islands would definitely not fit into the Atlantic basin between Boston and Bilbao. The Earth is rotating East to West, so as the Atlantic basin slid south leaving less room for the water that would continue to rotate around the Earth's axis as it expected to do, the coast of Europe would find itself ploughing into a pile of water that no longer fits in the ocean basin but which is determined by physics to keep rotating at some hundreds of km/hr. There would only be one place for it to go - over the land and into the Mediterranean. And as the speeded-up crust displacement continued over days, weeks and months the effect would continue until slowly the displaced seawater would find its way back to where it should be. I can imagine a massive flood of water hundreds of metres high rushing along the Mediterranean destroying all before it.

The same will of course happen in the Pacific. The water from further south in the Pacific will find itself trying to fit into the smaller ocean bed where Alaska almost meets Siberia. And in this case it would be Alaska racing into the extra water. The Alaskan muck deposits that contain "50 per cent ice and vegetable material as well as an abundant Pleistocene fauna" must have some cause, some reason why the torn remains of vegetation and animals have been mixed into the many feet thickness of this mud layer.

And as the extra speed imparted to the crust would take at least days or weeks to slow down the effect would be cumulative. And as it did slow down the water that had been swooshed one way would come surging back the other way.

This scenario of an asteroid crashing into the crust might also do something else. The asteroid that killed the dinosaurs is reckoned to have been about 6km wide and it presumably crashed on land, because it was vapourised into fine dust that spread all the way round the world. This dust was rich in iridium and this layer of dust can be identified everywhere. Fine dust high in the atmosphere can stay there many years, blocking sunlight, killing vegetation and hence killing animals. There is now good evidence that it was an asteroid or comet impact that started the younger dryas period and that it hit the North American ice sheet. The initial effect would have been to vapourise huge quantities of the ice into steam putting water into the atmosphere. Ice that was not vapourised would melt and become water that created massive flooding, the results of which can be clearly seen in North America (see Graham Hancock's Magicians of the Gods).

To all this I reckon you can probably add a couple of other things. A massive impact would create a very large earthquake across the whole of America. At the Atlantic coast this would create a massive tsunami that that would race across the Atlantic to Europe, exacerbating the effect of the crust displacement, similarly in the Pacific. Then the shock waves would probably travel through the crust and might trigger volcanoes at the margins of the continental plates, possibly all over the world, adding greatly to the dust being ejected up into the higher levels of the atmosphere

Such a sloshing around of the ocean from the crust movement, the ejection of water into the atmosphere, and major volcanic activity would certainly justify the worldwide myths of a flood, rain for forty days and forty nights and the skies going black obscuring the sun and moon. If you were there you would certainly feel that this was an event that almost extinguished mankind. The story you would tell would be the same as the main elements in the Noah story.

This would also be a reason why the imagery found at Gobekli Tepe is suggestive of the builders being very concerned with the doings of comets, of which more later.

No matter how it happened, a major flood appears to be part of the fairly recent history of mankind. And of course of the gods. So how did the gods and humans deal with these happenings. Let us pause for breath and consider the build-up to this Flood event.

****

Chapter 16 – Moving house.

During the whole period from 20,000 years ago to 12,000 years ago, many humans around the world will have had to move from where they lived. Rising sea levels are annoying. They flood your harbour works and houses that you have been thoughtless enough to build too close to the sea. But if it happens gently over time civilisations can cope with it. Or at least they could in days gone by.

In our current cities buildings come and go. We don't build much that is going to last 200 years. Sometimes houses are torn down when they have only been standing for 50 years, because they were not built to a high enough standard. Where there is trade and the buildings are there to facilitate that trade, what matters is the money the trade is making, which may be a lot more than what it costs to build the building. If you can increase trade by replacing a building or a harbour, then it is simply a matter of calculating how many years it will take to pay back the cost of the new building through increased trade. If the answer is only a few years then the old building is likely to go and a new one will be built. Capitalism is no respecter of the past.

Much more difficult for our modern cities is replacement of infrastructure, particularly infrastructure underground. Much of the New York subway is below sea level and is kept clear of water by electric pumps. When Hurricane Sandy hit New York in 2012, damage to the subway was severe as power was lost for too long and pumps stopped. Backup pumps only have fuel to operate for a certain length of time, after that they just stop. London has a looming problem with it's sewage system. In the 19th century the Victorians realised that the explosion of population in London was causing a severe crisis. The Thames river stank of sewerage and there were cholera epidemics that threatened the wealthy and powerful. Eventually the decision was taken to undertake major sewage works which cost a great deal of money. Those beautiful Victorian sewers are now, 150 years on, in need of major renovation. So far the political will has not materialised to tackle this in anything but a piecemeal fashion. London of course also has it's tube network, which like New York's subway is in danger of flooding if the Thames rises too far.

In the times we are discussing there were no such problems. There may have been surface systems to bring in clean water and take out sewage, but nothing like the technological cities we now have. There were no underground services such as gas pipes and electricity cables to worry about. If it became necessary to move dwellings and harbours to higher levels it could be done relatively easily, compared to our current problems with rising sea level. In England there are numerous places where ports used in Roman times only two thousand years ago are submerged, or are now miles from the sea due to changes in rivers and coastline. For the civilisations living around the world, on those flat and fertile plains that are now under the sea, they would have had to progressively move to higher ground as the ice sheets melted.

It is likely that human beings had no idea why sea level was rising. They would probably have worked out that tides were related to the moon and would have seen that the heights of tides varied over the year. One can imagine the arguments about where a town that was being flooded should be moved to but it is unlikely that a long-term view prevailed. Most people think short-term, so the move would likely have been of a few miles to the nearest ground that was 50 or 100 feet higher, rather than into the mountains to gain 1000 feet or more of safety from rising sea levels. It will be very interesting to see the pattern of settlements and how they moved as sea level rose, when archeologists finally begin to look seriously at the areas flooded after 20,000 years ago.

The gods' knowledge of Earth crust displacement.

We started this book with the assumption that the aliens that arrived were highly technologically advanced and highly knowledgeable. It is likely that they knew a lot more than our scientists and understood the dynamics of the Earth's crust and the processes of glaciation and de-glaciation. I have suggested that in their choice of home they would have taken account of this and the consequent falls and rises in sea levels. As they lived on Earth for many tens of thousands of years they would have carefully measured orbital changes, and the impact of changes in the sun, on the Earth's temperature and climate. They would also have monitored earth crust displacements. Slow melting of the ice and the consequent rise in sea-level would not have been a reason for them to move home, as they would have built their homes higher up. The Atlanteans might have had to move and build new harbours, but that would not be overly concerning to the gods.

Earth crust displacement is however rather more worrying than Earth temperature changes. If Hapgood is right and there have been several displacements of the Earth's crust, the gods will have lived through these and become accustomed to calculating when the crust was becoming unbalanced and where the poles were likely to end up once the crust started moving in a certain direction. The worrying issue is where the crust displacement will take your home. Hapgood's calculations of the first two pole shifts would have left Antarctica still viable as a home. It was only the last one that took Antarctica fully into the polar region.

If Hapgood is right about the timing of the last pole displacement, the gods would have measured the crust starting to move 17,000 years ago. That would have told them that their homeland was starting to move directly towards the South Pole. There would no doubt have been debate about how far the crust would slip and where the South Pole would end up. It is likely that this is far from easy to predict, as the weight of the crust in different places would change due to the things that happen during a crust displacement, that depend on precisely how the crust cracks. They would have known that there was a danger they might have to move out of Antarctica but would have been able to take a wait-and-see attitude.

There might however have come a point where they realised that the crust had accelerated to a speed that made it inevitable that Antarctica was going to end up where it now is, and would become a frozen continent. They might also have been able to predict this from where on the Earth's surface the imbalance of weight was and a knowledge of how close to the Equator this weight would be pushed by centrifugal force, before the friction between crust and mantle stopped it. It may be, once the mantle has melted, that the process only stops when the imbalance of weight actually gets to the Equator. Or it could be that you have to watch how long the crust continues to accelerate and work out that the time to decelerate and stop will be similar, with a similar distance moved.

The other factor I have invoked in causing the flood, a comet, is altogether much more difficult to deal with. Halley's comet was predicted by Halley to arrive in the solar system in 1758. This was on the basis of previous comet sightings in 1531, 1607 and 1682 that he guessed were the same comet returning again and again. In 1758 it was first sighted in late December and reached its turning point around the sun (perihelion) in early March. It therefore only spent around 5 months in the area where it was visible from Earth. Telescopes will obviously extend the period when a comet can be tracked, once you have first found it. Comets are dark when in outer space and very hard to find. They also go very far out and their orbit may be changed by objects in the asteroid belt that are also hard to track. The point is that the gods, even with sophisticated instruments, may have only got a few months or maybe a year or so's warning that a large comet was going to come very close to Earth and possibly hit. They would not have had advance warning of it, so would at that time have been focusing only on the impact of the crust displacement.

The gods' reaction.

Knowledge that Antarctica was going to become frozen would obviously cause the gods to look around the Earth for another place that could become their main base. They would then have some thousands of years to establish the Atlanteans there, to create a city that could support the gods in the style to which they had become accustomed. This would involve the gods living closer to the humans that had developed in other parts of the Earth, but having had many years' experience of controlling the Atlanteans this might not have been so frightening as they thought when they first assessed the capabilities of hominins from space, when they arrived.

The thought that the gods set about establishing a base elsewhere on the Earth is rather helpful to our investigation, as it implies that we may be able to find the remains of the city they established. They would have known that a corollary of Antarctica moving into polar regions would be that the North American ice sheet would be moved out of the North polar region and hence melt. So they would have been able to calculate that sea level would rise substantially. Their new city would have to be above any possible sea-level rise and hence will today be on land not submerged under the sea.

Considerations that we discussed in the chapter on how the gods decided where to set up home will still apply. An island that is sufficiently high with good water supply, a place near the coast but where the land rises reasonably steeply from the sea, and presumably in a place that would make it unlikely that a future pole-shift would move it into an inhospitably cold climate. They might indeed have established more than one city. There are a few candidates around the world where there are constructions that may date back to this period. My top three are the Middle East with Baalbeck and Giza, Cusco in South America, and Gunung Padang in West Java, Indonesia. One can imagine instructions being passed to the Atlanteans to get on with establishing these new home bases, which would then proceed over some hundreds or thousands of years in the period leading up to 12,800 years ago. This would be 'business as normal' with nothing traumatic about it.

Knowledge of a large comet heading towards Earth would be an altogether different matter. Our reaction to knowledge that a large comet or asteroid was likely to hit Earth would first of all be prayers that our calculations were wrong and that it would miss. Then if collision become more certain we might attempt to build rockets and nuclear warheads that could be exploded to deflect its path. This would be very scary as we would have to ensure we deflected it away from Earth and not towards us. It is also not easy to change the path of a large and very heavy asteroid traveling at a tremendous speed. It would need a huge force and we would have to wait until it got close enough to target accurately, which would not leave a lot of time if the first attempt went wrong. Then we would panic. The gods would have had another option. If they could still fit all the gods into their parked spaceship they could escape as the comet approached and wait to see if it hit or not. If their society had grown to a greater number than could be accommodated on their spaceship, they would have had to look at survival strategies for those who could not fly away.

As I have discussed above, floods from rising sea level are survivable, but the comet would pose an additional flood risk. Antarctica is on average the highest continent on Earth. It has high mountains that would be unlikely to be covered by sea even with huge waves thousands of feet high. But it is in the middle of the world ocean and therefore more at risk of flooding than places in the middle of the main landmass of Earth. The Earth is 70% covered by ocean, so if a comet did hit there is a 70% chance that it will hit the oceans and cause huge tsunamis and much ejection of water into the atmosphere. The survival strategy for any gods left behind would also need to take account of Antarctica anyway becoming uninhabitable in a few thousand years, and the likely onset of a difficult period climatically. The comet would likely cause some kind of younger-dryas period type event, at least for a few years. By far the best strategy would be for those that could to take to their spaceship as soon as the comet came close. And for any gods who could not fit into the spaceship, to move to the place that would give them the best protection from comet-induced flooding and the food supply difficulties of a period of cold and difficult weather.

What to do about the Atlanteans?

The Atlanteans however, and all mankind anywhere on the Earth, would just have to take their chances.

Things like the impact of a comet have a degree of unpredictability about them, no matter how good and accurate your instruments are. There are margins of error in all measurements. Even if you have great certainty that a comet was going to hit Earth, predicting precisely where would be hard. The Earth rotates very fast so only a small error in the time the comet would hit would make a big difference. Then there is the nature of the comet to contend with. The last comet to hit Earth over Russia exploded into several bits due to the stresses of coming through the atmosphere. The impact craters on the East coast of the USA from a cometary impact a very long time ago show not a single crater, but many smaller craters, presumably from a comet splitting into many bits.

The possibility of flooding caused by a comet impact with the inevitable move of Antarctica fully into the polar area could have been the trigger to set about re-homing the Atlanteans, from Antarctica to somewhere else. They would no doubt want to do this in a way that involved the gods themselves in as little effort as possible; a group of a couple of hundred gods could not move thousands of humans. Any Atlanteans who were not involved in the maritime trading activities and hence not already living on their ships would have to be encouraged to start moving to one of the established outposts around the world, or at the very least to prepare ships they could jump onto at the last minute when it became clear the comet would hit. The point to note at this point in the story is that this would provide a reason for a gradual influx of Atlanteans into the Mediterranean area. And then perhaps, if the gods got a couple of year's warning of the comet impacting, a reason for a more sudden influx of Atlanteans and a reason to conquer those civilisations at the eastern end of the Mediterranean, if Lebanon and Baalbeck were one of the chosen new homes for the gods.

The gods could also consider how they might transport to their new base(s) things of value that were then in Antarctica. I doubt they would have worried much about anything that could be re-made or re-built at their new base, they would only care about things that had taken lots of time to create, that had needed their intellectual engagement - such as breeds of livestock that had been developed in Antarctica and strains of crops. Mankind has over millennia selectively bred animals to improve them. If this was part of the gods' project in developing the Earth, saving these would be a priority. Shifting these would have needed some specialist transport, that might have taken several years to construct.

We have a story, quoted in both the Bible and the Quran, that suggests the gods made preparations to move livestock. The story of Noah. Noah was the tenth of the pre-Flood patriarchs. In other words, in the context of our story, he was the tenth leader of the Atlanteans. He would have had at least occasional 'audiences' with the gods, in order for them to instruct him on things they wanted the Atlanteans to do for them. If we believe the lifetimes quoted in the bible for the patriarchs, it is possible as we discussed that the gods had provided genetic treatments to create a family of long-lived leaders. It would have been important to move him and his family to the new base. And he would naturally have been put in charge of the process of moving valuables from Antarctica to the new base. The actual Noah story as it has come down to us probably contains a lot of post-rationalisation. The Atlanteans would have had to have been given a reason why they had to commit effort to building the Ark (or maybe several Arks?). The Ark as described was a large and complex structure that must have taken some considerable time and effort to build. It would need a greater workforce to build it than could be accommodated inside it when it sailed. So to keep the workforce happy and engaged with the ship-building project they would probably have been told that this was part of building their empire to new heights in other areas of the world.

That a comet should hit the Earth in such a way as to accelerate crust displacement may well have been something that even the gods could not calculate and predict. And if this speeding up of the displacement was a major factor in making the flooding hugely worse than would happen just from a cometary impact at sea, the gods may very well not have prepared the Atlanteans in the Mediterranean for this scale of disaster. They might have thought the Mediterranean would be relatively immune from a tsunami triggered in the Atlantic, which would not have the volume of water behind it to impact on more that the area just inside the Straits of Gibraltar. Most of the energy of the tsunami and the water in it would be dissipated on the coasts of Portugal and West Africa.

The gods may have thought that the Atlanteans sent off to settle elsewhere were going to have to survive a period of darkened skies and turbulent weather and maybe a tsunami if the comet landed in the sea, but had no idea that the crust could be made to slip sufficiently fast to slop the seas over huge areas of land, right to the end of the Mediterranean where we are told it destroyed the warring armies of Greece and the Atlanteans.

If so, then the gods got a surprise as well as humankind.

****

Chapter 17 – Life for humans after The Flood.

From here on in this story it doesn't really matter whether or not you believe the idea of Earth crust displacement. I like the idea because it would explain why the ice cover was where it was on the Earth at the last glacial maximum. It would also explain the rapid rise in sea level in the period 11,000 to 9,000 years ago (9000-7000 BC), if ice on North America had been moved into warmer latitudes. Such rapid melting of the ice does not fit with slow changes in worldwide temperatures anything like as well. And it would explain those uncomfortable facts of the frozen mammoths in Siberia and the ancient maps of the Antarctic coast.

The movement of Atlanteans from Antarctica to the Mediterranean 12,800 years ago would also explain where the strange gene pool with its distinctive marker came from, that later spread into the European hunter-gatherer population when farming practices spread into Europe from the Middle East. It might also explain why the Basque language is very different to the languages that surround it. The high mountains of the Pyrenees could have enabled the people near them to have escaped the Flood, which would have devastated the lower-lying areas of Spain and France. The Basque people might even be descendants of the Atlanteans. And it might explain Plato's story. I leave it to you to decide, but if Earth crust displacement combined with a comet impact is beyond your skepticism threshold, you will have to come up with another cause for a flood that nearly extinguished mankind.

From here in the book the two main ideas we are continuing to explore are the impact of the flood and evidence that could point to the continued existence on Earth of our Adventurers, the gods. It seems to me that they didn't fly away in their spaceship to another planet around another star. There is considerable evidence to suggest that they and their technology remained here on Earth in the period from 12,800 years ago.

A really big flood must have had a really big cause. Whether it was caused by a big cometary impact, with or without Earth crust displacement, or by multiple volcano eruptions and tsunamis, we now have a very unpalatable world. The re-glaciations of the younger dryas period are a confirmation of this, it was much colder and there must have been a lot of precipitation to rebuild the glaciers. The reason for the much colder climate must surely be huge amounts of material in the atmosphere, flung up by the impact of the comet and volcanoes. In the immediate aftermath humans would be living under cloud-laden skies, impenetrable to the sun, that had rained for 40 days and 40 nights. Any settlements placed next to rivers will have been washed away by the huge amounts of rain. The low-lying previously most productive lands have been drowned, the flora and fauna killed and the ground made hostile to plant and animal life due to the salt from the sea water. It will take many years of rain before the salt is washed from the soil and the land made productive again. The majority of previous civilisations placed near to pre-flood coastlines have been destroyed. It will be dark and cold so vegetation will only grow slowly. And as a final insult to add to injury one of the most productive sources of food, the sea, will now in many places be impossibly far from habitable lands free of salt. And something to be feared.

It may also have been a period of very wild weather. If crust displacement had been significantly speeded up, pushing the remains of the North American ice-cap into the current position of North America, and with rapid cooling in Antarctica and in the Arctic ocean, the temperature and pressure gradients that cause weather systems will have been upset and would need to find a new global stability. Those who study the younger dryas consider that it was an influx of cold fresh glacier water into the Atlantic that caused the weather systems to change, creating the cold period. The northern and southern jet streams would have been disturbed and high and low pressure areas in the atmosphere might have been much deeper, causing high winds and unusual amounts of precipitation.

To assess what mankind did in the aftermath of all this, the first thing we must do is to look for where there might be areas of the Earth that are still habitable and where there might still be sources of food.

Where would the Atlanteans go?

If we believe Solon's story the Atlanteans were already invading the Mediterranean when the Flood hit. The story has them in control of only the western part of the Mediterranean at this point. The Mediterranean does have some steep coasts on its northern sides leading up into the Alps and has the Atlas mountains in Northern Africa, so there is the possibility that some Atlanteans and the indigenous Mediterranean population managed to escape the flood. The hunter-gatherers in the middle of Europe would escape the Flood simply through their distance from the sea; though life will have been hard, analysis of modern Europeans' DNA shows that some did survive.

Atlanteans who were on ships at the time of the flood would be in a relatively advantageous situation, compared to those on land. Tsunamis and the swirling of the seas would have ridden under their boats. The impact of heavily cloud-laden skies would be much smaller in the oceans than on land. On land temperature will have dropped rapidly and the impact on plant growth would be immediate. Though the lack of sunlight on the oceans would slow down growth of organisms that live close to the surface and hence start to disrupt the food chains, the impact would be slower. If Atlantean families were used to living on their ships they would know how to provide themselves with food by fishing. Catches would be less but still possible. But any chance of hunting and gathering on coastal lands will have disappeared. Life will still not have been pleasant.

To live on board they would of course have had to have ways of getting fresh water. They might well have known how to create fresh water from seawater through evaporation and condensation. I would try a wooden bowl, with a smaller wooden bowl containing seawater standing in the middle of it, with a wooden cover fitting tightly into the big bowl. Burning the top of the cover to make it black would help it absorb more heat from the sun. Inside this closed container it would become hot enough to evaporate the seawater, that you could then persuade to condense by keeping the bottom bowl cooled, with a seawater soaked cloth around it. This would of course no longer be easy if there was no sun, but if it rained for 40 days and 40 nights that would provide ample drinking water at least for that period. They might have stayed on their ships for quite a long time while they worked out what had happened through visits to ports they knew, that would now be ruined and infertile.

Once they decided to land somewhere the question would be where. Or more probably they didn't have a lot of choice and the real question is where in the world they might have landed and survived. This question is basically asking where flora and fauna might have survived to feed them. Obviously the answer is high ground, but distance from the sea also matters. If there were hundreds of miles of flat land between the coast where they could land and the hills where plants and animals had survived, they might never have made it to those places.

Looking at the atlas, possibilities for survival include the eastern sides and middle of the Rockies and Andes. The Rockies would still be heavily glaciated. The western sides would have been flooded to a great height by the huge volume of water in the Pacific. Floods coming from the Atlantic onto the East of the Americas would probably have surged over the Appalachians and into the Amazon basin and drowned hundreds of miles of land, but could have left habitable land in the middle of North or South America. In Africa the safest place would have been around the great rift valley, protected from Indian Ocean water by the mountains of Kenya and Ethiopia and the many miles from the west coast of Africa. For such a world flood the coasts of China and India would have been devastated for many miles, leaving people surviving only in the middle of these areas and where they rise up into the Himalayas and the mountain chains of what is now Indonesia. Mongolia and Siberia would have become too cold.

There is a difficulty with all these suggestions so far; distance from the coast. Getting to the middle of North or South America involves either going over the Rockies or Andes, or traveling overland for thousands of miles from the West. The same is true for Africa. We have described the Atlanteans as a 'powerful empire' but we are not suggesting they had any amazing technology. The gods would have reserved that for themselves and made sure that metal technology for instance did not fall into their hands. The Atlanteans would still have been stone age people, albeit very competent stone-age people. Their main mode of transport would be by boat. They would not be equipped for very long overland journeys. So the real question is what is the place safest from major sea floods, that you can get most of the way to by boat.

In an earlier chapter you read the statement "for this sea which is within the Straits of Heracles is only a harbour, having a narrow entrance," and you may not have considered the significance of this at that point in the story. The Middle East would not be immune from massive sea floods, which would make their way up the Red Sea and the Persian Gulf, as well as up the Mediterranean itself, drowning coastal civilisations. But the volumes of water available to submerge the land are a lot less than in the Atlantic, Pacific and Indian oceans. The sea water would therefore run out of energy sooner and submerge less land.

The Mediterranean offers a few places where high ground that may have escaped the flooding is not too far from the sea, much shorter a journey than to trek into the middle of Africa or the Americas. If they went along the south coast of the Mediterranean the Atlas mountains would have been a possibility, but the northern coast provides more opportunities. The first opportunity is the eastern end of the Pyrenees. The western end would have taken the brunt of surging Atlantic waters but the eastern end might have been clear of the flood. However the land to the north and south of the Pyrenees would have been flooded and hence infertile due to salt. The next possibility is the Alps. However the southern side of the Alps is steep and hard to live on, and to get to territory in Austria where flora and fauna might have survived would entail crossing the Alps. Eventually the Atlanteans still sailing would get to the eastern end of the Mediterranean and the steeply shelving coast of Southern Turkey. These slopes lead to a much larger area where animals and plants may have survived the flood. Eastern Turkey and the north west corner of Iraq are likely to have survived without flooding, with the Mediterranean flood waters being deflected into Syria and Iraq.

In thinking about where the Atlanteans may have ended up in the world we should also not ignore the fact that they may have been instructed by the gods to head for the Mediterranean, and particularly its eastern end. If there really was an ancient maritime nation capable of traveling the world, the captains of the ships would have been excellent navigators, probably using coastlines as much as they used positioning from the stars (that would have been obscured after the Flood). Hapgood in his book "The Maps of the Ancient Sea Kings" suggests that maps to guide worldwide voyages have come down to us from this period. A famous maritime nation, the Phoenicians, did later develop in the eastern Mediterranean - could this have derived from knowledge passed down over the centuries?

That this area at the eastern end of the Mediterranean, known as the 'fertile crescent', was one of the main areas on the Earth where agriculture developed and civilisations bloomed in the ten thousand years after the Flood and the younger dryas period would tally well with its natural ability to survive a world-wide flood. Agriculture did also develop in some other areas of the world in this period, but the fertile crescent is considered the most important.

What would the gods do as mankind started again?

For the gods their whole approach on Earth would have changed once they decided to start creating bases in parts of the world other than Antarctica. The techniques they had developed to keep the Atlanteans worshiping them and serving their needs would have to have been made to impact more widely on humans. They would need the human beings in the areas where they established bases to worship them, and for humans further away to fear and respect their power so that it was unthinkable to conceive of the gods in any other way than as all-powerful gods. Though the Atlanteans may have done the major work to establish bases the gods would have needed to be hands-on in guiding them and in ensuring that creation of the gods' palaces and places if security was a priority. They would also need to have made themselves and their power visible in some ways to the surrounding populations. Solon's story as told by Plato suggests that at least some of the gods were involved in educating mankind in the arts of agriculture, health and procurement of food, and war to protect themselves from neighbouring groups that sought to take over the civilisations the groups the gods worked with had established.

Now that mankind was desperately in need of help there would no doubt have been a discussion about the degree to which the gods should help. The gods in their spaceship may not have wanted to return to the Earth until they saw what kind of state the Flood had left the Earth in, but it would be quite difficult to assess this from space with the whole Earth covered in deep clouds. They would have had to send a scouting party to land and investigate, to see if mankind had survived in any numbers and to assess what they might do to help, and probably to assess if it was worthwhile. The fact that the Earth was going to be considerably colder and very cloudy for perhaps many tens or even hundreds of years would have been a factor. Gods that had been closely involved with humans might have been more willing to do this than gods who had kept themselves more aloof from humans.

This assumes of course that all the gods could be accommodated in the spaceship. If not some would have had to stay behind and suffer the same as mankind. If there had been one group of gods riding out the Flood and its aftermath in the luxury of their spaceship, while another group had to endure the conditions on Earth, one can imagine some differences of opinion developing about what to do next and how fast. The gods in their spaceship might have felt little urgency, gods on Earth would want mankind to re-build a civilisation and regain their productivity as fast as possible. If the gods' society had by this time grown to a number greater than could be accommodated in the spaceship to fly to a different planetary system, at least some of the gods would have had no alternative but to make the best of the Earth as their home. To return to the kind of lifestyle the Atlanteans had supported them in would need rapid action to stop mankind slipping into uncivilised behaviours and a population collapse from even the diminished numbers left after the Flood.

If we believe the story of Noah in a literal sense, and go along with the supposition that the 'god' referred to is one of our Adventurers and not a 'real' God who had spoken to Noah in some mystical experience, it suggests that our Adventurers, the gods, desired mankind to survive – or at least some of them. It is after all possible, if aliens did come to Earth, that their mission was to seek out planets and accelerate the development of intelligent life. If that were the case, they would be roundly cursing the fact that astronomical processes had led to a disastrous change that might have destroyed all their work so far. And they would seek ways to rescue what they could. It is possible to interpret the part of the Noah story about the Flood having been brought down on mankind to destroy them, because they had become evil, as a story invented after the event - more on this thought later.

Or it could be that the gods were simply using what the Earth could offer to support their own lifestyle, with no concern to develop mankind beyond their own needs for manpower.

Stories have been handed down to us from this period that may shed some light on how closely involved with humans at least some of the gods were, if we believe the stories. One the main sources is the bible. Genesis 6 has some words on the subject (from the King James translation):

1 And it came to pass, when men began to multiply on the face of the earth, and daughters were born unto them,

2 That the sons of God saw the daughters of men that they were fair; and they took them wives of all which they chose.

3 And the LORD said, My spirit shall not always strive with man, for that he also is flesh: yet his days shall be an hundred and twenty years.

4 There were giants in the earth in those days; and also after that, when the sons of God came in unto the daughters of men, and they bare children to them, the same became mighty men which were of old, men of renown.

5 And GOD saw that the wickedness of man was great in the earth, and that every imagination of the thoughts of his heart was only evil continually.

6 And it repented the LORD that he had made man on the earth, and it grieved him at his heart.

7 And the LORD said, I will destroy man whom I have created from the face of the earth; both man, and beast, and the creeping thing, and the fowls of the air; for it repenteth me that I have made them.

8 But Noah found grace in the eyes of the LORD.

And it goes on to tell the story of Noah and the ark. This is suggestive of a growing closeness between some gods and mankind in the times before Noah. It doesn't make sense to interpret 'the sons of God' as human men. Men have been mentioned in the previous line, as the fathers of daughters. And they can't have been producing daughters without taking wives who were the daughters of other men. 'The sons of God' must refer to some beings that would not normally take the daughters of men as wives. 'God' in this context might refer to a ruling or chief god, the sons being part of the chief god's extended family. Or it could be that in later transcriptions an 's' has been omitted and that it originally read 'the sons of gods'. It is interesting that Genesis refers to 'the Lord' as well as to 'God'. Why use two words if these are the same entity? Was the Lord the chief god?

If we put these statements into the context of our story, they suggest an original small group of Adventurers, gods, had produced children who would be genetically gods. These 'sons of god' had then produced children by mating with humans. As the bible has it that these sons of gods mated with the daughters of men, we can only assume that the gods were biologically somewhat similar to early forms of human. Or that genetic manipulation to create home sapiens had made gods and humans sufficiently biologically similar to be able to produce viable offspring. Whereas the gods who had arrived in their spaceship were probably mature adults, their children born on Earth would suffer the raging hormones of teenage years; that they "saw the daughters of men that they were fair" sounds to me like a reference to lust. The bible is stating as fact that they mated with the daughters of men and produced offspring. If the gods had used some of their DNA in genetically engineering mankind, they are unlikely to have used all aspects of their DNA. So we would then have had on Earth three types of being, pure-blood gods, human beings and beings that had resulted from mating between gods and humans, with some additional god DNA and some human DNA, who were presumably the 'giants'.

The wording in the book of genesis is rather revealing if we take it literally, saying "There were giants in the earth in those days; and also after that,…". It is stating that the giants were on the Earth prior to the flood - 'in those days' - and also post flood - 'after that'. So either the giants survived the flood or new giants were born because the 'sons of god' continued to mate with the daughters of men.

This makes it worthwhile to re-think what happened as the likelihood of a major planetary disaster and flood approached. The gods may have restricted the size of their society and the number of true-blood gods they allowed to be born to the number that could be accommodated on their spaceship. They could have had rules controlling the rate at which true-blood gods could produce offspring. But that number would not have included the 'giants' who were half god and half human. When the first sons of god started this behaviour and produced offspring their progeny may well have been seen as being of no importance and entirely inconsequential to what the gods might want to do. But these offspring would not have been of no importance to the sons of gods who had fathered them. One can imagine some fierce arguments developing between the elders of the gods and the young gods.

There is a statement in the book of genesis that may well refer to this. "And the LORD said, My spirit shall not always strive with man, for that he also is flesh: yet his days shall be an hundred and twenty years." This could be an acceptance by the chief god that mankind is of the same flesh as the gods and not some inferior kind of being, and the drawing of an interesting distinction that mankind will be restricted to a maximum life of 120 years, whereas the gods and presumably the giants had much longer lives.

The phrase '…shall not always strive with man….' suggests that a degree of strife had already developed. This might be because the elder gods could see that they had created in mankind a really difficult problem. The younger gods were being attracted into mating with a creature that the elders had created to be a slave and an inferior being. And they would by this time see that the humans they had created had the intelligence and capability to breed uncontrollably and live out of ecological balance with the rest of the Earth's flora and fauna. This might of course have been inevitable but the gods might have felt some responsibility for speeding the process. Or the elder gods might have tried to control the actions of 'the sons of god' and to destroy the half-blood children that had resulted from the sons of god mating with the daughters of men, which would certainly have caused a great deal of strife.

There are other ancient texts that refer to a group of beings that had close contact with the gods but also with mankind. They are called various things including the Fallen Ones, Watchers, Nephilim and of course Angels. As mentioned, one ancient book that was excluded from the bible, is the book of Enoch. This goes into more detail about their activities. Andrew Collins in his book on Gobekli Tepe relates a story drawn from one of the Enochian texts, the book of the Watchers. This is about a group of two hundred Watchers who came together in an assembly on top of a mountain and swore an oath of loyalty before descending on to the plains below, where they took mortal wives and hence became rebels and outcasts.

Andrew Collins does not follow up this phrase 'rebels and outcasts' and indeed specifically distances his book from theories of aliens on Earth. I seem to remember his earlier books were not so antagonistic to the idea, but in the book on Gobekli Tepe he is aligning himself with serious archeology and hence probably does not want to upset the archeology thought police. If this group of people became 'rebels and outcasts' they must have rebelled against something and some other group, that they then became outcasts from. Could this be a story about an argument amongst the gods, where those who had taken mortal (human) wives rebelled against the elder gods who wanted to keep gods and mankind separate?

This is of course speculation based on pretty thin evidence of a few lines in ancient texts. If we are going to take this seriously we had better investigate whether there is other evidence available to us that can support the idea in any way.

Mankind's development after the flood and the (re)establishment of agriculture.

Life for the survivors of the Flood would have been very hard. Just as in any extreme situation, the first priority would be shelter and security from animals capable of harming humans, that would have been very hungry due to the decline in grazing animals as plants died. The weather could have made this particularly difficult. We have the story of it raining for forty days and forty nights. After that, with skies full of cloud and winds possibly very high further water may have been dragged up into the sky by low pressure areas in a way similar to hurricanes. The evidence of the cold younger dryas period suggests that cloud cover was maintained for many years, keeping the sun from the Earth. With the Earth cooling there would be more likelihood for precipitation to be hail or snow, rather than rain. If phenomena such as golf-ball sized hail happened not having a shelter able to withstand this would be pretty dangerous.

If the people who had survived had fled from lower-lying land, or were Atlanteans previously living on ships, they would have no existing shelter and would have had to construct what they could. And remember this would all have to be done with whatever stone tools they had or could make. By far the best form of shelter in this kind of climate would be caves. Those who found caves would feel themselves very lucky. There is of course also the thought as to whether it is possible to make a cave.

There are in Turkey some very intriguing sites of ancient habitation, carved in the relatively soft volcanic stone in the area of Cappadocia the central plain of Turkey. These include Derinkuyu, Özkonak, Mazıköy, Kaymaklı, and one recently discovered in 2014, below the hilltop fortress of Nevşehir. Unfortunately for this story, there is no way to date when these fabulous underground towns were initially created, and there is considerable evidence to suggest that they were extended and developed at much later periods than the time we are now at in this story. So I can only leave the thought dangling that creating the first stages of these places would have been a very tangible way for the gods to have helped humans after the comet impact and the Flood. And if some of the 'sons of gods' had remained on Earth, they too would have needed shelters urgently, until they could organise mankind to construct some new 'houses of god' for them.

Rather more productive for this story are some other sites in Eastern Turkey, which have been excavated and shown to have been inhabited at very early periods relative to the development of human activity in the fertile crescent. These sites include Catal Huyuk, Caydnu and Nevali Cori. These sites have provided many of the 'first examples' of important developments, such as animal husbandry, woven cloth, agriculture and sculptures.

These are of course 'firsts' in the conventional history of mankind that the majority of archeologists believe. These things may have been happening at numerous places now below the sea, and woven cloth and sculptures we know were happening in Dolni Vestonice thousands of years before we find the fertile crescent evidence. Any early agricultural civilisations that humans had developed prior to the flood would probably have been on the flatter lower-lying land and would have been drowned. Now humans would have been totally dependent on what they could gather from vegetation on higher slopes that had survived and on hunting animals. The animal populations themselves would be under stress as the growth of plants would be much reduced by the climate and lack of sunlight. Access to seafood would have been somewhat difficult as they would be living at fairly high altitude, as much from fear of the sea as to avoid salt-laden soil. The land available to animals would also have been much smaller areas than formally so animal stocks would be much lower because of this as well. If ever there was a time to start to develop more intensive food production then this was it.

A quick check on About.com:Archeology suggests that archeologists believe that food animals started to be domesticated from about 10500BP (8500BC) onwards, but with suggestion that dogs may have been domesticated considerably before this. One obvious use of domesticated dogs is to help in hunting so people that followed herds and hunter-gatherers would have found them useful. A study by Love Dalen of the Swedish Museum of Natural History concludes from genetic considerations that dogs and wolves split into different lineages between 40,000BP and 27,000BP. So the idea that animals could be domesticated was certainly not a new idea. In the development of mankind things then started happening pretty fast, relatively speaking, from around this time of 11,000BP and onwards. The first wheat is believed to have been grown in South Eastern Turkey around 11,000BP, and the wild rice in China, that was part of human diet 11,000BP, had been domesticated by around 10,000BP to 8,000BP. The dates for domestication of animals listed in Wikipedia are sheep between 13,000BP and 11,000BP, pigs by 11,000BP, and goats and cows by 10,000BP. Pre-pottery civilisations were appearing in Mesopotamia by 9000BP, with settlements growing in size from then on, until by the Uruk period 6000BP (4000BC) the Sumerian civilisation took form.

All these dates being so close together, relative to the whole life of humans since cro-magnon man appeared, seems to me to be a little suspicious. The alternative story, that some or all of these things happened much earlier and were now being re-established, seems to me much more plausible. Mankind, and the predecessors of mankind, have been hunting animals for millions of years. During this time they will certainly have come across baby animals that they might have kept alive for a while, so the idea of domesticating animals can hardly have been new. In quite recent times the people living on the northern tundra areas have lived mainly through hunting wild reindeer, but have also kept a few tamed reindeer as draft animals. Mankind may have had to re-learn some things, though some memory of past practices might have made these practices possible to imagine and hence easier to achieve

When the hunter-gatherer's life was pretty easy there was no need to turn to farming with its day-in day-out routine of looking after animals and crops. It has been estimated that hunter-gatherer peoples work much less hard than farming peoples. Where human populations are low and there is plenty of land in which animals can roam, the hunter-gatherer lifestyle works well. It is still practised in areas such as the Amazon basin with it's rich vegetation and animal life, and by the inuit who cannot grow crops. Farming is only needed once human populations grow so that the exploitation of the local area for food needs to become more intensive, or as in the case of our story, the available land has declined. So though animal domestication may have developed before the flood farming in the sense of growing crops in fields and intensifying yields perhaps didn't. The development of crops is now being traced back genetically to the ancestor plants from which they are derived. This is tending to confirm dates for development of modern cereals around 8000 or 9000 years ago, though there is evidence of grain seeds being part of human diet back to well before the flood times. The Warwick University website quotes research saying that the best example of grain seeds in human diets is the archaeological site Ohalo II in Syria, where more than 90,000 plant fragments from 23,000BP show that wild cereals were being gathered over 10,000 years earlier than previously thought, and before the last glacial maximum.

If it was quite possible to get useful amounts of food by harvesting wild cereals, there would be little incentive to selectively breed them to get higher yields. But successful harvesting depended on those lush low-lying areas now made so inhospitable by sea flooding. With only small areas in more hilly or mountainous country available for wild plants to grow in abundance, starting to cultivate food plants and to help them compete against non-food plants would have been a priority, as would getting higher yields from them.

The question we must ask is whether mankind received help to do this?

****

Chapter 18 – Did the gods return?

There are suggestions that the gods were 'hands-on' helping mankind in various books and stories that have come down to us from ancient times. Consider what Plato wrote in that section in Timaeus we looked at earlier, particularly the bit I have italicised:

"Solon marveled at his words, and earnestly requested the priests to inform him exactly and in order about these former citizens."

"You are welcome to hear about them, Solon, said the priest, both for your own sake and for that of your city, **and above all, for the sake of the goddess who is the common patron and parent and educator of both our cities. She founded your city a thousand years before ours, receiving from the Earth and Hephaestus the seed of your race, and afterwards she founded ours**, ...

.....(see chapter 14 for the full text).....

... Then as to wisdom, do you observe how our law from the very first made a study of the whole order of things, extending even to prophecy and medicine which gives health; out of these divine elements deriving what was needful for human life, and adding every sort of knowledge which was akin to them. **All this order and arrangement the goddess first imparted to you when establishing your city; and she chose the spot of earth in which you were born, because she saw that the happy temperament of the seasons in that land would produce the wisest of men. Wherefore the goddess, who was a lover both of war and of wisdom, selected and first of all settled that spot which was the most likely to produce men likest herself.**

There are legends from elsewhere that also describe gods that help mankind, such as Viracocha in the Inca mythology. Viracocha was not seen as a distant god, being described as a white man, who after the great flood taught mankind what plants were edible and how to practice medicine. I feel it is quite a reasonable assumption to make that even if the gods' initial relationships with mankind might have been different, by the time of the Flood there seems to be a degree of consensus in the legends that gods had a strong role in helping mankind develop.

It really seems to me rather perverse that we don't take more literally what these legends and religious texts such as the Bible, Quran and Hindu texts say about gods. The reason of course is because of the way the term 'god' is interpreted nowadays. The religions, particularly those that arose in the Middle East, have taken ownership of the term and have used it to focus worship by the religion's adherents, of the 'one God', who must be worshiped through the religion. Hence the existence of any other gods has to be denied. Where an individual such as Jesus Christ is used as a key focus of the worship, he is defined as 'the son of God', so the focus is still onto the 'one God'. The pantheons of gods of previous civilisations are dismissed as invented stories.

I have no wish to deny that there may be some higher guiding force for all mankind and other creatures. Neither do I want to deny that human beings can have truly spiritual experiences. The spiritual side of mankind would take a complete book on its own to discuss. Perhaps that might be a next project, because in reading books about ancient archeology you will inevitably come across an awful lot of information and speculation about spiritual belief systems. Human beings have quite a lot of inexplicable experiences and as we seek to understand these, spiritual beliefs are created. I think that what has happened over the 10,000 years or so of our recent recorded history is that some stories that have a real basis in real happenings of long ago have been mixed up with stories that have been propagated by religions for religious purposes.

The difficult word here and the cause of much of the confusion is the word god. As stated earlier, in this book, if I wish to refer to some truly higher spiritual entity that may be our maker and the ultimate source of life, the universe and everything, I am referring to this as God. With a big capital G. Where we need to talk about beings that appear to have god-like and apparently miraculous powers through the fact that they are different, though vaguely man-like and much more technologically advanced beings, then I use god, with a little lower-case g. I am stressing this point again because I don't want you to think in sections that follow, that I am in any way trying to undermine religious beliefs, what you believe is up to you. But I do want to help separate those things that should be central to faith and those things that have ended up in religious texts for other reasons.

It could well be that spiritual thoughts about the higher force and 'one God' may have become inextricably mixed with stories from the past about gods. And with how human beings have been taught to think about gods. This may indeed have been done on purpose as a cynical tool to control humans, or as a way to bring them together so they could be helped to survive. Any Atlanteans surviving the Flood would have a clear concept of the gods and would be pre-disposed to worship and obey them. For humans who were hunter-gatherers, previously living without any contact with the gods, it would be necessary to instill beliefs that would create an allegiance to a religion and a desire to worship the gods - in order for the gods to ensure sufficient control to guarantee their safety while they tried to help them survive.

It is likely that humans wherever they lived in the world would have naturally developed spiritual ideas and would have related them to what they could see. The sky would have been a nightly source of wonder. They would see the backdrop of the stars, in a way that we never now see them because of the light pollution in our cities, and might have conceived of them as being in some 'heaven'. In this 'heaven' they would see some lights - the planets and of course the sun and moon - that moved around in this 'heaven'. They may well have thought this is where their ancestors had gone when they died and left their bodies behind. The heavens were intimately connected to life on Earth, but humans could not reach to heaven. The gods on the other hand could, they had flying machines. So it would be obvious to humans that the gods could come down to Earth from heaven and could ascend into heaven. And if the gods had chosen to take Enoch or any of the other patriarchs on their spacecraft, there could well have developed a tradition that it was possible for kings and patriarchs to reach heaven before they died if the gods wished them to.

Whatever these pre-existing spiritual feelings might have been, the coming of the comet and the Flood would have caused a major re-assessment of how humans thought about heaven and their relationship to the spiritual world. People would need some kind of explanation that would enable them to rationalise what had happened. Think about what they would know. Before the Flood they would have seen a very bright sun-like object appearing in 'heaven'. They would see it rapidly getting bigger as it came towards the Earth from 'heaven' and then finally even those who did not actually see it crashing into the Earth would probably have felt the shockwaves and earthquakes as it did.

They would then find that pretty much immediately the sun was extinguished and the Earth became dark, as the immense amounts of dust and water pushed up into the atmosphere caused thick clouds to spread around the world. Heaven was no longer visible. A few people might have related this phenomenon to an extremely cloudy day but when the darkness persisted and the sun and stars failed to return into view their lone voices of reason would soon be drowned out by those who thought of this calamity in terms of heaven having fallen to Earth.

Next they would experience huge amounts of water falling out of the sky. They might easily surmise, if they had not worked out how clouds are formed from the seas, that this water had also come from 'heaven'. That more water had arrived on Earth would be reinforced by water flooding over the land and in later years by the height of sea-level, now covering previous homelands, that they would know about from the stories handed down. It is likely that the stars and maybe even the moon would be obscured for years after the Flood. If there was very high-level cloud even the sun may not have been a distinct celestial object, being instead a diffuse brightening of the sky. If this was so then humans might easily believe that the whole of heaven had fallen to Earth and that the stars were no longer there. It would only be after many years that heaven would be restored to its former glory, as the clouds and dust layers in the atmosphere finally dispersed. It might even be that the cloud cover lasted for generations and that the existence of the moon and the stars became a story about what the world used to be like, passed down from parents to children.

If this was the case we may be able to find references to this in the myths and legends. For example the Egyptian stories of Isis and Osiris and the conflicts they contain, that eventually result in the resurrection of Osiris and the birth of Horus might conceivably be linked to this. Horus is seen as a sky deity, with his right eye said to be the sun and his left eye the moon, and the story talks about the theft of his eye. The stories are however very complicated and have obviously been embellished and embroidered, and used to help people confront death. The scholars are trying to unravel the roots of these stories but so far have no agreement as to how they originated.

This is something I will continue to explore, as it is logical that there should be some folk memories if I am right that a comet evaporating a significant part of the Laurentide ice sheet would cause very high cloud layers persisting for decades. We know that volcanoes can obscure the sun with dust for years and are pretty sure that the comet that ended the reign of the dinosaurs ejected sufficient dust to bring the cold and lack of vegetation that probably caused their demise. We don't know what the effect of a large comet hitting ice instead of the ground would be, because as far as I know no climate expert has worked on this scenario. I am speculating here but with some support from physics. If fine dust can remain in the upper atmosphere for decades, water vapour which at that height will be dis-associated molecules will be lighter than dust particles and might persist longer. Water vapour in the lower atmosphere is a greenhouse gas and warms Earth, the question is whether globally-spread water vapour high in the stratosphere might have the opposite effect. I don't know, but it strikes me as a question worth conjuring with.

Getting back to the reality of a cataclysic impact starting the very cold younger dryas period, the people trying to survive this and make sense of it will have needed some comforting explanations. There might have been some secret knowledge held by a very few that knew the truth about meteorites and the nature of the solar system and universe, but for the vast mass of the people and even for the kings and higher functionaries a simpler explanation would have been needed. The explanation of what had happened would have to be based on the myths and stories built around what people at the time would have seen. Even today many people have difficulty getting their minds around the nature of the universe as we now understand it, with it's incredible distances and timescales. It would be far easier to get most people to believe in a well constructed story about the wrath of the gods being brought down on mankind, because mankind had sinned.

If you try to understand this period by un-picking the stories that have come down to us from the Sumerians, the Egyptians, the Bible and stories from other cultures, you will rapidly find all sorts of strange ideas that often contradict each other and which don't link into any kind of sensible story. Scholars have over the ages attempted to find the basis for the stories. You can find numerous books that promote one theory or another, probably with some grains of truth but also with a lot of speculation about what the texts mean and no clear conclusions. I suggest you approach this the other way. Think what you would say to humans if you were a god who knew clearly what had happened and who wished to ensure humans continued to worship you and the other gods, while retaining a belief in the need to work together and support each other, not just descend into fighting for survival and maybe even cannibalism..

Before the Flood the story could be quite simple. Humans could see heaven, that the gods could reach and they couldn't. They could see the gods were hugely more powerful than humans. When priests asked deeper questions about where the Earth and the stars came from, there would be no conflict if they were told that an original God had made heaven and Earth and everything in it, and if they were given an idea that this was a process, as described in Genesis. The truth about the universe initially being dark until stars formed, and the other things described in Genesis, would sit quite comfortably with the gods describing themselves as gods, who lived in heaven with God and hence should be worshipped. This is quite a simple story that it would be hard for the priests to find flaws with and it would need little elaboration to explain such things as why the sun and moon move. Only for very intelligent people with probing minds would it be necessary to provide more detail. These people would be initiated into the priesthood and taught the secret knowledge only once they had been fully conditioned never to reveal these secrets to the un-initiated.

It would be quite different after the Flood. A much more complicated story would be called for. If humans were going to continue to believe in and worship 'all powerful' gods, there would have to be an explanation of how and why all-powerful gods had allowed such a disaster to happen. The idea of a protector god looking after humans would be hard to believe, given what had happened.

The first step would have to be to explain why an all-powerful god had allowed so many humans to be killed in the Flood. This would obviously have to be an act of god, because god was all-powerful. But it couldn't be the fault of god, again because god is all-powerful and doesn't have faults. So the only way to explain the Flood is to make it the fault of humans, something god had to do because of human faults. And the obvious way to promote this story is to introduce the idea that the Flood happened because humans had 'sinned against god', because this would reinforce the idea that humans needed to obey the gods at all times. The initial Flood survivors would be told that it was their belief in the gods that had saved them.

Some generations later, when the stories of the Flood were getting less personal, the question might arise why god had failed to kill all humans, given that god is all powerful. Rather than a story that the righteous were saved and the non-believers killed, it might have been desirable to focus the story more strongly and precisely. If they allowed humans to perceive of the Flood as it happened, hitting some areas and not others, it would be seen to be the more random event that it was, which would tend to deny that it had been sent to destroy mankind.

So there would be a need to introduce the idea that some human and his family were saved when all of the rest of the world was drowned, because they were particularly good and righteous, and god having created mankind did not want to destroy his handiwork completely. And the story would have to include saving the animals too, as a full global flood would obviously kill them too. We will never know what name this saved person went under in the original story and whether it really was Noah or Gilgamesh or Utnapishtim. Over the hundreds of years that followed the stories will have been embellished and embroidered by the priesthoods, probably as instructed by the gods. In the days before writing, and for many hundreds of years after the advent of writing, the priesthoods carefully maintained their esoteric traditions. The stories that were purveyed to the vast mass of the people were coded and not the whole truth. Priests would only get to know the secret knowledge of what the scriptures really meant as they progressed up the ladder of initiation. To maintain this idea of hidden secrets there was every incentive to embellish the publicly available story so that over time it became more and more complicated, and more and more distanced from the real story. It is highly unlikely that any scholar will be able to interpret the stories that finally got written down and end up with the truth, because the stories are the creations of the priesthoods. They made complicated stories that they could sell to their public as the basis for complicated (and expensive) rituals that would keep the priesthood in business.

I feel the most we can expect to get out of looking at all these stories is some clarity of the key elements, that may well have come from the original story that the gods invented after the Flood. Namely:
- There is heaven where the gods live and Earth where mankind lives.
- Heaven, or a part of heaven, fell to Earth.
- What fell from heaven entered into the Earth and entered an underworld.
- From heaven there also came water.
- Eventually heaven emerged from the underworld into which it had fallen and heaven was restored.
- That the Flood was the fault of mankind.
- And that God, or one of the gods at least, decided to save mankind because god had originally created mankind, and did so by saving a human family that were sufficiently good and righteous.

Then, whenever you read about the stories invented by the priesthoods, of Gilgamesh, Osiris and Horus, or Noah, you can hopefully separate in your mind the grains of truth from what I believe are essentially invented stories, invented to control people and as a basis for rituals.

I appreciate that this is rather a bleak and cynical way of viewing many thousands of years of religious thoughts and scholarship. But I can fully believe there may have been many honest priests who have viewed these stories as the best way to get ordinary people to think about the higher things in spiritual life and to behave according to good moral codes. I wonder how many priests silently question the tenets of their faith and personally do not believe in many of the details of the stories they use to convince people to worship. Perhaps now that we are sufficiently distant from the actual existence on Earth of 'the gods', the spiritual feelings and insights of humans can be re-focused and a better understanding of whatever higher force there may be can be gained. I actually think that unscrambling the way the idea of God and ideas about gods have been mixed might make it easier for many people to come to a better understanding about their spiritual selves, but as I said earlier that is a topic for another book.

As part of this assessment of how the Flood story may have come about and in proposing that the gods returned to help mankind after the Flood, I am of a mind to give more credence to the people who wrote the ancient texts. While the story about the Flood being caused by mankind sinning may be an invention, I think it is possible to believe that other stories about the actions of the gods may well have been the truth, about the beings they referred to as gods.

It is our confusion around the term god that has led our interpretation of what they wrote going astray. In truth I guess that I am currently 70:30 or maybe 80:20 biassed towards believing that 'the gods', our Adventurers who I am writing about, did actually exist. The whole point of writing the book is to help me to pull together the various strands that have pushed my belief about this up to this point. And I want to help you to do likewise and discover what you should think about the ways gods and God have been thought about and talked about over the centuries.

However, to carry on with our speculative story, we potentially have some gods, and/or half-gods, actively helping mankind from immediately after the Flood, because they stayed on Earth and they too had to feed themselves from what the Earth could provide. But we also have other gods, perhaps the elder and more senior gods, who we are assuming have retreated to a spaceship. If they are going to stick with Earth and not fly off to another star system and another planet, they will eventually have to start thinking about coming back down to Earth.

We have now reached an exciting time in our story, because we can start to look at hard tangible evidence. There is no longer the possibility of the gods sequestering themselves in Antarctica where any evidence they left will have been largely destroyed and anyway made inaccessible. If the gods remained on Earth they will have to have been in places we can now get to, to look for evidence they may have left. And the gods no longer have the option of remaining separate from the growing hordes of mankind. They would have had to decide how to keep their privileged position and lifestyle while remaining in close proximity to humans generally, not just the specially privileged and closely managed group that became the Atlanteans. The gods were few in number relative to humans. Even if the post-flood human population was small they would have seen how it had grown over the previous ten thousand years and would know that mankind had the potential for similar population growth once the traumas of the flood have passed.

The problem for the gods is how to exert sufficient and widespread control for their security and to get mankind to remain sufficiently their slaves to produce and provide what the gods wanted. We will have to see if any of the evidence we can find sheds any light on this.

****

Chapter 19 - Humans and gods together.

Where should the gods land?

We have once before in this story considered the gods, our Adventurers, orbiting the Earth in their spaceship, considering where to set up home, but the parameters are now very different. Antarctica is rapidly becoming uninhabitable as it freezes. The only large habitable land area that is separated from the rest of the world's land area by sea is Australia. We are pretty sure that humans had reached Australia by 40,000 years ago and some must have survived the Flood as they are there today and have their own legends about 'Dreamtime'. The amount of sea between Australia and New Guinea would have grown since the times before the flood when the aboriginal people arrived, but the gap is not wide; human beings could still cross it even if humans in Australia had been wiped out. The opportunity for the gods to live separately from mankind was no longer really available. There are a few islands of some size that are separated by a reasonable amount of sea from the mainland, such as Madagascar, but nowhere as well separated as Antarctica was.

While living in Antarctica it was possible to let mankind develop at its own rate. I have suggested that the gods stimulated trade, using the Atlanteans to carry it out. Though I suggest the development of the Atlanteans had been stimulated to some extent, to become a 'powerful empire', they would have had been kept at the level of stone-age technology. Though humans elsewhere would see their ship technology and hear stories about the Atlantean civilisation, Atlanteans would not have been able to accelerate the development of other humans around the world very much. If you are trying to control populations of humans the danger point is when they develop metal extraction and the ability to construct metal weapons. Up to this point the machines they can build are limited. Working wood in complex ways is not very easy with stone tools, though boats were made. The romans did build ballistas in wood, which were pretty dangerous, but used metal tools to do it. The furthest distance a stone age person could project a weapon was with bow and arrow, which does at least require you to be within sight of your target.

If the gods were going to land and live somewhere accessible to human populations, or maybe in the middle of them, how would this play out in influencing human technological development. How long would it take for human beings to accelerate their technology to the point where they became a real danger to the gods? Looking at this logically, the gods would have had to re-assess what they were on Earth for. The point that had been arrived at in the development of mankind may have been by design or accident. Whichever way it happened the question would be whether living alongside human beings was sustainable into the future, for the thousands of years I have assumed the gods need to consider, due to their long lives.

Reappraisal of possible futures would suggest some possible outcomes that could result from the gods living close to human beings:

i) Human beings might be persuaded to see the gods in perpetuity as proper Gods and to keep them inviolable and free from harm. One of the joys of being a real God, if such exist, is that of having incalculable power. That is, really incalculable power. The Romans, Greeks and other ancient civilisations thought of Gods as able to reign thunderbolts down from heaven and to intervene miraculously in the doings of individuals. This kind of power is a different order of magnitude to the power the gods actually possessed. They no doubt had power that could appear to be incalculable to non-technological beings, but which would soon be seen to be not so powerful if really tested by strong rebellion against the gods by large numbers of humans.

ii) The gods might be able to separate themselves from human beings and establish a ring-fence around where they lived. This would hold until mankind acquired sufficient power and capability to break through the ring-fence. An assessment of the nature of human intelligence would soon bring the realisation that such a fortress would be hugely attractive to many humans. Inquisitive humans would want to find out what was inside the fortress and would work away at the problem of how to do so.

iii) They could just fly away in their spaceship to another planet and start again, leaving behind any gods or half-gods that they could not accommodate in their spaceship.

iv) Or they could combine options (i) and (iii), land and see how it went living amongst the developing human beings, reserving the option to fly away if humans proved too dangerous and uncooperative. They would need to devise the best possible ways to control and manage humans.

The home of the gods.

If the aim is to help mankind through the traumas of the post-Flood, younger-dryas period, then the place to land and set up a new home would be somewhere within reach of the main groups of human beings who had survived the Flood. If the gods' aims were purely selfish, of wanting to re-establish a workforce of slaves to grow their food and provide for other needs, this too would necessitate being close to where the surviving humans were. Humans must have survived in many areas of the world because we can trace the genetic histories of different races of humans to times well before the flood. However by far the most interesting area archeologically in the period of 11,000 years ago (9000BC) to around 5500 years ago (3500BC), when we started to get written records, is the Middle East. It is interesting both for the archeology in and on the ground and for the legends that are recorded in the religious books of the area. The area stretches from India with its hindu texts and legends, across Iran and Turkey, the 'fertile crescent', over to Ethiopia, which is maybe high enough to have been an area where people survived the flood. It contains Egypt, the source of the Atlantis legend and the home of the priests who obviously had access to very ancient texts. The loss of the library at Alexandria really was a disaster for historians. The earliest civilisations that we know of are here, particularly the Sumerian cities. As we come into the Mediterranean there are the Greek and Roman pantheons of Gods, that were derived from older religions.

There are other areas of the world that might contribute evidence for the existence of the gods on Earth in this period, that I will mention later, but we will start in the Middle East.

The most fascinating ancient site in the whole world for me is the megalithic platform at Baalbeck. The Great Pyramid in Egypt is fascinating too but it is just possible to imagine stone age humans making most of it, except for the kings chamber and the massive blocks above it. The Great Pyramid is one amongst a whole range of other constructions in Egypt, and the complexity of the pyramid and the whole area makes it possible for there to be many conflicting theories, which are hard to untangle. We will however look at some of these theories later.

The platform at Baalbeck is fascinating because of its simplicity and because of where it is. Ignore all the Roman temples and other constructions that have been added later. Imagine the very first phase of construction at

Baalbeck. The platform is an area the size of a football pitch, 90m by 60m, that has been leveled and taken down to the bedrock on top of which the major wall has been built. The major wall is quite obviously a lot older than the temple walls that have been built on top of it. The base part of the wall, standing on the bedrock, is 10m high. The three biggest stone blocks each measure 19 metres long x 4.2 metres high x 3.6 metres deep. They weigh 870 tons each. The layer these stand on is 19 blocks of granite, each weighing between 350 and 400 tons each. The blocks have been cut with very high accuracy so they fit together extremely closely.

Our view of the remains at Baalbeck today is confused by the subsequent building of the temple. The megalithic stones were obviously in place already when those who built the temple arrived. If you imagine the site with only the megalithic blocks, it would have been a flat rock platform with a massive wall at one end. There must have been a reason why the three blocks of stone known as the trilithon stones were used as the top layer of the wall. The similar block that was cut and left in the quarry was presumably a reject. And the even larger block that has now been found in the quarry may have been left there because it proved not to be necessary, the trilithon blocks that are in the wall satisfactorily doing the job they were required to do.

From pictures you can find on the Internet it looks to me as though the rejected stone may have a crack that might have caused it to break in transit or in use. Instead of it being cut into smaller blocks that would still have made a good wall, it was rejected and left there. The size of the trilithon blocks must be important. That might be because of how they looked visually, or it might have been because that was necessary because of the purpose of the wall. Cutting and placing blocks this size is an awful lot of trouble to go to for visual effect.

The key point is that there are two possible reasons for building in blocks that are so big and difficult to handle. The first reason is just because you can and it's easier that way. The second reason is because you need blocks of that size for the purpose of the construction you are making. If it is a just a matter of being able to cut and move large blocks easily, then why isn't the whole wall made of these large blocks? And if you have some large and some small blocks because of the ways it is possible to cut the stone out of the quarry, it would surely be more sensible to use the biggest blocks in the base of the wall and the smaller blocks, which are easier to lift, higher up. But this wall has the biggest blocks on top. If you are using large blocks because you want to make a high wall, why make the wall so deep? A wall of this height could easily be built with much less depth and still be stable, particularly when it is being built on top of bedrock. This is not a region particularly prone to earthquakes which might be the reason for a super-stable wall. If these were foundation stones for a really high wall, why aren't there decreasing size large blocks built on top of them. It looks as though the top of the ancient structure was the trilithon blocks.

I just don't believe such large blocks were used for visual effect. If you want visual effect to impress and you have very large blocks then the sensible thing to do is stand them up, as was done with the T-shaped stones at Gobekli Tepe, and maybe balance one on top of the others, as was done at Stonehenge and the numerous megalithic stones elsewhere. And I reckon if these were foundation stones for a much higher wall, there would surely be some evidence of megalithic blocks that had been on top of the trilithons, lying around the site if not still in place. My bet is that there was an engineering purpose why the blocks on the top of the wall had to be so big. As the blocks don't do anything except sit there, the engineering purpose can only be something to do with their mass.

A mass on Earth does two things. The first is that it is pulled towards the Earth by gravity and hence it squashes and holds down anything under it. The second is that mass has inertia, in other words it takes force to move it sideways. This is not just the force needed to overcome the friction between the block and what it is sitting on, it is the force needed to accelerate the mass and make it move. The bigger the mass the greater the inertia and the bigger the force needed to move it.

Now imagine that you are the owner of a large spacecraft, that you need to bring down to Earth because you need to live in it while you build other accommodation or because of other facilities that it has. You need to be able to land it and then be able to take off again and you need a suitable space for this. Small spacecraft like the moon lander can hover around to find somewhere sufficiently level and solid to land and you only need a small space. For a very large craft you need a very solid very level base. You don't want there to be any chance that the ground below it could subside or that the craft might sink into it and make a hole that it is difficult to get out of when you want to take off again. Even if you have anti-gravity devices, you still need a force to get the considerable mass of the spaceship moving at a reasonable speed.

We have so far sent our rockets into space vertically, because the only way we have of creating a propulsion force is by burning rocket fuel and a very limited amount of fuel can be carried. We throw away booster rockets at each launch. However we are now seeing companies experimenting with space rockets launched from planes that can be landed and re-used. If we had a rocket propulsion system that could produce a hefty amount of force continuously from an amount of fuel that could be carried in the main rocket instead of needing a booster, we would very likely fire those rockets up at an angle rather than straight up. The continuously produced power can then be used to gain lift through the atmosphere and to get it up to a suitable speed for orbit. If you have technology to overcome gravity then you can get into space by projecting a force straight down and taking off vertically. But if you have a craft with wings or an overall wing-profile shape, then taking off at an angle gives you the added lift that happens through the Bernoulli principle, as the air in the atmosphere flows over the wing shape. (Air is accelerated as it goes over the top wing surface which is longer than the lower wing surface, and this lowers the air pressure above the wing relative to the air pressure below the wing, creating lift.)

However this force to get moving and into the air at an angle is produced, whether by liquid rocket fuel, plasma engines, huge lasers or whatever, the principle is the same. You push something of quite low mass out of the back of the spaceship very fast, and as every force has an equal and opposite reaction, the large mass of the spaceship starts to move forward slowly, accelerating as long as the force is applied. The fast-moving jet will be directed down on to the Earth behind the spaceship. If it is soil below and behind the spaceship this will be blasted in all directions. If it is rock that is below the spaceship the jet will spread out on hitting the rock to a very considerable distance. This would be very destructive to anything around the launch pad.

But if your spaceship is standing on a football pitch sized area and is going to take off at a relatively gentle angle into the air, what you ideally need to do is to direct the propulsion jet coming out of the back of the spacecraft up into the air where it can do no harm. The USA Apollo rocket jets were deflected sideways in a direction that was kept clear of anything that could be damaged. They couldn't deflect the propulsion jet vertically up into the air because the rocket was going vertically and would have been fried by its own jet. Going off at an angle allows you to deflect the jet upwards where it won't harm anything on the ground around the space-pad.

For this you of course need a very substantial wall around one end of the platform your spaceship is blasting up from. You will however have to make sure that the maximum force the jet can exert on the wall is less than is required to move the mass of the wall. We achieve this by constructing massive ferro-concrete walls to channel the propulsion jet. If instead you have built the wall from stones, the stones most in danger of being dislodged are the stones on the top of the wall. The lower courses of stones are kept in place not only by their own weight but also by the weight of the blocks above them. Whereas the blocks in the top course of the wall must each have enough inertia to resist being shifted by the blast. Inertia is measured in the same units as weight, so we can think of this as them being heavy enough to withstand the full force of the blast that could hit them. Is this why the three largest blocks at Baalbeck have been used in the top course of the wall? And perhaps why the cracked one in the quarry was rejected, because if used in two halves each half would only have half the inertia of the full block, and if half received the full force of the propulsion jet it could shift and fall? This would provide a good and very logical reason to go to the trouble of lifting the heaviest blocks you have onto the top of the wall.

Another interesting fact about Baalbeck is that it is around 3,800 feet above sea level. If the gods were returning to help mankind, they would need to be somewhere fairly near where mankind lived, above the areas that had been flooded and made unproductive. Baalbeck would have been a logical choice, high enough to have escaped the flood, not so high that few plants would grow. Local legends about the archeological remains at Baalbeck abound, stating that it was the home of the Gods. I am not going to repeat them here, you can go and find them for yourselves and decide whether or not you believe them.

You can also decide for yourselves whether the proposals various people have produced to explain that these walls at Baalbeck could have been constructed by human beings have any truth. Though I think these various stories about why and how humans constructed the Baalbeck trilithon wall are very much a side issue. It is the engineering purpose of placing massively heavy blocks on the top of the wall that carries the story here.

****

Chapter 20 - The gods' new home; 12,800 to 10,000 years ago.

I have latched on to Baalbeck as the possible new home base for the gods because it is one of the most inexplicable constructions in the world that I just don't believe ancient humans had the ability to construct. But I should back up this assumption with some deeper consideration of the task facing the gods, that of establishing a safe home base in close proximity to many different tribes of humans.

For their own safety they would need to exercise a lot of control over the immediate area around their new home base. This would be comparable to the control they would have exercised over the limited number of humans in Antarctica but with the added problem that humans could of their own volition move into their area from further away, where they had less influence. Once it became known that the gods were living close to certain groups of humans and bringing advantages to them of better agriculture or other help, there would be temptation for groups of humans further away, who had survived the Flood, to migrate to their base area. Thinking long-term the gods would have realised that as mankind developed over the coming thousands of years they would populate areas surrounding Baalbeck, as they had done before the Flood, once the lower-lying lands became suitable again for human habitation.

We are now seeing the global pressures of migration on countries where it is pleasant to live, from peoples in less pleasant countries who can now manage to travel thousands of miles. In the times we are talking of travel meant walking, so even for armies able to walk fast traveling 300 miles would take at least 10 days. But 10 days is not a lot if you are determined. The American settlers who trekked to California to find a golden land walked a lot more slowly but kept going for weeks and mostly got there. The human populations in lands from which humans could relatively easily walk to the gods' base would eventually need to be managed.

If they decided that 'a relatively easy walk to the base' was say 1000 miles, what area would that cover? It would be quite easy for groups of humans with hunter-gatherer skills to migrate 1000 miles, if it was considered worthwhile to leave their home area. It's only 3 miles a day for a year, or a matter of moving say 20 miles every other week for a couple of years. In the timescales our long-lived gods are working to that is fast.

A 1000 mile radius from Baalbeck covers current-day Libya, Egypt, Syria, most of Saudi Arabia, Iraq, half of Iran and all of Turkey. This is the area in which the gods would need to exercise some degree of influence over humans, if only to ensure they were sufficiently scared of what the gods might do to deter unwelcome advances by humans. The area of prime influence would obviously be those areas closest, as good control of humans in these areas would help stop marauding parties from further away. How the gods directed their efforts would also depend on where the humans would develop large populations as they emerged from the privations of the Flood, so there would be a focus on areas close to rivers for water supply and transport. Initially this would be higher up the rivers but then moving closer to the sea once lower lying areas became again able to grow crops.

You will no doubt realise that we have described here the areas that contain the ancient civilisations of the Middle East. This is the 'fertile crescent' where archeologists consider civilisations were first established and one of the main areas in the world where agriculture was (re)invented. It is also the cradle from which western religions developed, which evolved from the ancient religions in Sumeria and Egypt, through the pantheons of Greece and Rome to the rise of Christianity, Judaism and Islam. Though these religions have fiercely fought each other there are common roots that can be traced, shared prophets and stories, and shared concepts such as the necessity to worship in specific ways and the prospect of glorious heaven. Any theory proposing that our alien adventurers were on the Earth must take the growth of these religions into account. Many people have immensely strong allegiance to their religion. If this was not aligned with controlling the behaviour of mankind towards the gods it would be in competition with attempts to control humans made by the gods.

But what about the areas outside this base area? I have suggested earlier in the book that the gods may have seeded their genetically engineered humans into other areas of the world, particularly India and South East Asia. In these areas, from the point of view of the gods' safety, they could afford to let mankind develop without interference to control them. However if they wished to visit on occasion, either to check on development, to help and guide development, or to gain resources from these areas, they would have needed the human beings to respond appropriately and safely whenever they appeared. Humans in these areas may have had some knowledge of the gods already, but this would need to be reinforced. We should expect to find some mention of the gods in their legends and the stories of their origins..

I have also suggested that once the gods knew that Antarctica was moving into a polar region that they would have organised the Atlanteans to settle in some other areas of the world in addition to the eastern Mediterranean, and I have mentioned Java in this context. And the plateau areas in the South American Andes mountains. It would be an interesting exercise to compare the myths about gods from these areas elsewhere in the world with the way that whole pantheons of gods are referred to in the Middle East. The myths of Viracocha for example are all about a single god, though they also include mention of a couple of sons of Viracocha. The Greek and Roman myths are about a whole family of gods, who engage in internecine strife. Perhaps this reflects the majority of the gods remaining in the fertile crescent area, but a few supporting humans elsewhere.

How might the gods have helped the surviving humans?

At this period of the development of mankind there is rather a mystery about why farming developed and then eventually cities. This is a counter-intuitive development from the point of view of individual people because a farming lifestyle requires considerably more work than a hunter-gatherer lifestyle. It is true that farming can provide a more reliable source of food, but only if you can protect your crops from being destroyed by animals or stolen by other people. Farming needs a different kind of societal organisation. Hunter-gatherer groups that exist in areas of the world today tend to be small groups of people, essentially extended families. You need to have enough adults able to cooperate in hunting but if you have too many then there are too many mouths to feed. In the days before refrigeration an animal that has been killed needs to be eaten before the meat goes bad, so the ideal is that the kinds of animals caught in the hunt will be sufficient to feed everyone in the group for a few days. Native Americans did live in larger groups which fitted their food supply. By driving bison towards cliffs they could arrange for many to be killed. They then needed to rapidly butcher them and dry strips of meat so that it would last and feed them when the bison moved away.

Farming either needs to be managed communally with division of labour, some people tilling fields and others herding animals, or an area needs to be secured by people in authority - the Lord of the Manor in feudal times - and the available land split into small patches so that each family has its own area of land to farm. Ian Morris, historian and archeologist at Stanford University in California has written about how human values evolve in his book Foragers, Farmers and Fossil fuels. He proposes that though moral values of societies can differ radically even between societies that are physically close to each other, there are broad systems of values that are common across different kinds of society. Hunter-gatherers all have societies where everyone is treated more-or-less the same. And if members of the group subvert this and try to develop dominance over others in the group, they will be ostracised or brought back into line with the group's moral values in other ways. Farming groups on the other hand have moral systems that are hierarchical. The group accepts that some people will be richer and more important than others. People at the bottom of the pile may not like their position in society, but do still accept that it is fair and simply their lot. This is how feudal societies worked without the peasants revolting.

The question is why the people who ended up at the bottom of the social pile when hunter-gathering changed to farming allowed this change to happen. Ian Morris's investigations have found that hunter-gatherer groups resist this kind of change if individuals try to make it happen. So there must have been some external pressure acting against this tendency to maintain a very equal society. The Flood of course provides the likely context for this change, but the pressure to change must have been exerted within the society.

Here then would be the key priority for the gods in helping mankind. Farming was necessary to get a bigger food yield from less productive land. How could humans be induced to move from their hunter-gatherer lifestyle to a farming lifestyle? The answer may lie in the most enigmatic ancient site in this area of the world, Gobekli Tepe.

Gobekli Tepe.

Picture the situation in the Middle East after the Flood. People who lived in the lush, productive, low-lying lands that are now Syria, the Turkish coasts and Iraq, will have been flooded out of their homes. The combination of the tsunami-type waves pushing their way inland and heavy flooding coming down the rivers, from the 40 days and 40 nights rain, will have forced those who survived higher. There may have been groups of people living in these higher lands who will not have appreciated their hunter-gatherer areas being invaded. Very quickly severe competition for available food will have developed. There will have been famine and groups fighting each other.

There would not have been a lot that the small number of gods could have done immediately to help with this situation, except perhaps to protect a chosen group and to stop too many others invading the territory they needed to survive. But as soon as the immediate aftermath of the Flood and comet-strike subsided, there would be a pressing need to impose order on the survivors and to manage the limited food supplies available. This could not be done if individual groups carried on doing as they wished regardless of the needs of others. There would have to be a way to gather people together into a more coherent society so that order could be imposed. And so that they could be taught animal husbandry and farming techniques that would maximise food production from the land, in this cold, cloudy and very unproductive time during the younger dryas period.

One of the most important features of the Gobekli Tepe site is that it is the earliest major construction that we know of. It is currently estimated to have been built around 11,000 years ago (9000BC) and abandoned by 8200BC. As stone constructions are hard to date these dates should be taken as a guide, it might have been started earlier, during the younger dryas period. Even the accepted date makes it considerably earlier than the accepted dates for other megalithic constructions and dates it to the period just after the younger dryas period. At this point the climate would have made it possible to develop farming more strongly, and hence it was the point when the productivity of the land would have started to become sufficient to free up the amount of labour necessary for megalithic constructions. Prior to the megalithic constructions it might have been a much simpler religious gathering place.

The site is at about 2500 feet (approx 750m) above sea level. Given that it is in the middle of a high plateau we have to assume that the people that it served were also living at this height above sea level. The early settlements that have been found in the area confirm this.

The most puzzling feature of Gobekli Tepe is that there are a number of similar constructions on the site that appear to have been built sequentially, with the previous construction being filled in. There are reports that suggest that there may be many more of these constructions on the hillside that have not yet been properly identified or excavated, and similar construction elsewhere in the area.

The constructions that have been excavated look to me like sites used for the disposal of dead bodies through excarnation. This is the process of disposing of dead bodies by having animals eat the flesh, leaving only the bones which can later be collected and stored without fear of disease from rotting human remains. Vultures are the desirable creature necessary for this as they are excellent at stripping flesh from bones.

Excarnation may sound gory to us but it makes a lot of sense for stone-age peoples. Digging graves is hard enough work when you have spades to do the job and nice soft earth to dig in. On stony hillsides with only stone-age digging tools it would have been a lot harder. And there is unlikely to have been easily available wood to make cremation possible, quite apart from the effort needed when the only available tools to cut wood were stone axes.

Leaving bodies to be stripped to the bones by vultures and other carrion birds is quite a nice way to deal with the problem of disposing of dead bodies once you have linked it with ideas about helping your relatives' spirits fly away into the sky. If you want to get some idea of how this may have felt to the relatives, search YouTube for "Red kite feeding". You will find video of the red kites being fed at Gigrin Farm in Powys. As they are fed every day they know to gather at the right time and you can see many tens of birds wheeling in the sky. Then when the farmer has spread the meat out for them, they all dive for it presenting an incredible display as they avoid each other in the melee. Now imagine this happening with vultures, which are a much bigger bird than red kites. The practice of excarnation might have supported a flock of hundreds of vultures. It would have been a very impressive sight indeed.

For excarnation you need somewhere that can stop wolves dragging complete sections of bodies away, making it hard or impossible to find the bones that you probably want to dispose of with some reverence. The vultures may take some days to remove all the meat from the bones even if the bodies were butchered prior to being laid out. A place safe from wolves could be created by constructing a wooden platform as some native Americans did, but an impressive enclosure built of massive stones would no doubt help with grieving and the social issues around people dying.

Whether or not this idea of the use of the constructions for excarnation has any merit the main feature of Gobekli Tepe that needs figuring out is why multiple similar enclosures were built and previous ones filled in. This would take a lot of work. It would take so much work by so many people that one has to ask whether the work required is the main issue that caused this strange behaviour.

Some group must have led and persuaded the populace in the surrounding area to contribute time and effort to the constructions. That effort might have been gained using a lot of people for a relatively short period. Or it might have been gained using smaller numbers of people for less time but over a much longer period.

Suppose that the group that initiated the constructions wanted all the people in the area to gather together regularly for some purpose. Just demanding that this be done is not a very good way, even if you are a powerful leader with ability to punish back-sliders. You need the people to want to gather, willing to give the time it may need to walk to the site. Linking your gathering site with death rituals would be a very good start. Every family faces deaths and every community has to dispose of bodies safely. Once you had established an imperative for families to dispose of bodies at your gathering site, this could provide a potential workforce to further develop the site. Help in quarrying and transporting the stones could have been required as payment to send your relative to heaven in a proper fashion. A maximum two-day journey to carry a dead body to the site before it decayed too much would imply that Gobekli Tepe serviced an area of around 5000 square miles – fit adults can pretty easily walk 20 miles a day, even with a load. This is a decent-sized area that could host a sizable population.

Then as your design requires some sizable monoliths that need some big teams of people to transport and erect, you could establish an annual festival of the dead and make it a requirement of the religion you have created around all this that everyone should undergo a pilgrimage to the annual festival at least once in their lives. Or maybe that every community should send representatives to the festival every year. Either approach ought to be enough to guarantee a sizable crowd when you want to shift and erect the next monolith. The approach of community representatives attending each year would of course also provide a mechanism to send ideas about how to improve agriculture back to every community in the area. And perhaps send some gifts back as well, such as seeds of a better variety of wheat.

You can probably see where I am going with this line of reasoning. It must have been a powerful group that initiated construction and there must have been powerful incentives for the workforce required. If our story of the gods establishing themselves in this area makes sense then this site would provide a mechanism for them to regularly interact with humans and to spread new knowledge about plants or the domestication of livestock. And to police the communities and set laws.

Of course if you are using quarrying and construction as a payment mechanism for proper disposal of dead people, you have a slight problem when after many years your original construction is completed. How can people now pay respects to and honour their relatives who have died? The obvious answer is to create a rationale for renewal of the construction and hence a reason to start on a new one and to fill the old one in.

Until someone comes up with a better explanation for why there are so many similar constructions and why new ones were built and old ones filled in, I shall keep this bit of wild speculation in mind as a possibility that might conceivably contain some grains of truth, or even be the whole truth.

There is also some interesting evidence being found in Central America, at Ceibal in Guatemala, that might bear on this. They have discovered that construction of the pyramids that archeologists reckon were used for ritual purposes predates the construction of the surrounding city. If you are searching for this the work is being done by Takeshi Inomata of the University of Arizona. In other words, before the city and farming developed groups of hunter-gatherers were willing to commit effort to construct stone platforms. The religion that used these platforms is thought to have been the stimulus that brought people together and which led to the development of cities. It is of course quite possible to imagine groups of hunter-gatherers coming together at festivals to trade and to marry off daughters and for sons to find wives. The Romany (Gypsy) traveller people in Britain gather annually at Appleby Fair. They race and trade horses and generally have a good time. They haven't however felt the need to create a religion or religious rituals around this fair. They simply gather in the same area every year.

Did the gods create a religion and establish the site of Gobekli Tepe as the mechanism to bring the surviving humans together and to forge them into a society that would adopt the new approach of intensive farming, and the moral values that accepted a hierarchical society?

The re-establishment of mankind; the spread of farming.

Gobekli Tepe, once established, would probably have become a religious centre that people hundreds of miles away knew about. Once agriculture was established in the local area and the populace was stable, emissaries could have been sent out to other communities that had survived the flood. The first trips would have been along the southern edge of the mountains, all the way to the Zagros mountains of Iran. Archeologists are coming to the view that agriculture started at numerous sites in the fertile crescent, not just at one site. There is a cluster of early agriculture sites on the upper Euphrates close to Gobekli Tepe but archeologists have also found evidence of the growing of grains in sites such as Choga-Golan, around 500 miles away.

It is interesting to note when looking at maps of where agriculture started (see http://www.sci-news.com/archaeology/science-chogha-golan-agriculture-fertile-crescent-01203.html) that Baalbeck is separated from the sites around Gobekli Tepe by the low-lying land of Northern Lebanon and Syria, which would have been inhospitable for quite a long time after the Flood. However early agriculture sites did develop along the river Jordan by around 8000 BC. The earliest dates for the city of Jericho are around 7000BC, so we can imagine a period of maybe three thousand years during which the gods living at Baalbeck would have been well separated from humans, except for the few who might have survived in the mountains of Lebanon.

There is also evidence of early agriculture in India and China. It might be that similar pressures to those faced by humans in the fertile crescent might have caused them to independently develop agriculture, or it might be that the gods found surviving groups of humans and donated knowledge of how to go about farming and maybe seeds of domesticated crops. However I will keep the main thread of this story on the influence and activities of the gods spread out from their post-Flood base in the Gobekli Tepe area.

If the gods wished to dominate the whole world and once again have trading routes that brought back to them things they desired, they would of course once again look to sea transport to do this. Trading routes would now be a bit more complicated than they had been when the gods were living in Antarctica, but they would still be fairly well placed to establish them, except for journeys to China and the west coast of the Americas. The Persian Gulf leads out to India, the Red Sea to the east coast of Africa and the Mediterranean leads to Northern Europe and the west coast of Africa. Overland routes would still have been very difficult. When the silk trade developed in historical times, the caravan routes from China went through the reasonably flat steppe and desert areas of mid-Asia, as the more southern routes were blocked by forests and vegetation; overland travel was extremely difficult until civilisations started to create and manage road systems. The sensible way to travel was by boat.

If you take your map of the world and consider the sea routes that could return traded goods to the gods' home base in Baalbeck and the human civilisations they were helping to establish, there are three options. Bringing goods into the Persian Gulf or up the Red Sea would involve trans-shipment and overland carrying, though the Tigris and Euphrates rivers would have helped considerably. The only sea route that gets close to a base at Baalbeck is the Mediterranean; don't forget that the Suez canal did not exist. And without difficulty this route can be extended into more Equatorial areas by following the coast of Africa, and into more temperate areas by following the coasts of Spain and France, Britain and Scandinavia. In later times we come to hear of the trading prowess of the Phoenicians, trading from ports such as Tyre and Beirut in Lebanon, Beirut being only 40 miles from Baalbeck. Evidence for how seafaring started in this period is probably best derived from looking at early settlements on the Mediterranean coast. The Franchthi cave in the Peloponnese islands for example, and the area surrounding it, show evidence of agriculture from around 8000 BC. This comes after an interruption in this cave being inhabited during the younger-dryas period. Though the cave would have been some hundreds of feet above sea level at the time of the Flood, the flora and fauna of this area of many islands would have been devastated by the Flood.

It is also worth noting at this point that megalithic structures are everywhere along the Mediterranean, European and British coasts, from the Shetland Islands, to Carnak to Morocco and of course Egypt and the Middle East. Though most of the megalithic structures we know of were no doubt built by humans we will ask later whether there could be some link with the gods.

****

Chapter 21 - 10,000 to 7000 years ago.

Apart from Gobekli Tepe there are no other sites that conventional archeologists are prepared to date to this period. I watch with interest the developments in Indonesia. And I note all the discoveries made by Graham Hancock in his underwater expeditions. But let's stick with what is easily visible and ask whether the gods might have had a hand in their construction.

In the Middle East this was a period when settlements were developing. The archeology at Nevali Cori and other similar sites reliably dates their earliest levels to this period. The end of the period saw the earliest levels at Jericho. The interesting difference between these two places is their elevations. Nevali Cori is on the Eastern Turkey plateau not far from Gobekli Tepe. Jericho is in a wadi in the Jordan valley and is actually below sea level. We must ask why settlements in the fertile crescent started in the hills and only later came down onto lower lying land, eventually to develop on the river plains of Mesopotamia.

As the archeologists' view is that small settlements were developing in this period, with no major civilisations from which we have received written history, they are not prepared to countenance any large structures being built at this time. There is however one for which a good case has been made that it was constructed well before the date conventionally assigned to it - the Sphinx.

The sphinx.

There are many books that have been written speculating on the astronomical significance of the ancient constructions at Giza. Whether or not you believe these theories is up to you, but to me one of the undeniable facts, made undeniable by the huge number of examples worldwide, is that ancient peoples were very concerned about observing the heavens and about astronomical alignments. Just in Western Europe there are the major examples such as Stonehenge, Carnac, The Ring of Brodgar and Newgrange, which are supported by the 'local' stone circles all over the place. Other examples can be listed from all parts of the world. So it is not hard to believe that great care was taken with alignments when building such constructions.

Then we have the weathering evidence on the Sphinx. Robert Schoch the geologist has closely investigated the Sphinx and even for someone without his knowledge the weathering is plain to see. You cannot draw direct conclusions on weathering from current rainfall in Egypt, as the whole Middle East had considerably more lush vegetation right up until Roman times, which is a fact that is annoyingly not mentioned in many TV programs discussing this area. The latest culprit was Dan Snow who I saw on TV the other night, presenting a documentary about Petra. In describing the area that Petra is in the middle of he said "In this desert………". It wasn't desert when Petra was at the height of its fame as a trading centre. He and all the other presenters of history on TV should know better and should describe it as it was.

The evidence that the area was not desert as it is today is not just that North Africa was still the 'bread-basket' into Roman times, or that Petra itself could not have been built if it was desert, because there would not have been enough trade. There is evidence how green and productive the Middle East was all over the place. The realisation came to me in 1974 when I was assistant sound recordist with a Yorkshire Television film crew working on "The Arab Experience", a set of 3 documentaries. We were in Saudi Arabia and had flown north of Medina up to Madain Saleh, to film the ruins of the Hejaz railway, that was destroyed by Lawrence of Arabia in the first world war. We were on the side of a valley. The 'main road' along the bottom was just a track and the whole place was sandy desert. Except that is for a single small rectangle of dense foliage in the valley bottom. It may have been perhaps 100 yards wide, for 200 yards along the bottom of the valley, which amounts to around three acres. On one occasion we saw a truck leave and head up the road – it was a dwelling surrounded by lush crops and palm trees. More precisely, it was an artificial oasis with a borehole and a pump scavenging the only water source for miles around, an underground stream. Everywhere else was sand and bare rock. The reason we were at the side of the valley was because were filming some huge rock-cut tombs, carved into fifty-foot high outcrops of sandstone. They are somewhat similar to those you find in Petra and there are lots of them. You can find pictures on Google maps – follow the road north from Medina.

The immediate thought on seeing the rock tombs was to wonder how on earth they could be there. Where was the civilisation that had created them? It must have been wealthy to have been able to afford such effort to cut the huge decorated front faces of the tombs. These are tombs that have been built to impress. The answer of course is that the civilisation is long gone, because the water that flowed in the wadis has gone and the vegetation that fed the town has died. Like Petra it would have been in important trading post on the route down to the Yemeni highlands, in ancient times an important source of frankincense, myrrh and other goods. The valley would have been verdant and productive.

When considering any remains in the Middle East it is important to remember the area was generally not desert up to quite recently, certainly 2000 years ago and maybe even up to 1000 years ago. There will have been some desert area but wherever there are buildings you would be better advised to think of the surroundings being comparable to the vegetation of current-day Greece or Southern Italy. Though there was not by this time the heavy rain that caused the high degree of weathering on the Sphinx, there was sufficient for food plants to grow.

There was something else that trip taught me as well. There was no hotel, so that night we were provided with tents and sleeping bags. Myself and a colleague decided to sleep outside our tent and as we lay we gazed up at the sky. We were 220 miles north of Medina. There was no light pollution within hundreds of miles in any other direction, just occasional individual buildings well closed up for the night. There wasn't a cloud in the sky and there was no moon. It was very dark. But slowly our eyes adjusted to the dark and as if out of nowhere the whole sky started to sparkle with stars. I would never have believed it was possible to see so many with the naked eye unless I had had that experience. There is nowhere in Western Europe that you could go to get a similar view, because you cannot get far enough away from the light pollution of cities..

And I understood at that moment what the night sky meant to people who lived before electric lights were created. It is awe-inspiring and quite wonderful. Gods or priesthoods who could explain what it all amounted to and how it worked would have been very revered.

To come back to the Sphinx, even acknowledging somewhat higher rainfall in the past, the body of the Sphinx and the sides of the quarry it is cut out of are heavily weathered. I am prepared to accept Schoch's view that this can only have happened over a considerably longer period than since the accepted date archeologists believe it was carved out - they think approximately 2500 BC, by the pharaoh Khafre. I also feel that it is very unlikely that the proportions of the shape of the monument would have been originally created so wrong. The size of the head is far too small compared to the size of the body. If it was originally constructed with a pharaoh's head on top of a lion's body, or a lion's head, the head would have been considerably larger. This suggests that the current face was very likely a re-shaping of a much-weathered original head. Whether this was a pharaoh's head or a lion's head is almost irrelevant, the important point being that it pushes the original construction date back.

If it did have a lion's head - and the body most certainly is that of a lion - the key question is why this was the chosen animal for the construction. For which the most obvious answer is that it was built in the age of Leo, when the Leo constellation was the constellation the sun rose into at the vernal (March) equinox. So that the Sphinx would have been facing the sun at sunrise on this most important day, that represents the start of the growing season in the northern hemisphere.

This would put the construction of the Spinx back to around 10,000 years ago. And as the earliest stages of the Sphinx Temple and Valley Temple are acknowledged to have been built with blocks removed from around the Sphinx's body, this would date these constructions to the same time.

If you were a god who had lived through the younger dryas period, helping mankind to survive and develop after the Flood, until the point came when it was possible to start developing large civilisations, you would have been able to choose where these should be started. Baalbeck, your home base is not an option, partially due to it's mountainous territory and partially because you would probably want to keep a base that was more distant from the thousands or hundreds of thousands of humans of the civilisations you expected to develop. The two choices you would have, with reliable water supplies and productive growing land, are the Tigris and Euphrates valleys and the Nile valley.

As we have envisaged the purpose of the religious observances established around Gobekli Tepe as being the key control mechanism for managing humankind, a first step in establishing a civilisation would be to create the religious centre where the humans would regularly gather for indoctrination and to worship you. If you are setting out to build extremely impressive megalithic temples, for which you are going to quarry massive blocks, it would be a very nice idea and a very easy decision to quarry in such a way as to also create a massive monument that would be the talk of the whole region and a clear symbol of your power and omnipotence.

The Great Pyramid at Giza.

If you have established your first major post-Flood civilisation at Giza, this would become the obvious place for any other constructions you needed, that required large amounts of manpower to construct. I would like to suggest that the Valley and Sphinx temples, and the Sphinx, came first, and that the Great Pyramid was constructed a little but not much later. The conventional Egyptologists cannot explain why the technology of pyramid construction appears to have arisen spontaneously and then declined. Other pyramids that they are sure were built by pharaohs later than Khufu, who they credit with building the Great Pyramid, are of much inferior construction and nothing like as complicated.

I have read many books that talk about the great pyramid, with theory piled upon theory. One I particularly remember – though I am afraid I cannot remember its title or author – set out to de-bunk the many theories about aliens constructing it and did a pretty good job. The reason I remember this book is because of the closing comment from the author. Having convinced himself the great pyramid was built by Egyptians for Egyptian purposes, his final line of the book was "But how did they move those stones?".

He was referring to the very large megalithic stones above the Kings chamber. Despite all his careful thinking-through of what could have been achieved by the ancient Egyptians, those massive extremely carefully cut and placed stones above the Kings chamber stumped him.

The main book I suggest you read about the Great Pyramid is The Giza Power Plant by Chris Dunn. The internal arrangements of the great pyramid are so unusual and so unlike anything found in other pyramids that they demand an explanation. And I am afraid that suggesting that the shafts that go up at an angle from the Queens and Kings chambers are aligned to point to certain stars, when they cannot be sighted through and when anyway the Queen's chamber shafts don't reach the outside surface of the pyramid, stretches my credulity too far. The suggestions made by conventional archeologists and scholars of ancient Egypt just don't stack up in my view. I am talking here specifically about the great pyramid. With the large number of pyramids in Egypt in various states of disrepair and collapse it is obvious that the Egyptians did build pyramids. But nowhere else is there a pyramid built so carefully to such an intricate design.

The design is the message. There has got to be a reason for all aspects of the design. Chris Dunn looks at the great pyramid from an engineering point of view. He found persuasive evidence of ultrasonic drilling having been used to make the granite coffer in the Kings chamber. However that is just a detail suggestive that people with high technology built it.

The main theory that Chris Dunn has developed has a lot going for it in my view. The suggestion that is most persuasive for me is his description of the Kings Chamber angled shafts as microwave waveguides. This would make the pyramid a huge power generator, that worked by amplifying a low power microwave signal beamed down one of the shafts, into a much higher power signal beamed up the other shaft. That would imply that the power was received by something in space that was in a geostationary orbit, with a smaller satellite generating the initial microwave beam that was then amplified and given a much higher energy. He also makes the suggestion that the grand gallery was the resonating chamber that built up the energy in the pyramid, that was imparted to the microwave beam. I wonder if that suggestion might possibly throw some light on the purpose of the lobed schist bowl in the Cairo museum mentioned in a previous chapter?

One of the most persuasive pieces of evidence that to me supports Dunn's theory is the way that the copper pins through the 'Gatenbrink doors' have been corroded. The fact that the corrosion is different on the two doors indicates that the environment around them must have been different. This is not just corrosion from air circulating around them, which would have produced similar corrosion on them both. The way the two pins on each door have corroded tells the story. The left hand pin on the northern door has clearly had something deposited on it, whereas the right hand pin has not. The deposit must have come from somewhere. I find Dunn's theories about an electrical cause for the way these pins have been changed very convincing. There is however still a lot of mystery as the 'second doors' behind the first doors have yet to be probed by the Djedi Project. If these prove to be part of the pyramid structure with only rock behind them that will provide a challenge to Dunn's theory. But they may prove to be caps for the shafts with space behind them. Read his book for details of the chemicals he believes the shafts supplied to a reaction in the chamber and the electrolytic effects these would cause on the pins.

I think the only sensible comment that can be made about the great pyramid is 'Watch this space'; there is a lot more yet to be discovered about it. However there seems to be quite a lot of secrecy and politics around the further investigations into the great pyramid and the political situation in Egypt is not conducive to archeology as I write. My view is that on the balance of probabilities the great pyramid was built by some group that had much higher technology than was available in Egypt generally. And it is clear that this technology was not available to later builders of pyramids in Egypt. What the gods may have used it for is a matter for a later chapter.

The evidence of ultrasonic drilling is more confirmation of a group with very high technology. If they were not the gods then some other explanation for who they were will have to be found. Or it will have to be shown that the characteristic marks produced by ultrasonic drilling can be produced another way. The granite container in the Kings chamber of the great pyramid at Giza has been drilled out; the drill marks are still visible inside it. Not only are they visible but according to Chris Dunn it is possible to see the feed-rate of the drill from the spiral lines that the drill has cut into the granite. The drill has also cut the harder parts of the rock more deeply than softer parts.

The only way Chris Dunn can rationalise these facts is if the drilling was done with an ultrasonic drill. The ultrasonic sound transmitted through the drill to the drill bit makes the rock resonate and essentially shake itself to dust where the drill contacts the rock, enabling the very fast feed-rate of the drill into the rock. Harder bits in the rock such as quartz crystals would tend to push an ordinary drill away making it cut a bit more deeply into the other side of the hole, leaving the quartz sticking out. But with an ultrasonic drill the hard rock vibrates more strongly than the softer rock, allowing this counter-intuitive fact of the hard rock being cut more deeply.

It is possible to imagine the Egyptians in the copper age drilling granite with a copper drill, with quartz or other very hard rocks such as gemstones embedded in it, but it is not possible, at least for me, to imagine that they were using an ultrasonic drill. They might have been able to invent ultrasonic whistles such as are used with dogs, but how would they know ultrasonics were involved? The reason sounds at this frequency are called ultrasonic is that they cannot be heard by humans. And anyway, how could they transmit the ultrasonic sound into the drill bit?

Chris Dunn works from the very careful observations of Flinders Petrie so I am prepared to believe the basic facts that cutting lines are visible in the granite and that harder parts are cut more deeply. And none of the explanations proposed by the archeologists as to how this granite box was created come close to believe-ability.

Other developments in the 10,000 to 7000 years ago period.

This is a period where not a lot seems to have changed once development started again after the younger dryas period, until towards the end of the period the first signs of city civilisations appear. Archeologists can distinguish layers in their excavations that they assign to this period. because during the period pottery slowly developed. And they can find artefacts that enable them to gain insight into the development of farming, for example to see how farming spread from the fertile crescent into the rest of Europe.

From the point of view of the gods, this may well have been a calm period when life was returning to how it was before the Flood. Human beings were carrying out their business in their usual stone-age ways. Seafaring may have started again as agriculture produced sufficient surplus to feed the shipbuilders without them having to grow or hunt food for themselves.

But overall we have remarkably little evidence that can tell us what was happening in this period. It is likely that more evidence of what was happening will come from genetic studies, of plants and animals as well as humans. For example is is thought that in the middle of the Americas, beginning as early as 7000 BC, there was domestication of maize, beans, squash and chili, as well as the turkey and dog, causing a transition from paleo-Indian hunter-gatherer tribal grouping to the organization of sedentary agricultural villages.

If we feel that the gods may have had a hand in these developments, this would suggest that they were active in other parts of the world as well as in the fertile crescent.

Of course the real problem in knowing what went on in this period is that we cannot easily date when stone constructions were built, though some techniques are being developed. And any wooden constructions, that might have happened at an earlier period than stone constructions as they would have taken less effort by the relatively small populations, will have decayed. We have only been able to date the constructions at Gobekli Tepe because they were filled in, and the materials used to fill them contained carbon-dateable material. Considering buildings such as the megalithic temples in Egypt, it is possible that these were constructed in this period, but we have no way of definitely knowing.

****

Chapter 22 - 7000 to 3500 years ago

This is the period when the development of our technological capability seems to have taken off. It started as the copper age and then became the bronze age, as the metal workers realised that adding other metals into the copper produced alloys with useful properties. Copper tools were being made in the area that is now Serbia from 4000BC onwards. By the end of the period quite large amounts of tin to make bronze were being mined in North Wales in the Great Orme tin mines, and in Cornwall, the south western part of Great Britain.

I suspect that this development might have been rather unwelcome for the gods. Co-existing with growing numbers of stone-age people, who very largely are awed by your powers, is not a particularly frightening prospect. Co-existing with people making progressively better and better weapons out of metal is a different thing altogether. I cannot write a scenario in which the gods would wish to continue to live alongside humans with the capability to make guns, unless they had completely 'gone native' and decided to live in human societies. Even cross-bow technology would be pretty dangerous because of the speed of the projectile. I can imagine the gods having laser weapons capable of dealing with arrows from long-bows, and beam weapons capable of stopping quite large numbers of humans in their tracks should they attack. And of course weapons capable of mass destruction should whole cities-full of humans get out of control. I can imagine them having force-field systems of some kind, but these are very different from beam weapons because they would need a lot more energy. There are carvings that are believed to show 'gods' where they are carrying hand-held devices. Graham Hancock in Magicians of the gods compares carvings from different areas of the world as to the similarity of the 'bags' the gods are shown carrying. These might be personal safety devices capable of emitting beams of different kinds. But a force-field of the kind beloved of science-fiction writers would need to project energy onto the whole surface of a sphere, continuously, rather than zapping troublemakers with a very short burst of energy. So if they did have force-field technology it could only have been used around their main base or key buildings. And it would need a powerful energy source, maybe perhaps a microwave beam sent back down to earth from a satellite?

So the only scenario I can write at this point, hopefully without spoiling the last chapter (if you haven't already sneaked a look at it!) is one where the gods stop trying to live alongside humans as soon as they develop sophisticated iron metal-working and explosives. That gives us a final date for gods in Asia of 900 years ago, when gunpowder was invented in China, and in the Middle East and Europe a little after that. However the Romans are known to have had very powerful weapons powered by wound-up ropes, and the Greeks are reputed to have used Greek fire, whatever it was, so it is clear that human beings were getting very dangerous by around 3000 years ago when the iron-age was well underway.

To come back to the times we are now discussing, at the start of the copper age, there would have been no reason for the gods to have moved on as yet and hence we may be able to find some constructions or other evidence that they were still around, as follows.

Stonehenge.

Stonehenge is a rather different kind of special place to constructions such as the great pyramid, the Egyptian temples and Baalbeck. It is special because of where it is.

The massive stones that make up the inner henge of Stonehenge are irrelevant to this story. They were a vanity project pursued by someone very powerful at a pretty late stage in the history of Stonehenge. The quarrying of the stones is nothing special. They are a fraction of the size of the Baalbeck stones and not well squared and dressed. Bringing them from the Prescelly mountains would be a task taking care and concentration, but not beyond the people of the time. The other stones are probably only there to make the henge more impressive, at a time when it was being used for religious gatherings.

The most fascinating part of the Stonehenge site to me is the circle of 56 Aubrey holes. These are very probably the earliest construction at Stonehenge and no-one really has a clue what they were for, though some people have speculated they relate to lunar cycles and prediction of eclipses. Whatever the underlying reason is for there being 56 holes, the more important fact that everyone agrees on is that Stonehenge was built as an observatory, to observe the heavens. Archeologists have attempted to date the Aubrey holes, but you can't actually date a hole, you can only date things you find in the bottom of the hole. Working from this the archeologists propose a date for them of late 4th millennium or early 3rd

millennium, in other words at least 5000 years ago. There is no reason why they could not be considerably older. The holes are on average about a metre diameter and 0.75 metres deep. Some people suggest they once held more stones, but for holes that size surely a much better suggestion is that they held wooden posts.

If you wanted to construct a ring of wooden posts you would probably want to make sure they were all set up vertically and you might also have wanted them to be the same height. If you are doing this for a garden fence you make the hole deep enough so that you can get stones under the post, to make it easy to adjust the height of the post with more or less gravel or sand underneath it, and for better drainage. And how deep you dig the hole depends on how high the post is, to ensure it is held securely. Half a metre depth of hole feels to me like a sufficient depth to hold a 2 metre post. You then make the width of the hole about twice as wide as the post, so that you can pack stones and gravel around it to keep it absolutely upright, adjusting this carefully as you fill the hole around the post. So this suggests to me that the posts were 30-40cms diameter and probably about 6 feet high, in other words the height of a person.

So what would you want a circle of posts like this for? Remember that the gods and mankind have survived a very nasty flood that we have suggested was caused by the Earth's crust slipping around the core of the Earth, combined with a comet impact. Keeping an eye on the Earth's axis of rotation could therefore have been rather important. It would be most important to pick up the signs of the crust shifting, and the future position of the pole that was moving to a new location, at the very earliest opportunity. The crust of the Earth has a huge mass. When the force responsible for the displacement first managed to start the crust moving, the movement would be very slow, assuming no external force such as a comet was involved. The force would however continue to accelerate the crust which would move faster and faster until the unbalanced mass on the crust approached the equatorial bulge, when it would start to slow down. If there was only a small population on the Earth that could move to other places, detecting the very earliest stages of crust movement would give time for people to respond. Any groups whose homeland was heading much closer to a pole and hence was likely to be inundated with snow, could be moved.

The way to check how the Earth is rotating is to watch how the stars appear to rotate every night. If you are at the Equator and look North or South you are looking along the rotational axis of the Earth, so the star currently in the direction the axis points will appear on the horizon. You might think that would be OK for checking that the Earth's axis is still perpendicular to where you think the Equator is, but the accuracy of observation would be very low. To check how the Earth's axis moves (and it does slowly through precession) you need to be able to see how the stars around the pole star circle during the night and when they rise above the horizon and set below it (i.e. when the turning of the Earth first gives you a view of the star and when it cuts it off). If you go all the way to the North Pole, the horizon never cuts off your vision of the stars around the pole star. At the Equator the stars around the pole are always very low on the horizon giving poor accuracy of observation as to whether their rising and setting positions are changing. Somewhere between the Equator and the pole there will be a position on the Earth that gives you the best chance to use the horizon cutting off the view of stars to observe the rotation of the Earth. I'm not an astronomer but logic suggests to me this is probably latitude 45 degrees, half-way from the Equator to the pole.

So the problem faced by the gods and mankind after the flood, if they wanted to observe Earth's rotation carefully, would be to build an observatory in the best place. There were no complex computer-based instruments available to humans at that time, so the process of observation would have to be a person standing in a field watching the stars rise and set and noting where this was relative to features on the ground. To make calculation easy it would be good if the horizon was flat in all directions, with no trees or hills sticking up higher than the tops of the posts. If you want to use the horizon as the check point for the time a star disappears from view, rather than when a star goes below the tops of the posts, for good accuracy of observation it would be good if the horizon is a long way away, making it less important to get your eye at precisely the same level every night. The posts would still be important because they would define precisely where on the horizon the star disappears.

So let's have a look at what the Earth is like at latitude 45 degrees or thereabouts. 45 degrees south is very wet. This latitude contains just about the maximum amount of sea possible, passing south of Australia and going over just a tiny bit of mountainous land in Patagonia. So this would not be a good choice for an observatory. 45 degrees north has more possibilities. Coming west from the Pacific this line of latitude passes over the mountains of Korea and North China and heads off across the Gobi desert; pretty flat but not a nice place to live. Passing the end of the Himalayas the land gets flat again by the Aral sea, but this is still pretty much desert. As soon as you get to the Caspian sea there are the Caucasian mountains, so the horizon won't be flat and this problem continues across the Balkans, the Alps and the Massif Central. I am going to ignore possibilities in America as we have decided the Gods and mankind were starting again in the Middle East, and crossing the Atlantic to get to their observatory is rather too far to go.

The Caucasian mountains do contain an ancient observatory, Zorats Karer. It is estimated to be 7500 years old. It is in a mountainous area but is a fair distance away from the peaks that stick up above the horizon, so the horizon is fairly level. It is more than 5000 feet above sea level, so in the Winter would be snow covered and a rather cold place to work.

As 45 degrees north does not look good for an observatory and coming a bit south is if anything more mountainous or sea, best option is to look a bit further north. Europe north of the Alps would in all likelihood have been covered in thick forest, which would have left the observers trying to judge when a star rose or set behind trees. Only at the coast would there have been grasslands, kept free of bigger trees by the winds carrying salt. The Lowlands of France and Belgium are precisely that, low lands and the view inland would have been wooded. But just over the Channel is England, and usefully close to the coast there are chalk downs that rise above the low lands, that similarly to the continent would have been covered by trees.

Chalk downland creates very harsh environmental conditions, including summer heat and drought, winter frosts and poor soil nutrient. Trees therefore don't tend to grow on the tops of the Dorset downs and Salisbury Plain. For centuries the landscape here has been further managed by grazing animals, which stops taller plants growing, but even in ancient times it is quite possible that Salisbury plain gave a view in all directions to a distant horizon. If you go to Stonehenge now you will find that the horizon is not far from being flat. And Stonehenge would have been pretty easy to get to, for the gods or for the priests they had tutored in astronomy. If their home base was in the Mediterranean they could have sailed up the coasts of Spain and France and then taken a fairly short sea crossing of only a couple of hundred miles to the Severn Estuary, alighting north of Bristol and then traveling along the Mendips to Stonehenge.

I suggest to you that Stonehenge is the major astronomical observatory of the ancient world. It is special because of where it is and how the site enables observation of the night sky.

Skara Brae and the Ring of Brodgar.

There are numerous stone circles in Scotland that have been carefully investigated by Alexander Thom. He demonstrated that what appear initially to be somewhat irregular circles are in fact combinations of circular and elliptical parts, indicating that they have been laid out mathematically and carefully. From his study of these circles and his measurement of them, he proposed that there was a standard 'megalithic yard' unit of length used in laying out the circles. A standard unit would imply a 'standards authority' and a degree of coordination of the construction of the stone circles that archeologists don't believe existed, resulting in them being dismissive of the idea of a megalithic yard. The debate still rumbles on. Whether or not Thom is right the importance of stone circles to the populace in Scotland is undoubted. And one of these Scottish stone circles is rather special.

The Ring of Brodgar is important. It's the 3rd largest stone circle in the UK, after Stonehenge and Avebury. As with all the stone circles the traditional explanation is that it is a ritual site. And indeed it may well have become such, but that may not have been its original purpose. Like Stonehenge when it was just the Aubrey postholes it may originally have been just an observatory, with the ditch acting in the same way as the wire fences we now put around scientific sites, to keep out animals. It was a pretty significant undertaking as the surrounding ditch is cut into the sandstone bedrock. It would have needed a lot of manpower.

Skara Brae is around 5 miles from the Ring of Brodgar, which is only a 90 minute walk – almost commuting distance! There are quite a lot of people nowadays who travel 90 minutes to work. The Skara Brae site and the Ring of Brodgar may very well have been linked. Between them Stonehenge and Ring of Brodgar are at the extremes of the British Isles, one south and one north. We of course don't know their original purpose but if they were astronomical observatories it sort of makes sense to have them well separated if you wanted to make comparative observations. Travel between the two observatories would have been by boat up the coasts of England and Scotland.

However it is Skara Brae that fascinates me more than the Ring of Brodgar. It may just have been a village. Or it might have been used as a village in later times, but I wonder if it was built as a normal village. The issue is that the excavated rooms are extremely high-status and virtually identical, built to the same design. And they are en-suite. They have a drainage system and even a kind of toilet. This is rather a startling fact. Now that in the western world interior plumbing is the norm it is hard to realise just how recently this has become so. When I was a student in Leeds in the early 1970s, the terraced house we lived in had the toilet in the back yard. And the house was certainly not at the bottom of the housing ladder. The houses the other side of the street were back-to-back houses and didn't even have back yards. They had a set of four communal toilets on the middle of the terrace that served all the houses on that side of the street. So instead of sneaking across the back yard in your pyjamas it was necessary for them to don an overcoat and to walk half way up the street if they wanted to go to the loo in the night. Hence chamber pots were still popular. In times earlier than the last couple of hundred years, it was only palaces and castles that had internal toilet facilities.

In a village it is natural that there would have been similarities between family dwellings but it doesn't strike me as natural that they would be built virtually identical. The extra effort to cut stones to similar sizes to make the cupboards, dressers, seats, and storage boxes would not have been worthwhile and surely there would have been some individual preferences if they were going to that effort. So why are they virtually identical?

The only place nowadays where you find identical very high-status rooms is in expensive hotels. Others have suggested that these constructions might have been homes to a 'privileged theocratic class' engaged in mounting rituals at the Ring of Brodgar. I suggest the inhabitants might have been a privileged scientific group, who visited every so often to check on the people engaged in the regular astronomical observations being made at Brodgar. Or possibly even visiting gods. You will have to make your own mind up as to what you think these rooms were used for.

Newgrange.

Newgrange in Ireland is almost as fascinating as Stonehenge and its purpose appears rather easier to unpick, as it is not a ring of posts as Stonehenge probably was at first. Stonehenge could be a multi-purpose observatory, but Newgrange appears at first sight to be single purpose. It was constructed about 5,200 years ago (3200BC). It was never a tomb as it is sometimes described, because the passage has to remain open for it to fulfill its purpose. On the Winter solstice the sun shines right down the 19 metre passage and illuminates the chamber at the far end very brightly for 17 minutes.

Confirming that the sun and Earth are continuing to rotate as they should and that Spring is on the way would be very important for the local community. Ireland is an island and if it had a sizable population it would be sensible for them to have their own observatory. The Sun being observed to be shining as it should would then confirm that all was well with the world. No doubt The associated rituals would confirm for the populace that the considerable effort in building Newgrange had been worth it.

But Newgrange does something else as well, according to Christopher Knight and Robert Lomas in their book Uriels Machine. Venus orbits in a 40 year cycle relative to the Earth. The pattern of the orbits repeats itself precisely every 40 years. There is also an 8 year cycle when Venus appears in the same place in the sky, but with some differences in the brightness with which Venus reflects the sun and how long before or after the sun it rises and sets on the day the cycle repeats. There are four occasions in the 8 year cycle when Venus rises before the sun on the Winter solstice, but on just one of those occasions, the time when it is brightest, its light passes through the same opening in Newgrange that lets the sun illuminate the end chamber. For about 15 minutes before the sun rises it is Venus that illuminates the chamber.

Knight and Lomas state that the Newgrange passage seems to be designed with curves to minimise the amount by which the coming light of dawn interferes with this effect. I am taking the authors at their word as the easily accessible information I can find on Newgrange focuses purely on the Winter solstice alignment and does not mention the Venus connection, so this is one of those things on the list for further research if I get the time. But assuming it's true, why would people in ancient times want to keep such a close eye on Venus? Was this actually designed in, or is it just sheer chance that Newgrange can confirm that Venus is in its correct place as well as confirming that the Sun is? If it was designed in to the structure it indicates some very advanced astronomical knowledge, so in this case it is certainly evidence of an advanced priesthood, and possibly evidence for the gods being around in this area at the time.

The end of the Old Kingdom in Egypt.

Archeologists talk about the earliest phase of high civilisation in Egypt as the Early Dynastic Period and the Old Kingdom. They are not really two separate periods. They count the Early Dynastic Period as starting with the unification of upper and lower Egypt under one pharaoh in 3100BC, with this period merging into the Old Kingdom in 2686 BC when a more powerful pharaoh came to power. The differentiation between the two periods is really just a matter of differences in architecture and the start, in the Old Kingdom, of much larger architectural projects.

What is of interest to this story is happenings around the end of the Old Kingdom, which happened around 2180 BC. There then appears to be a gap of 25 years or so during which there are no records of kings or pharaohs having control. Professor Fekri Hassan has researched this period, as has Dr Sarah Parcak who uses imagery from space satellites to detect the sites of lost civilisations. They propose that there was a sudden change in climate at the start of this period, which has been confirmed by the Earth Observatory at Columbia University. They reckon there was a change in the circulation of the Earth's weather systems, which led to a much drier climate in the horn of Africa - Ethiopia and the surrounding countries. The implication of this is that the Nile floods, which arrive predictably every year from the rainfall that happens in Ethiopia, could have very seriously declined. This would have led to the Nile valley being much less fertile and hence a collapse in food supplies.

Those who can interpret the hieroglyphs of Egyptian writing of this period report that they tell of terrible famines with people resorting to cannibalism and a complete breakdown of law and order. If the Nile valley at this period had a population of 2 million you can imagine the scale of the riots that may have happened as people desperate for food took the law into their own hands. Egypt would have been a very dangerous place to be at this time. Wikipedia discusses this as "The 4.2 kiloyear BP aridification event (which) was one of the most severe climatic events of the Holocene period in terms of impact on cultural upheaval.", and states that it also caused the collapse of the Akkadian empire in Mesopotamia.

Up to this point in our story we have the gods resident in this area of the world. In the light of this climactic disaster causing the population to rise up against their pharaohs and kings, with mass disorder happening, we must ask whether the gods remaining in this area was viable. No matter what degree of control the gods had over humans, willingness to worship gods that had allowed mass famine to occur would be very low. And whereas the gods may have helped humans in another period of famine, when the younger dryas period hit, that would have been a matter of helping small groups of humans that had survived the flood. The picture now would be very different. Strategies to help small numbers of humans would not work with millions.

The only response the gods could make to this development would have been to move away from the areas where there were large populations and to retreat to a safer place. There would be no safer places in Egypt or Mesopotamia, so the only choice in the Middle East would have been Baalbeck.

But perhaps this was the trigger that suggested to the gods that their time on Earth might be running out. As mankind became more technologically competent, as would inevitably happen once they got over this sudden climate change, the difference between the capabilities of the gods and humans would get progressively less. The techniques the gods had used to maintain a separation and worship by humans worked well with stone-age humans, progressively less well as mankind developed metallurgy - which by this time had progressed to bronze. It would only be a matter of time before the iron-age happened - around 700 years as it turned out.

Perhaps this was the time that the gods decided to move to another area of the world where mankind was still existing in a stone age?

****

Chapter 23 - 3500 to 2000 years ago; the Middle East and Europe.

However before I leave the Middle East and Europe in this story, to look at possible evidence of the gods in the Americas, it is worth considering whether the gods would have maintained a presence this side of the Atlantic. If they did it would very likely be a matter of them coming back to visit for some reason, to check up on mankind's development and maybe to continue to influence the leaders of mankind. It could also be possible that some gods did remain in this area of the world, despite the growing danger.

We can therefore ask whether there are any stories or other evidence that indicate that this might have happened. So the sections below make some speculations about hard-to-explain things.

I will start with the story in the bible of Ezekiel's vision of god. Ezekiel is reckoned to have lived around 600BC, in other words 2600 years ago.

Ezekiel's story.

Ezekiel's story fits into a category of evidence to which I give a reasonable amount of weight, stories with an inexplicable amount of detail.

If you set about creating a story to entertain or to deceive, and you want it to be easily believable, it is best not to add in detail that others might consider 'off the wall'. It breaks the believability of the story and you lose the attention of people while they weigh up how to think about that bit of the story. The best deceptions contain grains of truth which are then embroidered and developed in ways that are just believable. This is why stories of abduction by aliens tend not to get much coverage. Most people simply don't believe them so the stories only persist on the fringes of a society's stories of its history. So when I come across a story that has detail included that seems unnecessary and unhelpful in making the story believable, I tend to take notice and think a bit harder about it.

Try this section of the Bible as an example of a story with inexplicable detail (slightly edited to focus on what Ezekiel said):

Ezekiel's Vision of God:

"Now it came to pass in the thirtieth year, in the fourth month, on the fifth day of the month, as I was among the captives by the River Chebar, that the heavens were opened and I saw visions of God.

Then I looked, and behold, a whirlwind was coming out of the North, a great cloud with raging fire engulfing itself; and brightness was all around it and radiating out of its midst like the color of amber, out of the midst of the fire.

Also from within it came the likeness of four living creatures. And this was their appearance: they had the likeness of a man. Each one had four faces, and each one had four wings. Their legs were straight, and the soles of their feet were like the soles of calves' feet. They sparkled like the color of burnished bronze. The hands of a man were under their wings on their four sides; and each of the four had faces and wings. Their wings touched one another. The creatures did not turn when they went, but each one went straight forward.

As for the likeness of their faces, each had the face of a man; each of the four had the face of a lion on the right side, each of the four had the face of an ox on the left side, and each of the four had the face of an eagle. Thus were their faces. Their wings stretched upward; two wings of each one touched one another, and two covered their bodies. And each one went straight forward; they went wherever the spirit wanted to go, and they did not turn when they went.

As for the likeness of the living creatures, their appearance was like burning coals of fire, like the appearance of torches going back and forth among the living creatures. The fire was bright, and out of the fire went lightning. And the living creatures ran back and forth, in appearance like a flash of lightning.

Now as I looked at the living creatures, behold, a wheel was on the earth beside each living creature with its four faces. The appearance of the wheels and their workings was like the color of beryl, and all four had the same likeness. The appearance of their workings was, as it were, a wheel in the middle of a wheel. When they moved, they went toward any one of four directions; they did not turn aside when they went.

As for their rims, they were so high they were awesome; and their rims were full of eyes, all around the four of them. When the living creatures went, the wheels went beside them; and when the living creatures were lifted up from the earth, the wheels were lifted up. Wherever the spirit wanted to go, they went, because there the spirit went; and the wheels were lifted together with them, for the spirit of the living creatures was in the wheels. When those went, these went; when those stood, these stood; and when those were lifted up from the earth, the wheels were lifted up together with them, for the spirit of the living creatures was in the wheels.

The likeness of the firmament above the heads of the living creatures was like the color of an awesome crystal, stretched out over their heads. And under the firmament their wings spread out straight, one toward another. Each one had two which covered one side, and each one had two which covered the other side of the body. When they went, I heard the noise of their wings, like the noise of many waters, like the voice of the Almighty, a tumult like the noise of an army; and when they stood still, they let down their wings. A voice came from above the firmament that was over their heads; whenever they stood, they let down their wings.

And above the firmament over their heads was the likeness of a throne, in appearance like a sapphire stone; on the likeness of the throne was a likeness with the appearance of a man high above it. Also from the appearance of His waist and upward I saw, as it were, the color of amber with the appearance of fire all around within it; and from the appearance of His waist and downward I saw, as it were, the appearance of fire with brightness all around. Like the appearance of a rainbow in a cloud on a rainy day, so was the appearance of the brightness all around it. This was the appearance of the likeness of the glory of the Lord."

Ezekiel obviously only saw this once and it left him with an incredibly vivid vision, which he could recall but had difficulty describing. Josef F. Blumrich wrote a book called 'The Spaceships of Ezekiel'. Blumrich was chief of NASA's Systems Layout Branch of the Program Development Office at the Marshall Space Flight. He analysed Ezekiel's description to see if he could make any sense of it, really with the intention of disproving that it was some kind of spaceship, as Von Daniken and others had suggested. However he decided instead that they might indeed be right, coming to the conclusion that the builders of the craft must have had technology somewhat higher than our own. Needless to say various critics derided his efforts and you will have to decide for yourself whether Blumrich merely said that he found it convincing that Ezekiel had seen an extra-terrestrial craft, in order to sell the book, or whether he had personally convinced himself.

What Blumrich worked on was the amount of detail Ezekiel reported. We have to remember that Ezekiel is reputed to have lived around 600BC. If so, then at this time iron was in use for swords and other weapons and some domestic uses, but Ezekiel would never have seen a machine constructed of metal, or a powered machine. Imagine how he might have described a helicopter if he could not have seen the pilot. The only images that he has to use as metaphors are living things or the very simple wooden machines they would have had. He recognises wheels on which it moves, but they are 'wheels within wheels'. And he is very confused that it can move in different directions without turning the wheels, because all the things he knows of that move on wheels have to turn the wheels to move sideways, but this machine didn't. This led Blumrich to come up with a very ingenious 'wheels within wheels' system that would be able to move in any direction without turning, essentially a sort of circular wheel that could rotate and move along the direction it was aligned, that was itself made up of rollers that could move the machine sideways at the same time, independently of the forward/backward motion in the direction the wheel was pointing.

There is a wealth of material in ancient texts that might describe things ancient people actually saw but could not describe. Try describing a smartphone in action without using the concepts of display screen, touch-screen, button, speaker, radio, voice analysis, movement sensors, GPS or the Internet. I suspect your description will sound as confused as Ezekiel's.

If we believe this story, and if the bible is correct in describing when Ezekiel lived, this story suggests that the gods visited the Middle East in 600 BC. This is pretty much the same time as Solon was receiving the story of Atlantis from the Egyptian priests and presumably not questioning the idea that certain gods had been responsible for founding both Greek and Egyptian cities. But we don't find many stories of visitations by gods in the Middle East in this period, so we may have to come to the conclusion that they were no longer living at Baalbeck at this time. They certainly must have moved on from Baalbeck by the time the Romans built the temple of Jupiter there, in the first century AD.

Sodom and Gomorrah.

The story of Sodom and Gomorrah in the bible almost comes into my category of stories that have inexplicable detail. Unfortunately the amount of detail that has come down to us is very thin. The essence of the story is that two 'angels dressed as men' came to persuade Lot to leave the city where he lived. Presumably this was so that he was not caught up in the impending destruction of the two cities. The nature of the 'wickedness' that caused the cities to be targeted for destruction could be an invention by the writers of the story. Whatever it was it must have been very severe to require complete destruction of the cities. Then, in the process of leaving, Lot's wife looked back at the city, as it was destroyed with 'brimstone and fire' and she was turned into a pillar of salt.

The story is strange. 'Brimstone and fire' tends to refer to volcanic eruptions with great heat, material being thrown into the sky and then descending and acrid sulphur smells. But there is no evidence of volcanic activity in the area where Sodom and Gomorrah are supposed to have been, North East of the Red Sea. It sounds to me that the description of the destruction is of massive explosions in or over the cities. Imagine how biblical writers would describe the nuclear explosions that destroyed Hiroshima and Nagasaki. Searching online for 'ancient atomic warfare' will take you to numerous pages of speculation on this topic, looking at areas all over the world and utilising stories from ancient Indian and other sources – and of course material debunking these speculations. We must however remember that 'city' in those days would have meant what we nowadays would probably call a town, perhaps the size of the walled towns of York or Chester in England. Hence a blast that killed everyone in the towns might have been achievable with explosives that would not leave radiation behind. Though the bit about

Lot's wife is suggestive of some kind of radiation weapon.

The biblical dating for the story of Sodom and Gomorrah is around 1712 BC, just before the birth of Isaac. However archeological information that I sourced from Aish.com suggests a date of around 2300BC. The remains of cemeteries found in this area suggest there were 5 cities all with substantial populations. From information in the Torah, on the eastern bank of the Dead Sea there were apparently five cities, each with its own king, Bera, king of Sodom, Birsha, king of Gomorrah, Shinab, king of Admad, Shember, king of Zeboiim, and the king of Bela, which is also called Zoar (Genesis 14:8). This thriving group of city-states is referred to in the Bible (Genesis 13:12) as the Cities of the Plain. The five kings were under the dominion of a coalition of eastern Mesopotamian overlords. According to the Torah, with the help of the patriarch Abraham, the cities gained their independence, though their independence was only short-lived. A few years later, God destroyed the cities in a hail of fire and brimstone. So perhaps it was not just Sodom and Gomorrah that were destroyed, but the whole area.

The archeological evidence provides some other rather fascinating facts. Many of the skeletons found in the cemeteries were rather tall for an ancient people, between 5ft 9inches and 6ft 4inches tall. The archeologists attribute this to the excellent diet the inhabitants of these cities had, of which there is ample evidence in the remains of plants and seeds that have been found. As earlier in this story I speculated that there were both true-blood gods and the progeny of mating between gods and humans, could we be looking at the skeletons of the descendants of half-god half-human people? Make of this what you will, I just offer it as a possible component of a different way of looking at history.

I must also say that I find the phrase quoted on the Aish site, that "The five kings were under the dominion of a coalition of eastern Mesopotamian overlords." quite fascinating. The interesting word is 'coalition'. We are used to thinking of ancient civilisations being large empires ruled by pharaohs or kings, not of several overlords who trusted each other sufficiently to govern a large area as a coalition. And then also added into this mix is the role of Abraham, the Patriarch of the jews, who is said to have helped the kings of the 'cities of the plain' to gain their independence from these overlords. If a small group of true gods were living as overlords of cities of humans, who were kept in check and in awe of these gods by patriarchs, one can imagine the true gods not wanting any half-gods to be living amongst the humans, as that would tend to reduce the respect and awe in which the humans held the true gods. Perhaps better that any half-gods were made to live in places separated by quite some distance from the homes of the true gods. From the Mesopotamian cities of old to the area around the Jordan where the 'cities of the plains' were is some 500 miles.

Was the destruction of the cities of the plain really the destruction of a whole community of half-gods? Pure speculation of course and not something that I consider sufficiently on the right side of my skepticism threshold to be considered evidence to support this story, but something to keep in mind as an area of archeology to be watched.

Queen Hapshepsut's expedition to the land of Punt.

Hapshepsut came to the throne in 1478BC, approximately 3,500 years ago. This is right at the start of the iron age. Elites of this period would have had access to iron weapons but it is likely that armies still used bronze weapons. Large scale iron production did not start until around 1200BC, some 200 years after Hapshepsut's reign.

The reason for including mention of her is because of the stories around her expedition to the land of Punt, which was the major expedition of her life to a neighbouring civilisation. It is believed that Punt was a civilisation based in the horn of Africa, in the area that is now Somalia. It was a trade expedition, to establish trading links between the Egyptian and Punt civilisations.

The point of interest for this story, is that various of the sources that discuss her expedition state that Hapshepsut was directed to undertake the expedition by the god Amun-Ra. Hapshepsut is described as making a petition at the stairs of the sanctum of the god and hearing the command from the great throne to seek out ways to reach the land of Punt. At that time the treasures that Egypt got from punt, such as leopard skins, ivory, spices, precious woods, cosmetics, incense, aromatic gum, and frankincense came via a circuitous route through Arabia, presumably having been shipped from the horn of Africa to where Yemen now is. Hapshepsut's expedition established a new route by ship down the red sea, the overland route over the Ethiopian highlands presumably being too difficult.

The Ancient Origins website has a useful description of this but you can find other sources quite easily. Whether you believe that the story is true and that a god lived in an inner sanctum of the temple at Karnak is up to you. However this is not the only story of ancient kings being directed by the words from a god. The bible contains several such stories.

Vitrified forts.

Vitrified forts, like the last section, are not really part of the evidence base for the gods that I am presenting in this book, but they just might be. They are one of those mysteries that needs explaining. They may or may not have been forts, nobody knows. They are crude stone walls enclosing flat summits, many of them in Scotland but they are also found elsewhere. The mystery is that no-one knows how the heat was applied to vitrify the rock. It takes a great deal of heat to melt rock, needing temperatures of the order of 1000 degrees centigrade applied for a sufficient period.

Robert Schoch, one of the few people in archeology who does follow scientific facts of unexplained artefacts has written about these and postulated atmospheric 'plasma events' to provide the heat. The suggestions of other archeologists that the heat came from a great deal of wood piled around the walls and kept burning for a long time, or of wooden palisades on the tops of the walls having been burnt are almost laughable. Wood burns between 300 and 600 degrees centigrade, nowhere near hot enough. When wood is used to smelt iron it is first converted to charcoal and then blown with bellows in a confined kiln; you could not do similarly to a significant part of the top of a rampart around a summit. And it certainly does seem from the way that it is usually the top and tops of the sides that are most vitrified, that the heat came from above. However if Schoch is right and it was atmospheric plasma events why did this not affect rocks all over in different places? Why is the vitrification limited just to rocks surrounding flat summits?

The forts in Scotland are estimated to have been built between 900BC and 900AD. This was a period in the iron age when people knew how to create sufficiently high temperatures to melt rock, but no-one has any idea how this technology could have been applied on such a large scale. And if we were to take this as some evidence of the gods, we would have to find a reason why they wanted to land in so many places, in Scotland, Ireland, France and Germany.

****

Chapter 24 - 4200 to 2000 years ago in America

The Saksaywaman stone walls at Cusco.

Moving to the Americas, there is the site of the Saksayaman citadel at Cusco in the Peruvian Andes. There are plenty of images online of the walls of the citadel and those in the town, made of blocks incredibly well jointed at crazy angles. I find the walls in the town most persuasive. I can just about imagine humans going to the trouble of cutting crazy angled blocks for the citadel to make it imposing, but I can't imagine them going to the same trouble for ordinary straight walls along the sides of streets in the town.

The stones in these town walls are roughly rectangular and could have been stacked to make a wall without precisely fitting them. The fitting has either been done by incredibly careful measurement to cut blocks precisely before they were place, or it has been done by some kind of technology that cuts the surfaces of both top and bottom block once they are in situ, allowing the blocks to mould against each other.

When it comes to the wall built of polygonal blocks this issue is taken to the extreme. If you have ever done woodwork to re-furbish an old house, as I have, you rapidly discover that it is extremely hard to measure angles that are not right-angles. You can use templates that are cut by trial and error, but it is hard to get them completely precise particularly if you are dealing with more than one angle. I had to fit skirting board around a chimney breast that had both sloping sides and a sloping front. The only way to cut the joints at the corners was to put the boards in situ and mark-up where they needed to be cut relative to the sloping walls and the other board it had to join to. And then to very carefully align the saw and cut very slowly following the marked lines.

But I was cutting an outside corner that I could get at to mark. The stones in the polygonal wall have had their inside corners cut to very great precision. I could imagine doing this if the front surface of the wall was completely flat, so that a stone could be held against the outside surface and marked relative to the surfaces it would butt up against. There would have to be great care taken to make sure these were cut at right angles to the faces of the stone that would be on the exposed surfaces of the wall. But the stones don't have flat face surfaces against which to measure the angles. Again it looks very much as though these stones must have been cut in situ by some device similar to a laser that could remove and blast out of the crack any pieces of the stone stopping the stones fitting completely perfectly together.

And to top it all the stone used is andesite, which has a hardness of 7 on the mohs scale. It could only have been cut with something harder or with an energy beam.

Elongated skulls.

I have placed this section on elongated skulls in this chapter on the period leading up to 2000 years ago, because many of the finds of elongated skulls are in Peru and date to this period, but there is evidence from several parts of the world of skulls that are considerably elongated, over a long period of time. Statues of Egyptian Pharaohs and their children, and those thought to be of the Sumerian gods often have considerably elongated skulls, or headgear that could cover such a skull.

There are cultures around the world that are known to have practised deformation of infants' skulls, by binding and the use of boards to flatten the forehead. But there are also reports of a foetus found in a mummy with an elongated skull, where the foetus also had the elongation. And archeologists have reported on elongated skulls that appear to be natural and which show no signs of having been artificially deformed. The report of feotuses in utero with elongated skulls I found on the Ancient Origins website (http://www.ancient-origins.net/unexplained-phenomena/elongated-skulls-utero-farewell-artificial-cranial-deformation-paradigm-002526), drawing from Rivero and Tschudi'e book and stating:

"Rivero and Tschudi in Peruvian Antiquities (1851 Spanish, 1853 English) argue that the protagonists of the artificial cranial deformation hypothesis are mistaken, since they had only considered the skulls of adults". In other words, the hypothesis fails to take into account the skulls of infants and, most importantly, foetuses which had similar elongated skull shape.

It is worth quoting Rivero and Tschudi: "We ourselves have observed the same fact [of the absence of signs of artificial pressure] in many mummies of children of tender age, who, although they had cloths about them, were yet without any vestige or appearance of pressure of the cranium. More still: the same formation of the head presents itself in children yet unborn; and of this truth we have had convincing proof in the sight of a foetus, enclosed in the womb of a mummy of a pregnant woman, which we found in a cave of Huichay, two leagues from Tarma, and which is, at this moment, in our collection."

The author of the report provides various links and references that can be followed up if you wish. And on the web there are numerous images that can be found, some of which look to me pretty convincing. The skulls in videos made by Brien Foerster seem to me to be elongated to an extent that could not be achieved through deformation. I would like to know what the brain capacity of these skulls is. It is easy to imagine a young person's head being forced to grow into a different shape from a normal skull shape, but I see no reason why that should cause the skull to develop a much larger volume inside the skull. Yet some of these skulls don't seem to be much narrower than normal skulls which would mean the elongation also means greater brain capacity – the brain can hardly remain the same size as that for normal humans if the skull is much bigger, as even if surrounded by fluid it would bounce around inside the skull and suffer damage. There are reports that some of the skulls have a brain capacity 25% greater than normal humans and have some differences in bone structure.

However rather than pursue a lengthy process to try to validate whether the skulls found are the result of mechanical deformation or represent a genetic difference, I want to ask how the practice developed. What was the trigger to cause parents to do this to their children? If all these skulls were created this way, starting when a baby was very small and the skull still soft, what on earth made a parent somewhere start this process?

It must have been very important as it will have involved considerable trouble and quite possibly a fair bit of pain for the child. The usual reason given is that people with elongated skulls are presumed to have high status in the society and it was done to confer this high status on the children. This is a reasonable supposition once the practice had got going, but how did it start in the first place? Was there a race of humans who had elongated skulls but which has now died out, who had higher status than 'normal' humans? And if so where did that race emerge from?

You will find reports of DNA sequencing from these skulls, but it has been done privately and not fully released and has not been replicated by 'accepted' academic institutions. Which is of course the usual problem. 'Accepted' and 'reputable' academic institutions don't want to associate themselves with an area of study that immediately generates headlines about 'aliens', so the field is left to people who are willing to explore in more depth but who may or may not be reputable and who may not be after the desire for academic insight rather than profit.

I suggest you look at the available pictures and make up your own mind whether there was a human race who naturally had skulls that were elongated. That elongated skulls exist is not in doubt, and that we have images of gods and pharaohs that are depicted with elongated skulls is also undeniable. So the link between this skull shape and people of elevated status is also clear.

If our story is correct and there were gods with elongated skulls, it becomes relatively easy to imagine that a human king or leader might decide to try and prove their link to divine beings by subjecting their baby to skull deformation. People will do an awful lot for power. And if there was interbreeding between gods and humans, their progeny might well have had a mixture of skull shapes, some elongated and some not. Which might well cause the start of an artificial process to elongate the skulls of offspring with a human shaped skull instead of god-shaped.

****

Chapter 25 - 2000 to 1000 years ago.

The Inca God Viracocha.

You can find various descriptions of the Inca legends about Viracocha online. This one is from wikipedia - Cosmogony according to Spanish accounts:

"According to a myth recorded by Juan de Betanzos, Viracocha rose from Lake Titicaca (or sometimes the cave of Paqariq Tampu) during the time of darkness to bring forth light. He made the sun, moon, and the stars. He made mankind by breathing into stones, but his first creation were brainless giants that displeased him. So he destroyed it with a flood and made a new, better one from smaller stones. Viracocha eventually disappeared across the Pacific Ocean (by walking on the water), and never returned. He wandered the earth disguised as a beggar, teaching his new creations the basics of civilization, as well as working numerous miracles. He wept when he saw the plight of the creatures he had created. It was thought that Viracocha would re-appear in times of trouble. Pedro Sarmiento de Gamboa wrote that Viracocha was described as "a man of medium height, white and dressed in a white robe like an alb secured round the waist, and that he carried a staff and a book in his hands.

In one legend Viracocha had one son, Inti, and two daughters, Mama Killa and Pachamama. In this legend, he destroyed the people around Lake Titicaca with a Great Flood called Unu Pachakuti, saving two to bring civilization to the rest of the world, these two beings are Manco Cápac, the son of Inti (sometimes taken as the son of Viracocha), which name means "splendid foundation", and Mama Uqllu, which means "mother fertility". These two founded the Inca civilization carrying a golden staff, called 'tapac-yauri'. In another legend, he fathered the first eight civilized human beings. In some stories, he has a wife called Mama Qucha.

In another legend, Viracocha had two sons, Imahmana Viracocha and Tocapo Viracocha. After the Great Flood and the Creation, Viracocha sent his sons to visit the tribes to the Northeast and Northwest to determine if they still obeyed his commandments. Viracocha himself traveled north. During their journey, Imaymana and Tocapo gave names to all the trees, flowers, fruits, and herbs. They also taught the tribes which of these were edible, which had medicinal properties, and which were poisonous.

Eventually, Viracocha, Tocapo and Imahmana arrived at Cusco (in modern-day Peru) and the Pacific seacoast where they walked across the water until they disappeared. The word "Viracocha" literally means "Sea Foam."

The parallels with the story in the bible are obvious, suggesting at least a common experience and maybe a common source. It is worth noting that the elevation of Lake Titicaca is 3812 metres, over 11,000 feet, making it impossible for it to have suffered from flooding from the sea. However the lake is big enough to create a tsunami-like flood if shaken by a severe earthquake. As Titicaca is on the longitude that I have suggested experienced the most movement due to earth crust displacement, that the comet accelerated, this might be the cause of a flood severe enough to create the legends. If this is the case, it could mean that the earliest constructions at Tiwanaku predate the Flood, and could be evidence of consructions by the gods in an earlier period. As the next section discusses, the gods were certainly here at some point.

Puma Punku at Tiwanaku.

Searching online for images of drilled stone blocks will produce for you a huge range of pictures showing accurately drilled ancient stone blocks. The search will also produce links to numerous sites speculating about these blocks and whether they are evidence for the ancient aliens.There is a good video that will give you an overview of the Puma Punku site at http://www.youtube.com/watch?v=wPWbn8bn1VE.

If you try to get deeper than this and to find proper archeological investigations of these stones, information seems to be rather thin on the ground. It seems that not many archeologists want to do detailed investigation of how these stones were drilled. However despite this lack of solid investigation I am prepared to include them as evidence for our story.

I suggest you focus on just one of the stones and look carefully at the sharpness and precision of the cutting. It is obvious from all these images that whoever cut the stones had the ability to easily drill holes of varying sizes, from 6mm up to several centimetres in diameter. It is just about possible to suppose that some South American civilisation could do this. Though there is no evidence of the smelting of iron in South America before the arrival of the Spaniards, they did have gold and copper-working capabilities. Dating evidence puts the construction of Puma Punku at somewhere between 500AD and 600AD, though this might relate to later phases of construction, not when the drilled blocks were made. By this time there is evidence of the smelting of copper, not just the use of naturally occurring copper. I can just about imagine different sized rods of copper being made, and used with sand being rotated back and forth to grind the rather hard rock to make a hole. Once the hole was started a decent amount of pressure could be applied to the top of the rod as it was rotated and the sand grinding powder would stay on the hole. Note that in this process it is the hard quartz in the sand that is grinding the rock away, not the copper which is considerably softer than the rock.

Now look at the stone that has got four differently shaped holes up one side of it. It looks rather like a small child's shape-sorter. There is a five-pointed star hole, a rectangular hole with a rectangular shape cut out of one side, a rectangular hole with a circular shape cut on one side and a kind of stepped-pyramid shaped hole. You can't cut these by rotating a copper rod. You need something hard and sharp to hammer into the rock. Elsewhere on the Puma Punku site there are numerous stones with sharp cut internal corners. With these there is space to get a hand in to possibly hammer out these corners with sharp flint or other hard rock that breaks to give a sharp edge. It is not possible to propose this method for this block with four strangely shaped holes. The reason we would use a steel chisel if we were tasked with creating such holes is because it can be thin enough while still strong enough to be able to refine the shape deep into the hole. There is no rock that could do this. And copper is too soft. It would take a huge supply of copper chisels as they would have to be continually sharpened and would quickly wear away. Besides, no-one has ever found a discarded copper chisel in South America. Their metal working was almost exclusively dedicated to making decorative pieces.

I have to come back yet again to the argument I have used about other sites. Why on Earth would you want to make four strange-shaped holes in a piece of stone like this? The first part of the answer has to be because you can, easily and relatively quickly. The second part of the answer is either because you want to fit something into these holes, that need to be these strange shapes, or because you want to show off how clever you are in being able to do something that is going to seriously awe the people who will look at what you have done.

The challenge is there to the archeologists. Until someone seriously investigates how these and the other holes and angles were created, and comes up with a sensible theory and some experiments with rock to show it is possible with stone-age or copper-age tools to create similar holes, I think these are clear evidence that the gods were in South America. These stones don't give us evidence that they were there in the period up to 1000 years ago, as they could be earlier, but they might have been.

Suka kollu agriculture, Titicaca.

The suka kollu agriculture system involves very carefully constructed raised growing beds surrounded by irrigation channels. There are scholarly papers online that describe this in detail.

The Andean plateau is very high and growing food is difficult. There is intense sunshine during the day but with very cold nights during which plants need protection against the cold and frost, that the suka kollu system provides. The average potato yield in the area, for crops grown in normal fields, is around 5 tons per hectare. In trials of the suka kollu system the average yield was over 26 tons per hectare. (Figures from the New Zealand Digital Library paper on Traditional andean agriculture.)

There are two questions to ask. How did the inhabitants of this area learn to create the suka kollu growing areas. They involve a complex ecosystem that requires considerable scientific understanding to work out how the system produces better results. The second question is who the strong leaders were, who persuaded the inhabitants to commit the huge effort to creation of the raised fields and the irrigation channels. And when.

Nazca.

We are moving towards the present in our story. And I have already said that I don't believe we have gods on the Earth today. So it is probably already pretty clear what the central conclusion of the final chapter is going to be. Scholars think the Nazca culture that created the patterns on the ground existed between 1500 and 500 years ago (500BC and 500AD). So we are well into historical times. In those areas of the world where there is written history, for the years leading up to 500AD, it is clear that the gods were not active at this time. But in South America we don't have written history to confirm this, so there is the possibility that gods could have been there and their presence not recorded.

The Nazca plain is special because of the patterns humans have made on it that are only understandable from the sky. Huge effort was marshaled to carry and place stones, presumably over a considerable period of time, and those doing the work must have found it very hard to appreciate what they were creating. They may have had kites or even the technology of hot air balloons, but these would only have been used by the select few.

Whatever the patterns were designed to communicate, we can be sure that they were put there to communicate with something in the sky. This could quite easily have been ancestor spirits that were conceived of as living amongst the stars, in heaven. It really is not necessary to suppose the existence of ancient astronauts, our gods, to explain why these patterns were made.

But if by now, in reading this book, you have come to suspect that there is a plausible theory that beings with the ability to fly have been on the Earth in times past, the Nazca lines would fit well into that theory. It could be, like the cargo-cult natives, that they knew these beings flew in and they wanted to attract them to their area. Or it could be that these god-like beings had been important in the creation of their culture, and had then flown off into the sky.

If you wanted these sky-beings to come back, the only way you could send them a message to ask them to, would be lines on the ground.

****

Chapter 26 – So where are the gods now?

If you are sneaking a preview of the last chapter, to discover if I reveal some enclave of gods living amongst us unnoticed I am sure you knew before you got here that you would be disappointed. I am trying as hard as I can to avoid conspiracy theories. I don't think they help us in the search for truth. We now know so much about this planet that if there were a group of gods with technology considerably beyond our own, somewhere on Earth, we would by now have detected them. The electromagnetic radiation from their communications systems or machinery would have alerted us to their presence if they weren't easily visible other ways. I suppose if you want to play conspiracy theories you could imagine them skulking underground somewhere, or in the depths of the oceans, but that would be a pretty miserable life for gods used to lording it over humanity and all that the Earth can offer.

Conspiracy theories that might suggest the gods *are* still here, are in a different category altogether to theories that suggest they might have *been* here. I don't count theories that they were here as conspiracy theories, because the theory this book has been exploring is based on evidence. You may not agree the evidence is valid; I think quite a lot of it is very convincing. There are artefacts and stories that we just cannot explain without a high technology civilisation in the ancient past.

You can suggest that the stories are just imagined creations. It is clear that human beings like fantasy and that some delight in tricking others. We have known this in archeological terms ever since the Piltdown skull was revealed as a fake. And that is hardly likely to be the first outright fake, or invented story or artefact designed to put a gloss on the past. The Catholic church has been at this game for centuries, producing relics as foci for worship, the vast majority of which are unlikely to be genuine. Yet one or two might be. But in science you only need one rock-solid observation that is not explainable through the currently accepted scientific theories to provide a reason for a new and better theory.

So what do we have to draw some final conclusions from? The sheer volume of stories, ancient constructions and unusual artefacts that we do not yet have satisfactory explanations for does seem to point to a civilisation in many parts of the world, in the ancient past, with higher technology than we have. It seems counter-intuitive that this could have existed and then disappeared. But it is possible to lose technology. Only recently the US Air Force discovered that it had completely forgotten how to make a critical component of nuclear warheads. They had to set about rediscovering how to do this, which unfortunately they have. It is also possible for complete societies to die out, as witnessed by Easter Island and the Mayan civilisation.

However when human civilisations die out they do leave archeological evidence. And here we can draw some parallels with what we have had to do to reach our current technological level. Our journey to the ability to undertake huge construction projects and to cut hard rock to fine tolerances has involved mining and drilling for energy, the blasting of holes in the Earth and the creation of some things that will not decay for tens of thousands of years - radioactive sources in particular.

If we believe that the evidence of the stone constructions at Giza, Baalbeck, Cusco and Tiawanaka requires technology beyond our own, this cannot have been created by a large civilisation on Earth developing this level of technology over thousands of years, as we have. The lack of evidence of the kinds of damage we have caused to the Earth, pre-dating us, shows clearly that this didn't happen. So if our key conclusion is that evidence of ancient high technology exists, particularly involving metals and energy sources that could only be gained through mining, we must also conclude that it was brought here. The high technology must have been invented elsewhere and brought with beings that came from somewhere else.

I hope I have convinced you that a small group of adventurers, aliens or gods, whatever you wish to call them, could have existed alongside humans. If they kept their society small their impact on the world would also have been small, appearing just in those places they chose to use for specific purposes. The whole basis for their ability to exist alongside human beings, safely and with a privileged and luxurious lifestyle serviced by large numbers of humans, would depend absolutely on the difference of their technology, compared to that of human beings. Keeping their technology out of the hands of humans would have been just about their number one priority.

This would explain why we only find enigmatic stone remains. They would have guarded any technology devices very closely. If they moved location they would have taken everything of technological value with them. As we are talking of stone-age times, this means that they would not have abandoned anything made of metal if they could remove it. They would have become extreme recyclers. If the great pyramid at Giza was an energy machine, as Christopher Dunn suggests, if it was abandoned it would have been stripped of any metal or other technology before it was. Similarly if the carefully drilled holes in the stones around Tiawanaka were for metal connectors, we should not be surprised that there are not remains of the metal in them now.

If my scenario is correct, of a small group of beings from another planet coming here, it is a pretty easy conclusion to say that if they could come, so they could leave, and the only things left to conjure with are when and why.

Were they human? did they interbreed with humans?

But there is another issue that I have discussed that means it is not quite such a simple matter as a small group of gods jumping into their spaceship and leaving.

I started the book just theorising that they were alien beings of some kind. It was only in a later chapter, to propose how cro-magnon man may have appeared, that I suggested the gods' DNA might have been similar in many ways to ours. And then we started to look at the references in the bible to the sons of gods having children by the daughters of men. And we have looked at how on earth the idea of deforming babys' skulls started. Another possibility that must be in the frame is that at least some of the gods inter-bred with humans. Was this really possible? Could alien beings from another planet have DNA sufficiently similar to ours to make this possible?

There is growing belief in the theory of panspermia. This is the theory that it is possible for elementary forms of life such as bacteria to travel through space on comets, and to 'infect' planets that are capable of supporting life. If this is the way that life starts on a planet, as it cools from its hot birth, then there is a case to be made that DNA all over the universe may have a common basis. The basic double helix structure of the DNA molecule, with the four different nucleotides cytosine (C), guanine (G), adenine (A), and thymine (T) attached to code information and structure proteins, may be spread far and wide across the universe.

With a common basis for life, the next question is whether evolution on different planets could have proceeded along such similar paths, that the most intelligent creatures to evolve become very similar to human beings.

We do have one planet we can study in this respect - Earth. In the last few million years there have been several contenders for most intelligent lifeforms on Earth, the different kinds of hominin. And we keep discovering new ones. 100,000 years ago there were diverse forms of hominin on Earth, competing with each other. So to judge from what has happened here on Earth, the most intelligent creatures do tend to be man-like. More than this, we know that at least some of them interbred. Neanderthals and modern human beings certainly did, as neanderthal DNA can be found today in a proportion of the current population.

So the question we have to pose for ourselves is whether evolution took a similar path on other planets, to end up with man-like beings that could interbreed with humans becoming the dominant intelligent lifeform. The work of one extremely interesting scientist can perhaps shed some light on this.

There is a fascinating theory being advanced by Rupert Sheldrake. In his books he produces a considerable amount of validated experimental evidence that suggests his theory is true, even though nobody (including him) has as yet any idea as to how it works. His theory proposes that the way that things in our universe grow and evolve is guided by 'morphic fields'. Growing plants and animals develop into the final form of their species because their growth is guided by the morphic field of their species, by a resonance between the growing organism and the field. He envisages a hierarchy of these fields, with the morphic fields guiding the growth of individual cells being under the control of higher-level fields that guide the growth of the whole organism. In the context of human beings, he relates these proposed morphic fields to the ideas of a 'collective unconscious' and ideas that all things are linked. Most intriguing are his conversations with physicists that indicate that there could be links between observations coming from quantum physics and the morphic field theory. If you are interested in the leading edge of science I strongly recommend Sheldrake's books to you.

The point of introducing this idea is that Sheldrake has evidence that suggests that resonance with morphic fields operates completely independently of distance. For example, chemists who create new kinds of proteins that have never existed before, find that these new proteins are very difficult to crystalise out of the solutions they have been made in. Proteins are very complex molecules with many different clusters of atoms, and they crystalise by folding into a lowest energy state. These folded states are almost impossible to calculate as proteins contain thousands of atoms and can fold in many different ways. If you wish you can help scientists who are trying to work out how new proteins will fold, through the protein folding game, http://fold.it/portal/, which is crowd-sourcing help with this very difficult task. When eventually a new protein first folds, the chemists then discover that when they make more of this new protein, it crystalises much faster - all over the world. Sheldrake quotes the experience of one Pharmacy company that was successfully selling a new drug, when suddenly new batches they were making started to fold in a different way - and the drug lost its efficacy. Despite spending millions of pounds to try to get it to fold as it had, they could not and had to abandon it. The drug had found a new way to fold and something was everywhere influencing it to fold in this way.

In quantum physics it is possible to have particles that are 'entangled'. Don't ask me to explain how physicists entangle particles, it's complicated, but reading about these experiments with particles it is clear that physicists can do this reliably and repeatedly, so the existence of entangled particles is now an established fact. If you do something to one of the entangled particles, this instantly affects the other particle, no matter how far away it is. Einstein called this 'spooky action at a distance' and he really didn't like it. It indicates that some kind of influence can pass between particles completely independent of distance. Let me say that again - completely independent of distance. That means 'universe-wide'. The physicists know of no reason why entangled particles could not be moved into different galaxies and still influence each other, instantly.

Sheldrake has convinced me that his theory of morphic fields is true, though there is of course a huge amount to discover about it and how it works. If it is true it would provide a mechanism for evolution on different planets, no matter how widely separated, to be influenced in some way by the way evolution was happening on each. The somewhat different environments of the two planets and the evolutionary pressures would no doubt give rise to life-forms unique to each, just as on Earth we have lifeforms that are unique to islands, where evolutionary niches and survival of the fittest have worked alongside any influence from morphic fields, to create wildly different plants and animals. But when we are looking at how the most intelligent life-form climbs to the top of the evolutionary tree, there could surely be a degree of convergence, despite different environments on different planets. Human beings have spread into almost every ecological environment on Earth and are pretty much the same wherever they have evolved over the last 100,000 years. And all humans can interbreed.

I am of a mind to believe the stories of the sons of god producing children with the daughters of men.

What happened to the progeny of 'the sons of god and the daughters of men'?

What do you do when your children 'go native'? It is sometimes hard for parents to understand the choices their children make. Parents surround themselves with the comforts of life as they see them but sometimes find their children put little store in this and go off to a very different life. In the western world we have machines, readily available energy and lots of material goods to provide us with the comfort we want. When western colonialists went to other parts of the world they took only what they needed to enslave or employ local labour, that would then create for them the home comforts they wanted. Some colonialists then imported the luxuries of their home country and created fine houses similar to those they had back home. Other colonialists and missionaries made for themselves extremely pleasant lives in societies with much lower levels of technology, abandoning the products of high technology they could have had back home. They often inter-married and inter-bred with the native people, and essentially 'went native'.

In my scenario of an original group of gods that kept themselves as a small society distinct from human beings, but with sons that had availed themselves of the delights of the daughters of men 'that they saw to be fair', the parent gods would have had a difficult decision about what to do. As the safe existence of the gods over the long term depended on them staying distinct from human beings they would no doubt see this as potentially a massive breakdown in their control of mankind. If I was in the position of the elder gods, with a heavy heart I would have done two things. The first thing to do would be to make sure that the sons who had interbred did not pass high technology to the humans. Very little, if any, of the high technology of the gods would have got into the hands of the 'half-god' progeny. Colonialists tried not let western technology like guns get into the hands of the natives if they could prevent it and similarly the gods would probably have endeavoured to stop their wayward sons taking technology with them as they went to live closer to humans. One can even wonder whether that little episode of Sodom and Gomorrah could have been a 'nuclear option' with a group of wayward gods and half-gods whose actions were prejudicing the safety of the 'full gods'.

For the elder gods, they might have seen this as a matter of making difficult choices while still helping their younger gods, or they might have seen the inter-breeding as so heinous a crime against the society of gods that they had no problem viewing those who had decided to breed with humans as lesser beings. If there were some younger gods still remaining true to the blood line and eschewing any interbreeding with human beings, one can imagine them being forceful in wanting to cast-out their brethren who were despoiling the blood line. Introduction of human genes into the DNA of people descended from the true gods could have caused reduction in how long they lived. If you expect people in your society to live a couple of thousand years, having your son or daughter have children by a human and hence cause the grandchildren to die when they are only 300 years old would seem a desperately bad development. There is one aspect of ancient royal houses such as the Egyptian pharaohs that rather intrigues me, which is their desire to interbreed very closely, even marrying sisters and brothers. This is a bad idea if your gene-pool contains genes that can cause diseases and deformed children, but perhaps if it is possible to have a 'perfect' gene pool, from which all problematic or defective genes have been removed, interbreeding with close relatives may not produce these problems and instead may be a protection from diseases caused by defective genes. I have little knowledge of this so will just leave this thought hanging as an idea to be explored if you wish.

If there was this separation between the true-blood gods and those that chose to live with mankind, it is pretty easy to imagine what has happened to those that interbred. They may initially have maintained their god-status by living a lot longer than most humans, and maybe also by being sufficiently physically different to have been able to guarantee reverence, but over time this would have declined. The physical differences would have got less, perhaps causing the skull deformation trend, but eventually they would become indistinguishable from ordinary humans.

And hence they have gone because they have died out. Or perhaps we should say they are still here, because some elements of their DNA are still here in modern mankind, waiting to be identified as god DNA. There is an awful lot of the human genome that we have not properly investigated yet.

When did the true gods leave?

Imagine you are part of a small group of people helping the evolving intelligent creatures of a planet to become more civilised. I speculated at the start of this book on the reasons why a small group of 'adventurers' might have come to Earth. Such an expedition must have had some purpose, and given that their expedition would probably have required funding and effort by many of their kind who stayed home, it is easy to imagine some moral purpose in their mission, as well as adventure.

But whatever reason brought them to Earth, their purpose in staying after the Flood must surely have been to help mankind develop. Mankind does seem to be on some kind of journey. The ideas proposed by Robert Wright in Non-Zero suggest that this is a positive development that is moving mankind forward as a race. As well as societies of humans becoming more collaborative and mutually helpful it is also possible to describe a journey of spiritual development of mankind over the millennia and centuries. Our development as individuals in our globally connected world is now very different, and perhaps more advanced, than the kinds of moral and spiritual concerns that a peasant in medieval times, or a member of a stone-age tribe might have had. A concern for the state of the world and of the world's people is growing amongst many of the young people of today.

The gods may have been able to see this kind of development over the thousands of years they had been here, and hence perhaps could see that the time was coming when mankind would start to gain global control and global communication. This could have been the trigger that made the gods decide it was time to leave.

The legacy of the gods?

I believe that the gods have left us some artefacts that, if we could read properly what they are and what they mean, could give us much greater insight into our history, into our world, and into science that we have not yet conquered. The very existence of beings arriving at the Earth from elsewhere is a powerful piece of information, were it to become widely accepted. That those beings shared very similar DNA would also give us some powerful scientific insights.

Those artefacts left are here to be seen and wondered about, but they are part of the past. If we are to consider whether the gods have left us a legacy that is still shaping mankind today, we must look at things that still happen now because of what the gods did and that we did with their help. That we survived the Flood better than we might have done on our own could be one of these things. That we progressed faster in developing agriculture and animal husbandry could be another. However we might eventually have managed those developments by ourselves.

My suggestions about religion however may be a much bigger legacy, that is still affecting us today.

If I am right in my suppositions about the younger dryas period, imagine what the experiences of mankind during the period and at the end of the period were. My basic supposition is that the effects of the younger dryas period were caused by the Earth becoming enveloped in a complete and thick cloud cover due to the impact of the comet and the Flood. These clouds would reflect sunlight back into space and this would cause the sudden global temperature drop. Just for comparison, work by Ulf Buntgen on tree rings, at the Swiss Federal Research Institute in Birmensdorf, has concluded that just three giant volcanic eruptions starting in 536 AD caused a century-long drop in temperature with Summers up to 4 degrees celsius cooler. They attribute this to the volcanic dust in the atmosphere. With a comet impact and Earth crust displacement causing volcanic eruptions all over the world, and the Flood causing more water vapour to get into the atmosphere, I would like to suggest that there could possibly have been thick cloud cover over the whole world for 1200 years.

The amount of light penetrating these clouds and reaching the ground would be hugely reduced. The sun, moon and stars would have disappeared. Plant growth would have become very slow and many animals would have died as their ecosystems were disrupted, with food for all animals becoming very scarce. It must have been a truly miserable experience for the survivors of the Flood.

If the gods stepped in and helped mankind at this point their impact on the human beings would have been immense. With humans having no idea of the real nature of 'the heavens', or of Earth being a planet in a solar system and subject to impacts of comets, the explanations that the gods gave of what had caused the disaster would have been accepted and passed down. It would have become completely unquestioned that what the gods told humans was the true story of their history. The idea that it was the sins of mankind that caused God to create the Flood to destroy mankind would start the whole ethos of the Middle Eastern religions, that people are sinners and need to be saved.

Something made the younger dryas cold period end very suddenly. Imagine, if you can, that the complete cloud cover persists for the whole 1200 years of the younger dryas period. I don't know if this is possible, but I do know that weather systems are driven by the energy of the sun heating land and water, which heats the air above and evaporates water from the seas, creating the high and low pressure areas that drive winds. If there was very thick cloud cover the energy to drive weather systems would be hugely reduced. Because of climate change we are currently seeing 'stuck' weather patterns, that can give weeks of freezing temperatures or heatwaves, dependent on where the jet stream is. It flows west to east and the gradient of heat from Equator to Arctic determines how strong it is. With the Arctic warming the jet stream is at times slowing down and becoming more wavy. Areas can find themselves under a low-pressure for prolonged periods, while others get high pressure. Complete cloud cover over the Earth would not only reduce the overall energy, but would cause a massive temperature drop in equatorial regions, meaning that the temperature gradient between Arctic and Equator would be dramatically less. Could this cause the jet stream to almost disappear?

Is it possible that these effects caused the Earth's weather systems to become very much less dynamic, reducing rain and winds to very low levels, stopping the sun from evaporating clouds and minimising the speed at which dust particles and water vapour were removed from the lower atmosphere? And with such a lot of dust and water vapour up in the stratosphere that it took not just the century needed to overcome the impact of 3 volcanoes, but 12 centuries?

If so, the clouds at lower altitude might have slowly reduced, allowing a bit more light to reach the Earth, but with the water vapour and dust in the very high atmosphere still reflecting the sun and keeping the Earth cold. For generation after generation there would be no clear sight of the sun, no moon and no stars. Just a story that a long time ago a wonderful heaven had fallen to Earth and was destroyed.

There would then eventually come a point when the sun started to penetrate to the surface. Think about those foggy mornings that sometimes occur. It is dim and cold and you feel closed-in on yourself. Sometimes the fog lasts all day and your hopes that it will clear and let the sun through come to nought. But this would have been normality for humans in the younger dryas if it was caused by complete cloud cover. We know the younger dryas period ended very suddenly, perhaps in less than a decade. Can you imagine what it must have been like for people who lived through this period? The sky would get progressively lighter and the weather progressively warmer. Plants would start growing better. And then one day you would begin to see not just a bright patch in the clouds, that moved across the sky during the day, but the orb of the sun and sunlight making shadows.

You would have sought an explanation of this from your gods and they would probably have told you that the heavens were being re-instated - provided you continued to worship the gods and do what you should. And then, perhaps over only a short period of months or a year or two, the sun would become properly visible and you would begin to feel its heat on your back - what a wonderful feeling that must have been. And then the moon would appear, and blue sky, and finally the stars.

If the gods had convinced you that this had all happened through their agency and because humans had been worshipping them as they had been instructed to do, the very powerful tradition of giving thanks to the gods would be further strengthened.

I have depicted religion, you may think somewhat cynically, as a tool used by beings who were more technologically advanced than mankind, to control humans. It is possible these beings were also more advanced mentally, or maybe they had the same mental capacity as humans, but a greater insight into what it means to be an intelligent being. If they were very long-lived they might have reasoned that the creation of a religion requiring humans to worship in exchange for the help they provided was a necessary phase that mankind would eventually grow out of.

Religion is now being used cynically by some, who use it to justify conflict and the oppression of others. But we are also seeing both a growth in secularism and moral codes based on our common humanity, and a growth in spiritual awareness that does not need the rules of religions. It is instead based on beliefs about what is necessary to develop one's spirit, both in this life and in lives to come.

So as we come towards the end of this book I would like to draw once again the distinction between, religion, gods and God. Mankind has worshipped God in many ways and over the years we can see how this worship has changed, sometimes mediated by religions and sometimes as a matter of personal belief. The trend is generally away from the worship of whole pantheons of Gods to belief in a single God or an overarching life force and spiritual world that connects us all. Though some countries have tried to ban religions and worship of God, people seem to feel a continuing need and keep their worship going. Many who don't worship still express feelings of there being some higher power. As we transition from religions that dictate how to live and pray to personal beliefs that provide a guide in living a good life, some may have lost a strong moral sense and some may fear death as the end, with nothing surviving death. There is a need for a stronger debate about the spiritual side of mankind, hopefully a debate that is not polarised into competing religions.

This is subject matter that is not really for this book; it needs a whole book of its own. But it does provide an ending thought. If the gods came from a planet that had already travelled the kind of path that the Earth is on, and that had produced a more enlightened planetary civilisation, perhaps they arrived with a level of moral and spiritual insight that was far ahead of even current mankind. They could have had their own appreciation of the meaning of 'God' as something so far beyond us all that it is sensible to strive to be more like 'God'; to have the compassion and love to care for 'lesser beings'. And they could have appreciated the need for societies of humans to care for each other and the environment, to enable individuals to practice what is necessary to develop spiritually.

If that was so, perhaps the gods were instrumental in moving mankind along the path to development of their own sense of what 'God' is. And just maybe they knew that removing themselves so that they would eventually cease to be the objects of worship by humans was a necessary step in helping us move to the next stage, and a trigger for their leaving.

Finding your own God, whatever you conceive God to be, is something that you have to do alone. Avoiding worshiping false gods is the necessary first step.

The end.

****

Appendix 1 - What kinds of evidence of the gods to look for.

This appendix is the analysis I did of how we can differentiate between constructions made by humans and those that undeniably require technology considerably beyond that available in the past, and possibly also beyond our current technology.

You can find the full (27 page) appendix on the website www.GodsGenesandClimate.com.

In the appendix I consider the different kinds of building materials used then and now, and the quarrying and transportation methods available then and now.

The main conclusions which informed the body of this book are:

i) Buildings built by the gods are likely to be made from very large, very squarely cut stone blocks.

ii) Very level foundations cut into bedrock are likely to be the work of the gods, particularly if they extend over large areas.

iii) Transportation of very large stone blocks over relatively level land is achievable by humans, but transporting massive stones uphill in rocky territory, and raising them into place directly on top of other stones where there will be high friction, is very likely the work of the gods.

iv) Cutting hard stone to fit precisely against other stones at strange angles, cutting sharp internal corners deep into the stone, and accurately drilling deep holes is very likely the work of the gods.

And that the best way to assess what we find is to initially assume that everything was made by humans, until by assessing how they did it we reach the conclusion that the work is significantly beyond human capabilities - then and maybe now.

****

Appendix 2 - Acceleration of the Earth's crust due to a comet.

This is the 'back of the envelope' calculation that I made to convince myself that a comet impact, combined with an already slipping crust, could cause an acceleration of the slippage such as to create world-wide floods.

The calculation is only intended to give an order-of-magnitude assessment of this. The individual assumptions and figures can all be debated, the question I am trying to answer is only whether this is a possibility.

The key assumption is that the process of Earth crust displacement has been happening for sufficient time before the comet impact for all of the magma underneath the crust to have been liquified, through the heat generated as the crust grates over the underlying layers. This liquid magma will be a very thick and viscous liquid, though it will exert some drag on the crust, this will be a small fraction of the resistance to movement before the slippage started. So I have not included any allowance for this in this calculation.

The process below is:
- Calculate volume of the Earth.
- Calculate volume of the Earth without the crust.
- Hence find the volume of the crust.
- Multiply volume of the crust by average density of the crust to find its mass.
- Estimate the size of the asteroid or comet that hit and its volume.
- Calculate its mass from the average density of meteorites.
- Estimate the speed of the asteroid as the average speed of meteorites.
- Assume that when the asteroid hits all the kinetic energy it has is used to accelerate the crust and ignore the energy dissipated as heat or through ejection of material upwards.
- Assume that the part of the Laurentide ice sheet that the asteroid hit is sufficiently thick, that the asteroid blasts a 2000 metre deep hole in it.
- Calculate the time it takes for the mass of the asteroid to be stopped, from its speed and the fact that it is stopped after only traveling 2000 metres.
- Hence calculate the force exerted on the crust.
- And from that calculate the acceleration imparted to the crust in that time.

For those of you unfamiliar with mathematical notation using powers of 10:
- 10^{18} means 10 to the power 18, in other words 1 with 18 zeros after it. 10 is the same as 10^1 which is just 10, 10^2 means 10x10 = 100. 10^3 is 1000, 10^6 is 1,000,000 and so on. It saves having to count long strings of '0's.

So:

- Calculate volume of the Earth.

Radius of Earth = 6360 km.
Volume of a sphere in cubic metres = 4/3 x pi x radius cubed.
Volume of Earth = 4/3 x 3.142 x (6360 x 1000) x (6360 x 1000)x (6360 x 1000)
= 4.189 x 6.36 x 6.36 x 6.36 x 1,000,000,000,000,000,000 cubic metres (10^{18})
= **1.077×10^{21} m³**

- Calculate volume of the Earth without the crust.

Earth's crust varies in thickness from as little as 2km thick to over 70 km thick. The average value for the continental crust is approximately 35 km thick. Average thickness of the oceanic crust is 4.5km.

Approximately 70 % of Earth's surface is covered in ocean and so it is assumed that this is the proportion of the crust formed of the denser, but thinner oceanic crustal rocks whereas the remaining 30 % is assumed to be composed of the thicker but less dense continental crustal rocks.

So:

We can calculate the volume of the crust by taking the volume of the Earth without the crust away from total volume.

Volume of Earth without oceanic crust is 4/3 x 3.142 x (6355.5 x 1000) x (6355.5 x 1000)x (6355.5 x 1000)
= 1.075×10^{21} m³
So volume of crust if it was all oceanic would be 1.077-1.075 X 10^{21} = 0.002 x 10^{21}
We need 70% of this which is **0.0014×10^{21} m³**.

Volume of Earth without continental crust is 4/3 x 3.142 x (6325 x 1000) x (6325 x 1000)x (6325 x 1000)
= 1.06×10^{21} m³
So volume of crust if it was all continental would be $1.077 - 1.06 \times 10^{21}$ = 0.017×10^{21}
We need 30% of this which is **0.0051×10^{21} m³.**

- Hence find the volume of the crust.
So overall volume of the Earth crust is 0.0065×10^{21} m³ = **6.5×10^{18} m³**

- Multiply volume of the crust by average density of the crust to find its mass.
Density: It is assumed that the continental crust has an average density of 2700 kg/m3 and the oceanic crust a density of 3000 kg/m³.

Average density of crust = (2700 x 0.7) + (3000 x 0.3) = 1890 + 900 = 2790 kg/m³

So mass of the crust = 6.5×10^{18} m³ x 2790Kg/m³ = $18,135 \times 10^{18}$ kg which = **18.135×10^{21} Kg.**

- Estimate the size of the asteroid or comet that hit and its volume.
Assume the asteroid was diameter 12km, radius 6km.
Volume is 4/3 x pi x 6000 x 6000 x 6000
= 4.189 x 6 x 6 x 6 x 1,000,000,000 (10^9)
= 904×10^9 m³

- Calculate its mass from the average density of meteorites.
Iron meteorites have a density of around 7.5 g/cm³ and chondrite meteorites around 3.35 g/cm³
There are 100 x 100 x 100 cubic cm in a cubic metre, so we multiply these densities by 10^6 and divide by 1000 to convert to kg.

We will assume the asteroid is chondrite, so its density is 3350kg/m³

So its mass is $904 \times 3350 \times 10^9$ kg = 3028×10^9 = **3.028×10^{15} kg**

- Estimate the speed of the asteroid as the average speed of meteorites.
Meteors enter the atmosphere at speeds between 11km/s and 72km/s. A large asteroid would hardly be slowed at all by the atmosphere. I will use a figure of 35km/s for its speed when it hit.

- **Assume that when the asteroid hits all the kinetic energy it has is used to accelerate the crust** and ignore the energy dissipated as heat or through ejection of material upwards. If we wanted to take into account energy dissipated as heat and through ejection of material into the atmosphere this just means we reduce our final result by whatever factor we choose for this.

- **Assume that the part of the Laurentide ice sheet that the asteroid hit is sufficiently thick, that the asteroid blasts a 2000 metre deep hole in it.**
The Antarctic ice sheet is in places 4000m thick, so taking 2000m is a conservative estimate of the thickness.

- **Calculate the time it takes for the mass of the asteroid to be stopped, from its speed and the fact that it is stopped after only traveling 2000 metres.**
The asteroid presumably hit the ice sheet at a low angle if it did accelerate the earth crust displacement. This would make the time it took to stop a little longer than if it hit vertically but there would only be a small difference. So I will assume stopping time is simply how long an object traveling at 35km/s takes to travel 2000m.
= 2km / 35km/s seconds = 0.057 seconds.

- **Hence calculate the force exerted on the crust.**
Force exerted when an object stops is the rate of change of momentum, which is mass x velocity (speed) divided by time it takes to stop.

Momentum is mass x velocity, $(3.028 \times 10^{15}$ kg$) \times 35000$ m/sec $= 105980 \times 10^{15} = 1.0598 \times 10^{20}$ kgm/s

Force $= 1.0598 \times 10^{20} / 0.057$s $= 18.59 \times 10^{20}$ kgm/s/s $= 1.859 \times 10^{21}$ kgm/s/s

- **And from that calculate the acceleration imparted to the crust in that time.**

Force = mass x acceleration. So acceleration is Force divided by mass (of the crust)

So 1.859×10^{21} kg m/s/s divided by 18.135×10^{21} Kg.
= 0.1 m/s/s acceleration.

This acceleration is applied for the time it takes the asteroid to stop, 0.057 seconds.
So the crust will speed up by 0.1m/s/s x 0.057s = 0.0057 m/s = 0.57 cm/s

In 1 hour this speed will cause a movement of 3600 second x 0.57 cm/s = 2052 cm - a bit over 20 metres. In 24 hours = 480 metres.

In a week this amounts to over 3km.

This may not sound a lot but don't forget that at the Equator oceans are moving at 1668km/hr and the huge gyroscopic force the oceans exert will act to keep them rotating as they were, while the Earth slips under them.

I have no idea how long it would take for the very weak force that the bottom and sides of the ocean exert on the water to act against these gyroscopic forces and get the oceans back into the ocean basins in their new place. It might take a year?

The really unknown factor is what happens at coasts. Tsunamis in the middle of the ocean are just a gentle swell, but when they hit the shelving sea-floor close to land this causes them to raise up to huge heights.

It would need someone much cleverer than me to work out precisely what sudden acceleration of an Earth crust displacement would cause, but I think this back-of-the-envelope calculation is sufficient to allow the conclusion that severe flooding from the sea could be a result.

If you don't think so try playing with the figures. The size of the asteroid makes a massive difference, because the volume and hence the mass depends on the radius cubed. Doubling the size of the asteroid makes almost a ten times difference in how far the crust would move in a day, from 480 metres to over 4 kilometres.

****

Bibliography

Bibliographies that reference all the sources an author has used can be very helpful. An extensive bibliography is something I look for before purchasing a book, because it suggests the contents is not just pure speculation. But long lists of sources leave you with the problem of finding out which are worthwhile. In this area of 'mysteries' there is so much re-hashing of other peoples' work that it can be hard to get to anything that is real factual truth or solid research.

So in this bibliography I am mainly mentioning sources that do have checkable facts and/or original ideas and research. But I am also including a few that speculate, sometimes wildly, but which mention things you may not have come across that are worth a look.

Those who approach this area as leisure reading are unlikely to have the time to follow-up copious sources, but want instead books that are relatively easy to read, that will add to their knowledge without presenting huge depths of scholarship or undue speculation. This is what I am trying to provide you with here, a reading list of books I hope you will enjoy. With some of the reasons why I consider them to be worth reading.

You will find various other books by many of these authors, singly and writing together, through which you can follow how thinking in this area has developed since the early 70s.

The books are listed in alphabetical order of the author's surname. First author or editor where there is more than one author. Date is date of first publication.

Gods of the New Millennium. Alan Alford. 1996.
A compendium of the evidence for technologically advanced beings on Earth. It is a bit of a shock in pulling this book off my shelf, to realise that he was pulling all this evidence together 20 years ago, yet it continues to be denied by scientists and it is still academic suicide for scientists to actively investigate how the stonework in South America was created.

When the Gods Came Down. Alan Alford. 2000.
Alford explores the roots of religion. He makes much of happenings in the heavens and comets, and how these might have been the roots behind the ancient myths and legends that underpinned the religious thought of Egypt and other ancient civilisations. Some of his speculations go too far for me but I think his book contains some interesting pointers to things worthy of a closer look.

Ancient Traces, Michael Baigent. 1998.
A collection of examples suggesting humans developed earlier than was conventionally understood at the time, and exploring various mysteries of the past. Contains a useful analysis of the face of the Sphinx indicating it was not originally constructed with the face of Khafre.

Keeper of Genesis, Robert Bauval and Graham Hancock. 1996.
Bauval and Hancock start from Robert Schoch and Anthony West's views on the date when the Sphinx was built, based on the levels of erosion on it's sides. They go on to consider the astronomical alignment of the Sphinx and how that relates to Egyptian mythology and stories of origins.

The Spaceships of Ezekiel. J F Blumrich. 1974
Working at the time as Chief of the systems layout branch of NASA, Blumrich set out to debunk the idea that Ezekiel saw actual spaceships but ended up coming to the opposite conclusion. Considering how ancient people would describe high technology machines and systems led Blumrich to some very innovative ideas that he considered technologically very competent, but requiring technology a bit beyond what we are currently capable of.

Gobekli Tepe, Genesis of the Gods. Andrew Collins, 2014.
An excellent description of Gobekli Tepe and of the comet iconography found there that indicates how important a comet was to the presumably religious practices the Gobekli Tepe constructions were used for. He goes on to speculate about the garden of Eden and its location.

Forbidden Archeology, Michael Cremo and Richard Thompson. 1993
This is a 900-page source work looking at fossils and stone tools. Published in 1993 it made the case for humans and other hominins making and using stone tools some millions of years before archeologists of the time thought this had started. They also discuss anomalous artefacts that have been found in places that indicate they are millions of years old. This is more a book to use as a reference than to consider a good read.

In Search of Ancient Gods. Eric Von Daniken. 1974. One of the original books proposing Earth was visited by aliens, that set so many people off on searches. Von Daniken ranges very widely and includes lots of pictures of ancient artefacts that you may not have seen.

Guns, Germs and Steel, Jared Diamond. 1998.
As an anthropologist Diamond has studied the development of human societies in different parts of the world. He provides a brilliant description of how the landmasses and climate of the world, combined with the luck of where evolution of animals happened, has been a central determinant of how world history has developed.

The Giza Power Plant, Technologies of Ancient Egypt. Christopher Dunn. 1998.
A very detailed investigation of the engineering of the Great Pyramid in Egypt and the machining carried out on the granite box in the kings chamber, using Petrie's observations as well as more recent observations. He concludes from this that the granite was drilled out with an ultrasound drill. The book goes on to speculate that the pyramid might have been created to be a power source, speculation you can believe or not as you wish. The engineering and machining perspectives are however hard to deny.

The Atlantis Blueprint. Rand Flem-Ath and Colin Wilson. 2000.
A re-visiting of Hapgood's ideas of crust displacement with particular reference to Atlantis having been in Antarctica. They combine this with explorations around ancient secret knowledge and possible sites around the world that might have been linked as a global network of observatories and mystical sites.

Lost Ancient Technology of Peru and Bolivia. Brien Foerster 2012.
This is basically a tour of the sites and stone artefacts in and around Cusco. Brien Foerster's YouTube videos are the best place to start to get a feel for this area, but this book gives a more complete overview. It also has some interesting things to say about how and when the major ancient constructions at Tiwanaku were destroyed, which opens the possibility that the gods were active in South America before the Flood, something I have not had space to consider in this book.

The New Science of Strong Materials, Or Why You Don't Fall Through The Floor. J E Gordon 1991.
Fascinating if you want to understand the science of strong materials and how things break. Ahead of its time in discussing how perfectly made materials can be exceptionally strong, that we are now seeing in materials such as graphene and carbon tubes.

Graham Hancock.
Special mention for Graham Hancock, as he has done more than anyone else to create a solidly scholarly basis for discussion of the artefacts that undeniably exist, which mainstream archeology ignores or explains in unsatisfactory ways - as the four books below show. These are all essential reading.

Fingerprints of the Gods, Graham Hancock. 1995.
Where Hancock started, looking at the enigmas of Egypt and America.

Underworld, Graham Hancock. 2002.
The book that undeniably makes the case for advanced civilisations prior to the growth of civilisations in the Middle East from 10,000 years ago. He has drawn on the knowledge of geologists to chart the progress of the flooding of lower-lying land from the end of the last glacial maximum 22,000 years ago, which has deprived us of easy access to the archeological remains of these civilisations, that he persoanlly dived on to see.

Supernatural, Graham Hancock. 2005
Hancock explores how human beings describe strange experiences that they have but which they cannot explain. He looks at this across time and right around the world and finds some very intriguing commonalities across time and across geographies. You might think it impossible to link the cave art of 40,000 years ago, with reports of fairies in the middle ages and of abduction by aliens in recent times, to experiences people have in shamanistic worship.

To me he makes a pretty convincing case that there is a link. Important to me in making the case for the universality of human spiritual experiences and hence how religions have tended to focus people away from their natural spiritual experiences, towards explanations of these mediated through the religion.

Magicians of the Gods, Graham Hancock. 2015.
A very powerful pulling-together of the evidence for a race of technologically advanced beings on Earth, combined with the detailed evidence of the comet strike on the Laurentide ice sheet. It was this book that finally persuaded me to put pen to paper and create Gods, Genes and Climate, particularly as he pulls back from the next step of discussing where this technological race came from and why they disappeared.

The Path of the Pole, Charles Hapgood. 1958.
Before I read this book I considered the idea of Earth crust displacement interesting and maybe possible. After I read the book I was convinced. The quantity and quality of evidence that Hapgood assembles for crust displacement, which Einstein describes in the foreword as "...the extraordinarily rich material that supports his displacement theory." is to me impossible to deny.

Uriel's Machine, The Ancient Origins of Science. Christopher Knight and Robert Lomas. 2000.
An excellent overview of ancient astronomical science that makes it clear that ancient mankind were highly knowledgeable about astronomy and that their societies went to huge lengths and great expense to plot the movements of the heavenly bodies.

Lost Civilisations of the Stone Age, Richard Rudgley. 1998.
Rudgley pulls together a huge range of evidence that suggest intelligence far earlier than most archaeologists will accept. He even goes back as far as bones that seem to have been deliberately and intelligently scribed that date to 250,000 years ago. The archeologists who found them also found bones that they reckon are homo-erectus bones. He discusses sculpture, early writing, evidence of early medicine from bones and teeth, and development of language. He pushes the existence of intelligent beings back into the period between the first cave art and the early civilisations that have left records, so really begs the question about why there is not more evidence of early civilisations that were the pre-cursors to the civilisations that grew from around 7000 or 8000 years ago.

The Presence of the Past, Rupert Sheldrake. 1988.
Included with reference to how it might be that aliens arriving on Earth might be so similar to the hominins that had developed on Earth to be able to inter-breed, and as to why human behaviours established by the gods might still be influencing the behaviour of modern humans. Sheldrake's theories on the interconnection of all things through morphic fields are truly revolutionary and one day will cause science to develop a radically different view of the world we exist in. This is tangential to Gods, Genes and Climate except that it is about core mysteries of who and what we are. The fact that Sheldrake and Lee Smolin are now finding some interesting common ground in exploring the nature of time I find very hopeful. My thoughts on this will need a separate book - watch this space!

Inevitable Surprises, Peter Schwarz. 2003.
This is not a book about mankind's past, but about our future. Peter Schwarz looks at various issues in the world that are staring us in the face but which we as societies are failing to notice. Hence when they happen governments and organisations express great surprise, whereas had they been more analytical they would have seen the problems coming. One that he discusses is the likelihood of 'water wars', with various places in the world currently using water from aquifers at far too high a rate, and arguments happening between countries downstream and those upstream that are using too much water. The virtual disappearance of the Caspian Sea is one major example. What is refreshing and important about this book is his ruthlessly logical deductions from verifiable facts that are staring us in the face, which the vast majority of people are failing to interpret properly.

The Sirius Mystery, Robert Temple. 1976.
Temple, a Fellow of the Royal Astronomical Society, discovered from an anthropological study that a tribe in sub-Saharan Africa, the Dogon, have astronomical knowledge that they could not have obtained themselves - the existence of Sirius B. This star, in the Sirius system, is invisible without the use of a high-power telescope, but the religious traditions of the Dogon claim that their great culture-hero and founder of their civilisation came to Earth from Sirius B. They have such a precise knowledge of the Sirius system, which is a double star system, that Temple became convinced that this was prime evidence of beings from another planet having visited Earth in ancient times.

Egyptian Dawn, Robert Temple. 2010.
Temple theories about the Giza pyramids I found hard reading but the book does have two key points of interest for me. The first is his work with Ioannis Liritzis on thermoluminescence dating, which if correct dates Egyptian megalithic buildings earlier than archeologists reckon they were built. The second is his analysis that there were two completely different levels of stone technology in Egypt at the time, the very high technology demonstrated in the North, while in the South they were trying to build similar structures but obviously did not have anything like the same technology. He also has some interesting things to say about the extent of the 'Libyan' civilisation that existed alongside ancient Egypt, that extended right across the north of Africa to present-day Algeria and Morocco.

Earth in Upheaval, Immanuel Velikovsky. 1956.
Velikovsky's books were instrumental in starting many people on the investigation of those things ignored by scholars. Earth in upheaval was first published in 1956. The very first chapter details the many explorers who described the massive extinctions of mammoths in Siberia and fauna of all kinds in Alaska, the evidence for which has been preserved in the permafrost. This, and similar evidence from elsewhere in the world is very persuasive evidence of combined flooding and freezing. The book goes on to look at cataclysmic geology much more widely and across a much greater timescale. It provides lots of evidence that shows the current theory of ice ages is woefully incomplete and cannot explain either the glaciation that has happened at the Equator or the existence in the polar zones of fossils and coal that can only have formed under tropical conditions. Velikovsky wrote this book to provide evidence for the theories he had developed in his books Worlds in Collision and Ages in Chaos, that drew on the recorded histories of Egypt and other civilisations. Hence he does not relate the earthly evidence to Earth crust displacement, but to changes in Earth's axis wrought by heavenly collisions, that are unlikely to be true in my view. But still fascinating reading in the light of Hapgood's theories, published only a couple of years later.

Gods, Genes and Consciousness, Paul von Ward. 2004.
A book I came across only after I chose the title for Gods, Genes and Climate, but given that his book deals with many of the same ideas the closeness of title is extremely helpful. It is particularly good to see another author making the same connections as to the origins of religion and belief. However he relies pretty heavily on Zecharia Sitchin's translation of Sumerian tablets and takes the stories pretty much at face value, which I

have avoided doing as they could be embroiderings around some central true facts, or even inventions. The book provides useful links if you want to follow this route. He also lumps together with physical contacts between humans and gods the kinds of stories that we would now class as alien abductions or channeling of messages. However in the later part of his book he deals at great length with the impact contacts with 'Advanced Beings' as he calls them may have had on the development and current practice of religions, particularly the Indo-European religions. He goes on to discuss how this may be affecting our whole 'species consciousness'. If this is of interest to you I recommend combining reading Paul von Ward's book with 'The God Delusion' by Richard Dawkins, and Ruper Sheldrake's riposte to this, 'The Science Delusion'.

The World Without Us. Alan Weisman. 2007.
An excellent description of how rapidly the world would revert to nature, and evidence of mankind would disappear, were humans to be wiped out. Which also illuminates which parts of the evidence of our existence on Earth would not disappear. This is important to Gods, Genes and Climate in assessing why a technologically advanced race has not left similar evidence to that which humans are leaving.

Non-Zero. Robert Wright. 2000.
Wright propounds the theory that human society is on a path of development that does not follow the 'survival of the fittest' theory of evolution but instead that the benefits to humans of working together for mutual survival is the driving force. And that this mutual survival has been getting stronger through the different societal forms that have evolved. He makes the case that mankind is on a developmental path of growing collaboration for mutual benefit, despite the regular setbacks.

****

Reference Index

Sections

Introduction - Incredible ideas and crackpot theories............................1
Chapter 1 – Setting the scene...9
   How likely is it that aliens came to the Earth?..............................11
   Long lives..14
   The North and South Poles being in different places......................15
   How many aliens might have come to Earth?.................................17
Chapter 2 - Arrival of the gods...19
   What will our Adventurers be thinking on arrival at Earth?..........19
   What can our Adventurers see?...21
   When did our Adventurers arrive?...25
   Earth Crust Displacement – could it happen?..................................27
   Earth Crust Displacement – how would this make the Earth different?...33
Chapter 3 - Was Antarctica a potential home for our Adventurers?...34
   Where to land and make home?...35
   Considerations on what makes a good home................................37
   Where to find good water and food...38
   Where to find good shelter and security?..40
   Security from hominids and hominins...43
   Security from flood and transport considerations...........................46
Chapter 4 – Antarctica as a desirable home......................................49
   Climate, flora and fauna in Antarctica...49
   Creating the comforts of home; animal products..........................51
   Creating the comforts of home; furnishings...................................52
   Farming versus hunting and gathering...54
   Why did our Adventurers come?...56
   Possible impacts on the Earth and human beings.........................60
Chapter 5 – What kind of society did our Adventurers have?............62
   What size of society did our Adventurers create?..........................63
   Sex and procreation amongst our Adventurers.............................67
   How stable a society?..68
   Weapons and society..71
   How did our Adventurers achieved self-fulfillment?.......................75

Chapter 6 – From new arrivals to residents 77
   A transitional chapter 77
Chapter 7 – Sugar and spice and all things nice 80
   Spaceship food 80
   Better food 83
   Collecting plants and animals 85
Chapter 8 – The need for manpower; early development of humans. 87
   Cro Magnon man 92
   How evolution works - as far as we know 95
   The early movements of humans 96
Chapter 9 - Creating manpower 101
   Genetically modifying hominins 101
   Creating the first manpower 105
   Where was the Garden of Eden? 107
Chapter 10 – Developing manpower 109
   Human intellectual development 109
   The nature of early humans; nature versus nurture 111
   Controlling the tribe of intelligent humans 114
   Leaving the Garden of Eden 116
Chapter 11 - Using manpower 119
   How would the gods set about using their manpower? 119
   The problem with intelligent manpower 122
   Intrinsic versus extrinsic control 125
   The role of religion in maintaining intrinsic control and power .. 126
   Controlling leaders 129
Chapter 12 – Humans in Antarctica? 133
   Leaders of mankind in Antarctica 136
Chapter 13 – From myths and legends to written history 138
   Changing our perspective; looking for evidence 138
   The shape of history from 50,000 years ago to the present 140
   Myths, legends and history 141
   Should we believe sources literally? 143
Chapter 14 - The period 40,000 to 20,000 years ago 146
   The gods in the period 40,000 to 20,000 years ago 148
   Atlanteans before the flood 151
   The role of the gods in Atlantean civilisation 162
Chapter 15 – Floods and The Flood 165

Ice and sea level	165
Was it an ice age?	169
Melting ice – the effect on sea level	170
The cause of the Flood of the legends	172
What could make the oceans move?	174

Chapter 16 – Moving house..180
- The gods' knowledge of Earth crust displacement..........181
- The gods' reaction...183
- What to do about the Atlanteans?....................................185

Chapter 17 – Life for humans after The Flood....................188
- Where would the Atlanteans go?.....................................189
- What would the gods do as mankind started again?......192
- Mankind's development after the flood and the (re)establishment of agriculture...197

Chapter 18 – Did the gods return?.......................................201

Chapter 19 - Humans and gods together............................210
- Where should the gods land?..210
- The home of the gods..212

Chapter 20 - The gods' new home; 12,800 to 10,000 years ago........217
- How might the gods have helped the surviving humans?..........219
- Gobekli Tepe..220
- The re-establishment of mankind; the spread of farming............224

Chapter 21 - 10,000 to 7000 years ago................................227
- The sphinx..227
- The Great Pyramid at Giza...231
- Other developments in the 10,000 to 7000 years ago period.......234

Chapter 22 - 7000 to 3500 years ago..................................235
- Stonehenge..236
- Skara Brae and the Ring of Brodgar................................240
- Newgrange...241
- The end of the Old Kingdom in Egypt..............................242

Chapter 23 - 3500 to 2000 years ago; the Middle East and Europe..245
- Ezekiel's story..245
- Sodom and Gomorrah...249
- Queen Hapshepsut's expedition to the land of Punt.......251

Chapter 24 - 4200 to 2000 years ago in America...............253
- The Saksaywaman stone walls at Cusco........................253

    Elongated skulls..254
Chapter 25 - 2000 to 1000 years ago..257
    The Inca God Viracocha..257
    Puma Punku at Tiwanaku..258
    Suka kollu agriculture, Titicaca..260
    Nazca..260
Chapter 26 – So where are the gods now?..262
    Were they human? did they interbreed with humans?..................264
    What happened to the progeny of 'the sons of god and the daughters of men'?..267
    When did the true gods leave?..269
    The legacy of the gods?..269
Appendix 1 - What kinds of evidence of the gods to look for..........274
Appendix 2 - Acceleration of the Earth's crust due to a comet.........275
Bibliography..280
Reference Index...288
About the Author...292

About the Author

By day, Roger Broadie has been a stage-hand, carpenters' assistant, film sound recordist, physics teacher, teacher trainer in the days when computers were just being introduced to schools, Education Marketing Manager for Acorn Computers, Chief Executive of the European Education Partnership, prime instigator of the Naace Third Millennium Learning Award and an independent consultant, helping schools to develop connected-world learning.

By night he has read eclectically about a huge range of topics that are on the edge of accepted knowledge in science, ancient history and archeology, always trying to tie the ideas and facts presented back into a true scientific basis. Balancing an open mind with a 'skepticism threshold', to avoid the untrue and speculations that have no basis, in this book he has created a synthesis of facts and ideas propounded in the books and articles he has read. His 50 years of exploration of the edges of knowledge is now being extended by new studies being published, particularly studies about the human genome.

See http://www.rogerbroadie.com for updates to this book, links and further work by Roger Broadie.

www.ingramcontent.com/pod-product-compliance
Lightning Source LLC
LaVergne TN
LVHW051039080426
835508LV00019B/1604